Weave of the Ride

ANDY WELCH

Edited by Eva Arnold

ISBN-13: 978-1477531396

For everything

CONTENTS

ACKNOWLEDGMENTS

Thanks to everyone who helped, hosted, fed me, and shared their
wisdom and time with me on this wonderful adventure.
Thanks to Emily Chappell (www.thatemilychappell.com), Siobhan
Graham, and Lisa Barron for their additional help with editing and to
Pete Moffat (www.rooted-design.co.uk) for his fantastic cover design.
This book is an 'Open Product' in the sense that it was co-created by a
group of people, distributed through print on demand, and the ideas
are intended to motivate and inspire further adventures.

1

The Seeds

I am Andy.

I was brought up in a small rural village in Leicestershire and spent most of my childhood playing in the muddy fields and forests around my home, which contributed to my love for adventure and the outdoors. I've had a fascination with bikes ever since I bought a mountain bike magazine when I was thirteen years old. I would show pictures of bikes to my dad and he would say things like 'Wow, such beautiful engineering around the weld,' as he gazed at a picture of a shiny, silver Marin bike. I would update him with the latest technology in hydraulic disc brakes, Rock Shox suspension, or Shimano gear systems. For my fifteenth birthday, after constant nagging, I received a mountain bike with a polished, oversized aluminium frame, fifteen gears and Mavic wheels. I was incredibly proud of it.

In 2004, I went to the University of York to study Environment, Economics and Ecology – because going to university was what you did after completing your A-Levels. I chose the course based on the inherited notion that I couldn't make a living out of art. Other, respectable options were out: law was too boring and I wasn't interested enough in buildings to study architecture. My secondary school economics teacher, Mr

Dorran, talked about environmental economics during A-Level economics lessons; the value of the natural world seemed something I could relate to because of my countryside upbringing.

At the fresher's fair, I wanted to get involved in a sports club, but the rowing initiation entailed getting up at four in the morning to go swimming in my pyjamas, and drinking my own urine at the rugby initiation also didn't appeal. Instead, I joined the much safer option of the mountain biking club.

Every Wednesday and Saturday, we would travel away from the floodplains around York into the hills and fresh air of the Yorkshire Moors, Dales, and the Peak District, with weekend trips to Scotland. The biking experience was incredibly tough at first. I didn't enjoy it whilst doing it, but afterwards the sense of achievement was immense. I would go riding practically unprepared, but I soon learnt that I needed to organise myself, which meant preparing my food and my bike, researching the route beforehand, and turning up on time.

A certain level of survival skill, preparation, and self-reliance is important when venturing into remote areas by mountain bike, and with time I realised that there is something instinctively satisfying in the ability to be self-supporting.

Mountain biking became a way of life for me, but when I left York I found myself back in Leicestershire where the biggest hills are molehills in ploughed fields with wheel-clogging mud.

My attempts to get a job related to my degree in the environment sector were fruitless, due to a lack of availability in the area and the fact that you needed experience to get the jobs in the first place. Instead, I found any work I could get. I worked on creative projects making t-shirts, artwork and websites, but it reached a point where I got sick of sitting in front of a screen and continuously thinking amount about money. I hadn't done any proper mountain biking for almost a year so I got a job as a mountain bike guide in Croatia.

I flew to Zagreb, caught the bus down the coastline to the port of Orebic, and took a boat over to the Island of Korcula, just off the Dalmatian coastline, where I would spend the next five months living in a small village called Lumbarda.

I was late for work the first day after drinking Sambuca at the welcome night celebrations. I assured my boss that it wouldn't happen again (being late, not celebrating). I was determined to do a good job. It was a position that I was keen to keep because I could do what I loved in a sustained way, and be away from the distractions of everyday life in England.

The work was a disciplining experience. I took three rides per day, from complete novices to expert bikers. New guests would arrive each week and I began to see the bizarreness of the concept of 'going on holiday'. On average the guests were pale-looking, usually unfit, English tourists who each week were herded – for want of a better word – into the hotel, and set free to run riot: attempting to kill themselves doing intensive sports they weren't wholly prepared or conditioned for and then drinking and eating copiously in the evenings. At the time, this phenomenon seemed like perfectly normal holiday behaviour for an average Brit.

As far as working went, things were idyllic. I had a role of responsibility to play in a community of people, a group of friends, a beautiful girlfriend, and a picturesque natural environment to explore; but there was still something missing.

A couple of my friends hired a car and travelled around the island. On their return, I saw their photos and it looked like it had been a lot of fun: swimming in lakes and jumping off waterfalls. Once I'd seen what they had been doing, it planted a seed in my mind. I started to develop wanderlust and think beyond the bubble of the hotel's activities.

Two months into my time in the village, another mountain biker arrived to help me out with everyday tasks. Meng was a thirty nine year old retired businessman who had spent the last fifteen years of his life working for a multinational IT company in London, managing teams of software developers. He had earned enough money to buy a house in Brighton, which he rented, affording him a stream of income. He was eager to tell me that the world was his oyster.

We would sit outside the bike shed in the afternoon sun, mend punctures, and exchange stories. Meng would describe vividly wonderful cycling adventures in the Malaysian Jungle, on routes no one had ever ridden before, and dangerous encounters with wild exotic animals. He described how he had once jumped a cobra, which had reared up in front of him, and his calf muscle had missed becoming a fang-pin-cushion by a fraction. On another occasion, he found himself following, from a distance, a herd of wild elephants. Sensing Meng's presence, they diverted their course off the path allowing him to pass. Having tentatively done so, he looked back to see them slowly returning to the path; it was as if they were allowing him a safe passage and he had an unspoken communication with them.

One day, two adventurous guests and I were out on a ride to look for unridden trails. We got completely lost and reached a dead end. We hiked up a terraced hillside hoping to find an old farmer's path or track that would lead back to the main path. After an hour of battling thorn-covered bushes, spider's webs, and loose sharp rocks on the eroding path, hot and fed-up, we slumped down to rest in the shade of some overgrown shrubs. We sat for some minutes, stewing in the heat. The sweat poured down my face.

I was embarrassed to be lost. I wondered what to do. Should we turn round and head back? The decision was made to press on and, after a short distance, we found that we were only ten metres from the main track. This afforded me an appreciation for the maxim that you are most likely to succeed when you're just about to quit.

There was a particular hill on one of the mountain bike rides, which had been named 'Beer Challenge'. It was a near impossibly steep climb, strewn with loose boulders. If you managed to complete the climb in one go without dabbing a foot, everyone had to buy you a beer. No one had managed to ride it in the four months I'd been there.

One week, on my day off, I went for a ride on my beautiful steel-framed Orange P7 mountain bike. I passed the beginning of the 'Beer Challenge' route and, feeling like I had built up a good level of fitness, decided to give it a go. I positioned my bike in preparation and pondered possible tactics. It would require an equal combination of balance, power, and stamina.

Initially, I failed: three or four times. Each time I wheeled the bike back down the hill to try again and each time I felt a little more adrenalin pulsing through my bloodstream as I turned round to try again. I concentrated hard on balancing whilst pedalling powerfully with a steady motion. I leant as far forward as possible over the handlebars to keep weight forward and traction on the front wheel. Just a couple of pedal strokes further – the last push was the worst – and I crept over the brink. I had achieved it. No longer was it a brick wall ahead of me. At that moment, it felt like anything was possible.

I continued the ride and, by the last downhill, feeling exhausted and buzzing on endorphins, I started to dream. What if I didn't just cycle a loop? What if I had everything I needed with me on my bike? I would have ultimate freedom to go and do what I liked. Such a lifestyle change would undoubtedly tear apart the 'reality' I'd been conditioned to expect: a reality that involved getting an office job, and earning stacks of money. And yet, the idea seemed magnetic.

I had lit a flame inside me but the likelihood of following up such an idea seemed very low. I thought I might only consider it if I was desperate and had no other options. At that moment, as I pedalled passed the tranquil bays and traditional stone-built village houses on the way back to the hotel, I was content with life.

Nevertheless, the seed was sown. The holiday season ended in late October, the weather cooled, the tourists disappeared, and I reluctantly returned to the UK. I remember going to see some friends, feeling inspired and full of excitement. I wanted them to understand the thrilling lifestyle I had been experiencing but I soon realised that I couldn't just transfer my energy to them. I spent months at home applying for reams of jobs, to no avail, and I felt my energy begin to dissipate.

Eventually I secured a job in an office near my home working for a computer networking company. I jokingly said to my mother that if I wasn't happy after a year of work I would cycle off in to the sunset.

Each day I would get up at 7.30 am, travel to work by 8.30 am, walk down the stairs into the basement, and sit at my desk. On most days, I would only move to make instant coffee, buy (usually tuna and sweetcorn) sandwiches at eleven, go to the toilet or go to see the boss. By the end of each day, I would be caffeinated to the eyeballs and fit to burst with pent up energy. I would get home at six, fly into the house, run to my room, throw on my running gear, and tear off across the fields. A half an hour run was enough to neutralise the caffeine and get the endorphins flowing again. It all became terribly efficient. After running, I would bolt down the food my mother had prepared for me, and on most nights retire back onto the computer or meet friends for a drink at the pub in the small local town of Kettering. It was an enclosed existence and I found myself frustrated because I felt that life had more to offer.

My friend Tom had finished his Computer Science degree at university a year later than I had, and had taken a year out to get a skiing qualification. After finishing university, he worked on a few freelance web-design projects but didn't find a 'real' job.

Tom and I have been friends since I met him in secondary school. Our friendship hasn't always been on good terms because we have always cultivated a healthy sense of competition. On occasion, we would fall out and fight each other. Usually this was caused by shared personality traits, namely a willingness to go to extremes, a disregard for authority, and mule-like stubbornness.

I wanted us to challenge each other, to embark on and achieve something out of the ordinary. I'd always felt that if Tom and I could do a project together then it couldn't possibly fail.

2

Off The Rails

One morning in the summer of 2006, I arrived at work, and the previous night there had been a huge storm, which had flooded the basement office. We spent the rest of the afternoon carrying every piece of computer equipment upstairs to the boardroom, transforming it into a cramped temporary office, which we inhabited for the next couple of weeks.

The weather was spitefully wonderful and sunny and I was frustrated to be cooped up indoors. To make matters worse, the air conditioning was broken so we cooked in the scorching heat. The room was like a greenhouse. I grew increasingly disgruntled and eventually the feelings of dissatisfaction forced me to act. The idea for the cycle travel, which had come to me in Croatia, suddenly popped into my head. For the first time it felt like a feasible option. I sent a text to Tom: 'I'm going to cycle around the world.' That evening I spoke to him on the phone and I wasn't surprised when he agreed to join me because we had been discussing various ideas for an adventure for a while.

Over the next year, we turned the preparation for our big adventure into an obsession. With our combined energies focused, we got sponsors, a free stand at an exhibition in London, appeared in numerous news media, and even got on the six o'clock BBC news!

The process of finding sponsors was trial and error at first. I spent hours scouring the Internet for equipment shops. I would try to find out the name of the director or manager and send out an email detailing what we were planning to do, including links to photos and additional information that backed up our plans. Gradually the email evolved and we explained how helping us, might benefit them: through being advertised on our website, in the monthly news updates, and their having access to, and use of, our travel photos. It became rather like our own business for which we weren't getting paid, but the outcome, I hoped, would be exponentially more valuable than money: freedom.

At the exhibition in London, Tom and I spoke with everyone who was willing to listen, about our travel plans. It gave me a lot of confidence and inspiration to believe in the big idea. Hans Rey, the founder of the charity Wheels4Life.org, and a mountain bike legend, turned up with a big display board to put at our stand. The charity, for which we became ambassadors, would allow us to donate bikes to people in need of mobility.

Whilst wandering around the stands at the show Tom met two girls: Katie and Sally. They were promoting their businesses: 'The Book of Green' and 'Your Safe Planet', respectively. After hearing about our project, they passed our details on to an emerging film company called String Films. A couple of weeks later Tom received an email from James at the film company saying they were excited about our plans and inviting us to visit them in their office in Wimbledon where we discussed the possibility of filming the trip for a podcast series. Somehow, this process garnered sponsorship from Optical Express.

Tom acquired some free tickets for The Bike Show so we drove to the Birmingham NEC with our press packs (prepared at midnight the night before) and a couple of cheap t-shirts printed with the Ride Earth logo and website address. We spoke to many different organisations including Chain Reaction, Extreme.com, DT Swiss, *DIRT*, and *MBR magazine* and we met Steve Peat, the UCI mountain bike world downhill champion and freeride mountain biker, Gee Atherton.

Tom had worked the previous winter in a ski resort in France and had looked after the chalet for the family of JP who was a guest there. Tom talked of his plans for a cycle trip and JP revealed he worked for the WWF in Switzerland.

He took an interest in Tom's ideas and said he would be in contact when he returned to the UK. A couple of months later

Tom received an email saying that JP wanted us to go to Geneva to meet him and one of the managers, Jimbo, of mountain bike company Kona. Through an astonishing occurrence of serendipity, JP had met Jimbo when he sat beside him on a recent flight.

It's difficult to explain these coincidences but when you focus on a huge goal, prepare as much as possible, and launch yourself into the unknown, a momentous process ensues.

'Until one is committed, there is hesitancy, the chance to draw back, always ineffectiveness. Concerning all acts of initiative (and creation), there is one elementary truth the ignorance of which kills countless ideas and splendid plans: that the moment one definitely commits oneself, then providence moves too. A whole stream of events issues from the decision, raising in one's favour all manner of unforeseen incidents, meetings and material assistance, which no man could have dreamt would come his way'
– W.H. Murray

We sat on JP's balcony looking down over a beautiful Swiss hillside with the Alps and Mont Blanc in the distance and we chatted with Jimbo. He told us how he had been a broke ski bum working in a bar, and had got into the mountain biking movement as it was emerging into the mainstream. Turning to Tom and me, he said with a grin, 'But that's my adventure. Your adventure is just starting.'

Things were beginning to take on tangibility. I grew increasingly aware that it was going to happen but I still only had a pile of bike stuff that didn't yet resemble a complete bike, increasingly worried parents, and a lot of talk to show for my efforts. As time drew on towards the scheduled leaving date, I began to wonder what was going to happen after we left. I had done only a little travelling before in Europe and no cycle touring whatsoever, and any kind of training had yet to emerge.

I was inspired by the combined energy of Tom with James and Ben (from String Films) collaborating on the same project. What we had started had now become bigger than the initial idea. The cogs were turning and the idea was snowballing.

Having sponsors for the majority of the equipment had its difficulties. Most of the bike parts didn't start arriving until a couple of weeks before and the most essential items, the wheels, until two days before. I called Leisure Lakes cycle store and they didn't have the wheel rims I wanted (Sunn Rhynolyte). Someone had forgotten to order them. Instead, I settled for a particular model of Mavic rims with which I was aware other cyclists had experienced problems. However, had we waited for the perfect set of conditions to arise we would never have left.

The day before leaving, I was able to build the bike. Once it was built and loaded up with luggage, I was relieved, although it's clear to see how leaving on a long distance tour, on a bike you've never ridden, towing a silly amount of luggage, was not likely to pertain to the smoothest travel experience. The majority of the non-essential gear I had would be sent home or given away over the course of the next months.

Mark (a friend of Tom's from university) decided a few weeks before our leaving date that he would join us. Mark was much more stoical than Tom or I and we didn't really know if he would actually come until he turned up to the leaving party with his kit. I knew Mark from a cycling trip in Scotland the year before, when the three of us had mountain biked off-road from Inverness to Fort William. It had made an indelible impression because it was the first time any of us had attempted such a thing.

'An extreme thing,' said Tom's dad on film, 'to cycle around the world.' It never started as an idea to do that, and that's why it eventually changed so much from its initial objective. The idea of a world tour is the logical conclusion of a bike traveller's goals as much as it is for any traveller with a desire to see the world.

When I first considered travel and I tried to think about where I wanted to go, I couldn't, because I thought everywhere would be interesting when I left England. There was just too much choice and it was impossible to decide.

On the 7th June, we prepared a party, bought a keg of beer, and gathered at Tom's house. I arrived on my ridiculously heavy bike in the early evening. The air smelt sweet as fresh rain evaporated from the tarmac in the remains of the day's sun. I said goodbye to my parents and family with polite hugs. 'Take care of yourself,' said my mum. The wording didn't seem to match the gravity of the situation, but they thought I would be back in a week.

Throughout the evening, I repeatedly refilled my mug from the keg of beer. At some point during the evening, we decided that we would shave our heads. Clumps of hair fell to cheers from friends, family, and well-wishers.

Mark recited Lewis Carroll's 'Jabberwocky', creating a suitably surreal and poetic moment. In the vein of Alice in Wonderland, we were about to dive into the rabbit hole of life.

'Twas brillig, and the slithy toves
Did gyre and gimble in the wabe;
All mimsy were the borogoves,
And the mome raths outgrabe.
Beware the Jabberwock, my son!
The jaws that bite, the claws that catch!
Beware the Jubjub bird, and shun
The frumious Bandersnatch!'

The whir of the clippers vibrated against my skull as I watched the hair fall at my feet.

The party continued and the keg was drained. Joviality was all around. My memories are a haze of fragmented clips of sound and scattered images. Late in the evening, I fell from my seat at the table and onto the floor and lay horizontally underneath the chair. I began to slide around on my back playing a solitary game of human curling whilst 'Smack my Bitch up' by the Prodigy played on the stereo. At some point, a moment of realisation befell me that most people had left, that foolishness had surpassed the celebration, and so I retired somewhere to sleep.

In the morning, I had a huge hangover. Everywhere seemed peaceful apart from in my head. I needed to spend some time in my own company. I took my music player and collapsed on the floor in the basement garage. Warm morning sunrays flooded through the open doors. As I lay my head back, my thoughts were like stormy seas in which I was drowning. I moved my eyes from one side to the other and things started to spin. Focusing was a task, which I would remit to another day. I closed my eyes, allowing them to roll and eventually rest where they clearly desired to be: deep in the back of my head. I was too hung over to care about anything. If I wanted I could just walk away from this whole ordeal now, or could I?

The morning passed in a flurry of activity and last minute packing of kit, offering very little time for thought or contemplation of events. The atmosphere was exciting but I was trying to overcome the distractions of my poisoned brain. There was a cake-cutting ceremony just before leaving. Everything felt somewhat staged due to the presence of the cameras but it also served to create a sense of permanence.

It came to the point of leaving and it was reminiscent of being on the starting blocks for a swimming gala at the age of fifteen. Friends, family, and my grandparents stood on the quaint village green in usually quiet Middleton. Ben and James had rigged up a scaffold and crane to get a dramatic sweeping shot of us cycling past the start line. It all felt pretty ridiculous. My dad was talking inanely about some technical details of the suspension forks fitted on my bike. My mum cried as I hugged her and said goodbye.

3

Entering the Rabbit Hole

That was it. We started pedalling. The feeling of movement broke everything away like a cliff side eroded by the sea, finally collapsing into the waves, breaking up, and disappearing into the swell. The last year of preparation was over and that lifestyle had ended. I was utterly aware of this transition in my life occurring before my eyes, and I felt very self-conscious of my pedalling action, but it felt fantastic.

Within a couple of minutes the clapping, cheering, and people were gone, and it was just the three of us. We climbed the first hill through the village and just managed to make it to the top before needing a rest and collapsing on a bench. To make matters worse, my parents turned up in the car and enquired, with a wry smile, how we were doing.

Another couple of kilometres and we stopped again. I lay down under a sign for a village, which was close to where I lived, but which I had never visited before.

We managed a grand total of seven and a half miles on the first day. They weren't easy miles either because the bike was very heavy. I began to realise that the cycling wasn't going to be as easy as talking about it, and planning it, had been.

The spectacular idea didn't seem as attractive as reality set in, and my hangover took no prisoners. I cursed the binge drinking culture of England. Our plan was to camp that evening but none of us had the first idea how to organise that and tensions began to fray as the afternoon drew on.

We pedalled into a village called Deenethorpe. Mark and Tom decided that we would camp on the village green. 'It's about as exposed as you can get, overlooked by all the houses.' I protested. It just wasn't the proper thing to do: turn up in a quaint Leicestershire village and camp on the green. There was no category to describe us: were we homeless vagrants, hippies or perhaps even terrorists?

A man came over to investigate what we were doing. We shook in our boots, thinking we were probably about to be accosted or arrested but incredibly, after introductions, he turned out to be the husband of Tom's old primary school teacher. 'How strange,' I thought.

He invited us into his home. Mark and I sipped port and nibbled on cherry Pavlova, fruit salad, cheese, and oatcakes, grinning at each other whilst Tom filled our host in on the details of the story so far.

Afterwards we retired to our tents and the rain started pattering down. Droplets built up on the tree leaves above my tent and dripped down onto the roof making what sounded like a racket to me. I laid out my sleeping bag and thin polystyrene mat and attempted to scribble in my diary, soon realising that it wasn't easy to write whilst lying down. I felt cold and uncomfortable and I couldn't get to sleep. I was used to getting into a nice comfortable bed and disappearing into a cloud-like duvet at night.

The next morning I felt miserable as I poked my head out of the tent door to be greeted by drizzle and depressing grey skies. The weather affected my mood. I felt cheated, as though I expected it to be sunny everyday. Already I was fulfilling the stereotype of the Englishman on holiday complaining about the weather.

The damp road stretched ahead. Often one of us would stop to change a piece of clothing, go to the toilet or have a rest. More time seemed to be spent doing this than actually moving.

We reached the town of Stilton, south of Peterborough in Cambridgeshire; a place well known for its cheese. It lies on the Great north road seventy miles from London. It was an important coaching stop in the days before motorised transport.

It was a novelty to visit Stilton. Ordinarily there would be little reason to visit the town, as any Stilton I ate normally came from the Supermarket. It looked like an average English place with pub signs, galvanised railings, a WH Smiths newsagent, steady traffic, HSBC bank, and a Marks and Spencer. Was I expecting the town to be made of cheese?

We bought a crusty loaf, cheese, and chutney from a souvenir cheese shop (the cheese is actually factory-produced in Leicestershire, Nottinghamshire or Derbyshire). Tom propped our video camera up and filmed us stuffing our faces. Being as we were in Stilton we felt that we absolutely had to eat loads of cheese as if it was a rite of passage. Not just a little, but an entire wedge. Once I had consumed an enormous amount of this mouldy foodstuff, I could have sworn that I began to mildly hallucinate. I told myself I needed to remain open-minded because it was to be expected that I would come across mind-altering substances whilst travelling.

I couldn't fathom what was going on in Tom's head. Perhaps the cheese was causing him some psychological issues. He seemed uptight whereas Mark seemed to be calmer and more relaxed. You could tell by Tom's expression that he didn't feel good about leaving his family and friends behind. Equally, I couldn't fathom my own feelings. We had only cycled seventy miles away from home and I'd seen my family only two days ago. I couldn't get emotional about the future or what I planned to do because I had no idea what would happen. I found it difficult to vocalise my thoughts and feelings. I wondered if Tom had more of an idea about what to expect.

Tom had meticulously planned a GPS route through England. He carried the maps and appeared happy to take control of the navigation. However, it soon became demoralising to follow him. At the beginning of each day he would say where we were heading but neither Mark nor I would receive any other information. If we didn't reach the destination, which we never did, then it felt depressing that we weren't covering enough distance and were underachieving in our own goals.

Tom seemed to see it as his responsibility to navigate. I saw his single-minded determination to take control as a negative for me because it meant I had no opportunity to work things out myself, which I liked doing, and needed to do in order to learn. I felt like my contributions were on the back burner. I felt that I had the choice of keeping quiet or muscling in to take part.

I was happy to be leaving England but I was taken aback by the beauty of the country roads so close to my home that I'd never explored before. It looked somewhat familiar, quaint, and homely, but also strangely alien. England unfurled before my eyes and I saw it in a very different light. Along with the ugly grey industrial warehouses and excessive signage and regulations, I was seeing a buzzing population going about their daily routines and I was floating through like a ghost.

On reaching Huntingdon, a grimy little town where John Major and Oliver Cromwell were born, we bought soggy fish and chips and sat in an ugly market square surrounded by high street stores. I began to notice that, on the face of it, the high streets of English towns looked very similar with the same shops and layout.

A man came over and spoke to us.

'Hello, where are you going on your bikes?' he enquired.

'We are looking for somewhere to camp. We have tents and sleeping bags.' Mark replied.

'There is a big park down there,' he pointed, 'you might be able to camp there.'

His assistance was one of the first occasions on which a random human being had helped us. I thought at the time that this was a significant occurrence for England. His visibly Japanese ethnicity was also exciting. I was only in Huntingdon but already I was meeting a Japanese person.

I felt so conspicuous that we may as well have been disguised as Mujahideen. I was worried about a park warden taking offence to our intention to camp there and getting us arrested. I felt like a tramp. It wasn't a feeling I liked although admittedly it was an intriguing experience to sleep in a park. That only happens acceptably in society's eyes if you're a tramp or a stray dog. I had a new place in society. That was at least whilst I was against the backdrop of this particular society without – I thought – doing anything particularly subversive. I felt framed differently in the eyes of others. Of course, this was happening mainly in my own thoughts because for the moment we still just looked like a bunch of recreational cyclists, albeit, with our new cycling gear, extremely well prepared ones. It was the idea and intention of sleeping in the park that was affecting the way I felt.

I'd never seen so many rabbits before and we joked about different ways of killing them in multiples and cooking fresh meat over a huge, crackling, open-fire. By experiencing the landscape from a different point of view, and much more closely, we were seeing ways to exploit what was there for our own benefit. Rather than buying a rabbit from a butcher or gamekeeper we could just hunt one ourselves, although we didn't because we had no idea how to.

We loitered at a picnic table, clowning around, taking photos of each other. There wasn't a lot to do so I ended up observing others. I watched afternoon dog walkers, runners, and people strolling and making the most of the sun. I wondered where they were going and couldn't help but think they were probably going to sleep that evening in a nice warm bed with a book and a cup of tea back at their homes … Or, perhaps, not at their homes, but I imagined that would be less likely to involve the book and tea.

It felt utterly bizarre and unnerving to sit waiting for people to leave the park and the light to fail enough before plucking up the courage to find a good camping spot. To the outside eye, my behaviour perfectly conformed to that of a tramp. I told myself I was just camping, but then normally I would have gone to a campsite, right?

The next night's quest to find a place to sleep began with Tom bluntly stating that sleeping in the centre of a 'sponsored' grassy roundabout would be a good idea. I was not as keen as I watched the cars zooming around the circular patch of land. A church beside the road provided a dry porch for shelter as it began to rain again. Mark and I went to see if we could find the churchwarden to ask about taking shelter in the church. We walked along a suburban street and knocked on door after door. After a couple of rejections, a man directed us to a house across the street. We opened the little gate into a front garden, which was replete with many overgrown plants and shrubs. 'Knock, knock, knock!' A young woman opened the door.

'We are looking for the Church Warden.'

'He's not here at the moment.'

'We are cycling around the world and looking for a place to camp this evening.'

'Okay, my back garden is not very big, but you can camp there if you want.'

'Wow, really! Thank you. That is brilliant!'

It was exciting to camp in someone's back garden and I felt privileged to enter their private land. We pitched our tents around an apple tree in the centre of the grassy plot.

A storm bucketed water onto my tent in the night as the drumming rain clattered down. I hadn't pitched the outer sheet well so moisture began to develop on the inside of the tent. I wondered how the process of my life had got me to this point and caused me to take such drastic action to find excitement and meaning.

I had expected life to be a smoother process. Maybe I was adapting to the present state of society. Was I looking for love, knowledge, danger, or all three? I was definitely over-analysing things, but it seemed like the process of travel was making me ask myself the bigger questions in life.

I woke in the morning, my tent was full of earwigs and I had slept in a puddle of rainwater. The earwig was a small creature I hadn't looked at closely since I was young. In the summer when it was hot, my mum used to put water inside a toy inflatable dinghy and I would sit in it and play. I once sat on an earwig and it gave me a nasty nip with its pincers. From then on, they became a target of my vengeance and an object of curiosity. I would squash them at every opportunity and be surprised by how they could survive multiple foot stamps or beatings with a toy. I think that over time they began to earn my respect. I would flick them away into the grass so they could continue their lives of whatever earwigs do.

Whether due to the rain, an urgency to make progress or an increase in fitness we made better distance the next day. As the afternoon drew on, the clouds cleared, and the sun shone a gratifyingly gorgeous glow upon the summer leaves. Tom suggested we find somewhere to sleep. We cycled off the main road into a little village.

A lady was cleaning leaves off the pavement outside her house. A regular task of keeping her patch of land clean, tidy, and looking neat for onlookers and the local neighbourhood. I wondered whether this was her way of consciously doing her bit to contribute to the local community, or a pointless routine bred from the nature of the built environment and surrounding cultural pressures.

'Would it be possible for you to fill our water bottles?'

'Of course, no problem' she replied.

'We were wondering if you knew somewhere around here where we could camp?'

'Erm … I'm not sure, let me have a think'

The lady, a middle-aged Scottish woman, lead us to the house of an eccentric man who ran an animal sanctuary in his back garden. He had a slight hunchback and wore a red shirt and flat cap.

His garden contained many wooden huts with different animals: a giant turkey, pigs, chickens; and a veritable menagerie of rodents, mammals, and birds. He told us he often had school groups come to look at the collection but it was privately funded (by himself) and he was worried about being shut down by the health and safety department of government. His strange creation felt a little like the result of an obsessive collector or hoarder. It certainly was not the sort of thing the average English household has in its garden. He had a bit too much sovereignty over his project to make it a viable resource for the community. Undoubtedly, it would need to have various bureaucratic surveys done to clear it for 'proper' use.

He was a kind-hearted man with good intentions and I felt a little sorry for him. He gave us seven fresh eggs for breakfast. We pitched the tents on a spot of land that was relatively free of animal droppings, ate dinner, and got into our tents. I lay down on my roll mat, feeling huge relief as my vertebrae stretched out after being compressed. My back was not used to leaning forward over the bike all day. I hoped that it would improve.

The next day we passed through the county of Suffolk. Many yellow fields and quaint villages later, we arrived at the sea. We stopped at the typically English-looking seafront with quaint, pastel-coloured beach huts. Seagulls floated up and down in the thermals. It was tranquil and quiet and I felt aware of the sound of the sea and the sea breeze on my face.

We pedalled to the port and Tom and I took the video camera into reception to 'blag' a discounted ticket.

'We are doing a round the world bike ride for charity and making a film about it, can you offer us a discount?'

'Hold on let me call the manager.'

I had become used to receiving things for free from sponsors so I felt disappointed that we could only get a discount. I knew I could never afford to do what I was planning if I had to pay for everything. I was relying on the generosity of people so that I could experience travel. Perhaps because of my experience I might become a better person and be able to return the favour by helping others. Our budget of five Euros a day was probably not going to be sufficient in Europe but one could live quite happily on that in India.

Ben from the film company drove down to film us riding onto the boat. He stepped out of the car, grinning, and shook our hands, bidding farewell and good luck. He then filmed us as we cycled away on to the ship. It felt good to be leaving the island.

4

Leaving the Island

The cabin on the boat felt incredibly luxurious. In an enclosed space, I suddenly noticed how much I stunk and took a delightful steaming hot shower.

We went down to the ship's restaurant to drink a beer. As we bantered amongst ourselves, I noticed the croupier dealing cards on the table in the games area. She was a tall, slim and wore a pencil skirt and red shirt. I started thinking about meeting girls on the way.

The following day I rolled off the boat to a grey Hook of Holland. Mark exclaimed, 'Ride on the right, ride on the right, ride on the right, or die!'

A grey car park, a grey road, a grey sky; in general, Holland looked grey. We pushed on to Amsterdam. The cycle paths LP1 passed across the undulating coastal scrubland, which stretched out for miles, and we passed other cyclists and walkers en route.

At a little café, Mark and I wanted to stop for a coffee. Tom was not happy. 'I don't intend to waste my travel budget on coffee'. It seemed an extreme length to go to, to save money. Mark and I bought a coffee anyway in defiance. However, the atmosphere soon became uneasy as Tom made it clear that he wanted to press on. Being stingy was obviously going to be beneficial to make the funds last but it would be a pointless exercise at the expense of enjoying the experience. Tom was motivated to 'Make the Distance'; I was intrigued by my surroundings and wanted to take things slowly. Tom saw the cycle paths and flatness as an opportunity to cover large distances.

For a couple of days we rode on an abundance of flat cycle

paths. It was a good aerobic introduction for less geographically challenged countries ahead.

One lunchtime we didn't eat properly and instead snacked on wine gums and nuts. I soon felt the effects of the undernourishment and chemicals in the sweets. My energy crashed and I became so hungry it felt like my insides were going to come out of my throat. My moods swung from soaring happiness to debilitated lethargy and I became dizzy. The technical term for this experience is called 'bonking' and it either happens when a cyclist runs out of energy because they haven't eaten enough or if they eat a lot of very sugary foods. The sugar energy is used up very quickly and energy levels crash. It is important to eat enough carbohydrates to ensure a slow release of energy and avoid crashing.

I told Tom and Mark I needed to eat. I was begrudgingly given a banana. I wasn't supposed to eat more than them, but it was possible that I needed to. When I ate the banana, it felt like I could taste the energy itself and feel it being absorbed into my bloodstream.

I looked around me at the landscape as I cycled. The houses, streets, people, and weather seemed similar to England, but subtly different. Dutch is closely related to English; the tone of the speech is so similar that it could be that the people are speaking English but all the words are scrambled, distorted, and rearranged. Having left England, I felt myself more attuned to look out for what was different. How should I act in a different country? How do Dutch people feel about English people?

We saw a castle and went to see if it was possible to look around. We cycled into the gateway and were quickly met by a rotund, balding, middle-aged man shouting 'Fuck off English!' who then chased us out of his driveway. His house was so impressive that we had thought it was a tourist attraction.

The countryside was flat and agricultural with many cows. People had incredibly well kept gardens. I concluded that the rural Dutch are avid gardeners because there doesn't appear to be much visual excitement offered from their environment so planting flowers and keeping impressive gardens alleviates visual boredom.

5

Amsterdam

We cycled through the outskirts of Amsterdam. We had reached our first destination of significance. I'd been looking forward to visiting the city since Tom had told me of a hitchhiking trip he had made there whilst at university.

The first thing that struck me in Amsterdam was how widely used bicycles are for everyday transport. It looked like a blueprint for the ideal system for a modern city. We cycled through a park with lush greenery. There were hundreds of cyclists flowing along beside us. Some people commented on our bikes and kit and offered words of encouragement, which felt fantastic. Scores of slim girls in tight jeans rode city-style bikes with curved back handlebars, purposefully and gracefully gliding along.

The plan was to find a hostel and we had the address of one called 'Inner Amsterdam Tourist Hostel'. It began bucketing it down with rain, which started instantaneously, like a sprinkler had been turned on. Tom gave me a look, and gestured to the sky as if to say, 'What the hell is going on with this weather?' Having spent much of the recent year indoors, I wasn't used to being subjected to the weather. I could control the weather by staying indoors. Weather is something which exists elsewhere unless you go on a bike tour. We pedalled along the streets through the torrential downpour as temporary rivers were created. It was a lot of fun, almost like pedalling on water. We found the hostel and were able to get a discount on the price.

We were paranoid about leaving the bikes locked up outside and the way to get the bikes to the safety of the courtyard at the back of the hostel was to wheel them through a busy bar, packed with drunk tourists. This wasn't ideal, as I was shattered, freezing cold, smelly, soaked to the bone, and wearing shoes with SPD clips which had no grip on the slippery floor in the bar. I tentatively shuffled along whilst a group of drunken British tourists laughed at us.

I was stressed out and tired. I changed out of my wet clothes and retired to my bunk bed in the dorm to wind down for a few minutes. Tom and I were sharing the dorm with two backpackers who were completely stoned. In fact, I don't remember them moving for the entire time we stayed.

We walked into the centre of Amsterdam. I had an idealistic vision of getting involved in an amazing night of clubs, parties, and meeting beautiful girls. When many English people think of Amsterdam, they think of Marijuana because of the coffee shops. Although cannabis is not legal in the Netherlands, the Dutch policy-makers believe that if a problem has proved to be unsolvable, it is better to try a different approach instead of continuing to enforce prohibitive laws with mixed results. By contrast, most other countries take the point of view that drugs are detrimental to society and should therefore be outlawed, even when such policies fail to eliminate drug use. The significance of the approach of the Netherlands is they choose to mediate the situation rather than impose an ideological system, which might not be effective when matched up to the actual experience.

For me, smoking cannabis didn't fit with the philosophy of the trip, which was a natural detox. The drinking culture in the UK is so heavily embedded with social activities that it sometimes seems difficult to do anything sociable that doesn't involve drinking. The binge drinking culture in the UK is a reflection of people using alcohol for its affect, as a means to escape the constraints of everyday life.

I think that alcohol is great in moderation. I've had many valuable experiences whilst intoxicated and I like to try the wealth of interesting local, homemade, independent brewed varieties to test, and refine my knowledge. The mass-marketed, mass-produced, profit-driven drinking culture annoys me. It exploits the fact that some people drink for the outcome rather than the qualities of the product, like a connoisseur might.

On first impressions Amsterdam wasn't living up to my expectations. I felt out of place. Looking around me, I tried to feel motivated to pursue my typical idea of the night out. Instead I saw seedy, tacky bars with neon lighting; groups of leery swaying, drunken week-enders; stag dos; American tourists; and drunken Brits, noisily scattered about the streets. It seemed like the people I saw had money to burn and I didn't. The built environment looked like an attempt by businesses to try to satisfy the preconceptions of tourists. My personal idea of what I thought I wanted from a night out was physically manifested in front of me, but I no longer wanted it anymore; I wanted something different. My preconceived idea had come from my experiences of nights out in England but was heavily affected by seeing Amsterdam in various different media, films, television, and the Internet. I felt cheated. I felt like the real Amsterdam was hidden under the plastic façade which was there to sell this invented notion of Amsterdam to people who were on a fleeting visit and then moving on to the next place by plane or other fast means of transport.

On a positive note, we found a rustic Italian restaurant in a basement and ordered three massive Calzone pizzas. The restaurant was like a cave and it felt good to take refuge and get some good food. The pizzas were huge and the tomato sauce was nicely seasoned and had a satisfying tang.

After eating, we went to the 'Bullseye Cafe', written in neon green and pink lights above the basement door. It was a dingy place with nauseating pale green lights. At the bar sat a scruffy man. As he turned to me, I noticed his face sported a large scar across the cheek and there was dried blood around his nose. He asked me if I wanted a joint and I said no thanks, but he gave me a half smoked one anyway. We sat in the corner of the bar passively inhaling other people's smoke as I watched the joint burn down to the butt.

I was tired from the cycling and I wasn't used to the smoke.

This, combined with the atmosphere of the bar, began to make my head spin. We left the bar, and there was a band playing Caribbean music on a float. The music seemed to reverberate more than usual and the noise in my head became increasingly louder until it felt like it was at brain-exploding levels.

On the bike, I had spent hours in the countryside in the company of nature but now I was being subjected to a sensory overload; an unnatural bombardment of disordered information couched in an intrinsic language of popular culture which I was unfortunately familiar with from years of television, Hollywood films, and news. My travel was opening my eyes to some of the anomalies and hypocrisies in the fabric of this shallow culture.

On our way back to the hostel, we were making a lot of noise, and not paying any attention to where we were going. Tom was babbling excitedly about something but I couldn't hear what he was saying because it seemed like white noise. The din of the city centre was soon behind us and was replaced by the damp echo of the back streets, sided by terraced town dwellings, and lit by dim orange lamps. We soon realised that we were completely lost and Tom became quite angry.

Eventually we found our way back to the hostel. I climbed into my lower bunk, put some music on, and lay back. I could see colours on the insides of my eyelids. Tiredness overcame me as I began to relax and fall asleep. Although I was exhausted, I could feel a sense of freedom and happiness starting to bubble inside me.

I had previously ordered some new, hopefully more comfortable, handlebars to the address of the Post Restante in Amsterdam. The Post Restante is an address, to which you can send things, usually located at a city's post office. Mark and I walked to find it. On the way, we met a tramp with dreadlocks and a guitar. He seemed to be crazy, talking loudly and waving his guitar around as he spoke. I grinned, nodded, and smiled politely. This street dwelling man didn't make sense to me.

We reached the Post Restante and found it was closed until

Monday. Mark wanted to find a bike shop to do some repairs. We found one tucked away down in a basement. If Batman had a bicycle instead of a batmobile, his cave would have looked like that one. Hundreds of pairs of handlebars hung on the wall, crates of chain-rings, wheels, and other spares sat on the floor. It was a toolbox for creating wonderful vehicles.

We walked along the busy street and headed back the hostel. A cosmopolitan crowd of tourists, business people, and shoppers scuttled along the pedestrianised street beside souvenir and high street shops. Mark and I chatted about the experience so far. He said he was missing his girlfriend.

Tom insisted that we left the hostel and we went to find somewhere else to sleep in order to save money. It wasn't difficult to motivate ourselves to leave the stuffy hostel with its resident stoners.

We cycled to a campsite in a park on the outskirts of the city. It wasn't exactly wild camping and we paid seven Euros for the pleasure. We would save a lot of money if we could get used to camping wild, especially in Europe, although it wasn't easy or directly obvious where we would find places to sleep.

Tom and Mark asked at the campsite if there were any big parks we could camp in. The surrounding area was parkland but it wasn't permitted to camp. We decided that if we headed further out of the centre we could find more secluded places where it would be easier to pitch a tent unnoticed.

On the way, we came across an event where hundreds of spectators were watching a boat race. Tom got talking to a tall, wiry, middle-aged man called Richard, with short grey hair, and spectacles that he peered over with energetic eyes. He was wearing a green sailing jacket and yellow shirt, jeans and brown deck shoes. He was carrying two shoulder bags, strapped across his chest. One looked like a camera bag and the other was overflowing with paper documents. He was incredibly inquisitive about us, our bikes, and especially the trailers. It was impossible not to be enthused and intrigued by him. He shifted his weight between his feet whilst talking and fixed your gaze when he spoke.

Richard didn't give much away about himself, but he immediately seemed to know how he could help us. He said he had a friend who was a harbour master at a nearby quay who might be able to help us with a place to sleep. We were lead past many private jetties with many different sizes and shapes of boat. We crossed over a little bridge and stopped next to a green gate. 'I think it's here,' said Richard. 'I can't promise anything, but I've known this friend for a long time. We used to go sailing together and I had a space on his Jetty. He's a cyclist too; he's done some cycle touring.'

I felt apprehensive but there was a sense of 'seeing what happens' in Richard's way that was infectious. We wheeled the bikes along a path to the harbour club bar and met the harbour master. He was a tall, sturdily built man wearing navy-coloured overalls and a knitted beanie hat. He told us that when he was younger he had cycled up to Norway carrying only fifteen kilos of luggage and only a blanket to sleep. It made me realise how over-prepared I was. Considering the numerous mini-adventures we'd had in our adventure so far, I imagined he must have had many more, and I was in awe of his stories.

We drank a coffee with him and then he showed us to a long, corrugated-tin-roofed building. He beckoned us in. Inside, there were sailing boats of various kinds. I was awestruck; it was a boy's dream. There were piles of life jackets, rolled up sails, dinghies, lasers, and toppers. More importantly, it was a dry place to sleep.

Tom was in a foul mood at dinnertime. I don't know exactly why but I had a feeling it was to do with me. I wasn't being sensitive enough and Tom was too prone to being wound up. We were both stubborn to boot.

I was making it worse. I wanted him to calm down but we needed our space. I was determined that the mood-swings would not spoil the travel experience, but it was difficult to act differently. Tom was determined to do things his way and I was determined to have my say but things did begin to improve as time went along and we got used to life on the road.

I lay in my sleeping bag, smelling boat varnish and looking around at all the different coloured boats. What an adventure! It was amazing what was to be witnessed behind locked gates and closed doors. I felt like the bike travel was opening up new ways of looking at the world. I was beginning to see the possibilities of the journey compared to a static lifestyle.

The next morning we cycled to the Post Restante to pick up my handlebars. On enquiring about the whereabouts of the parcel, I was told that it had been redirected to a depot on the outskirts of town. I had a preconception that trying to find anywhere in a city by bike was futile. Normally if I was going to a place in a city, I would have printed out a Google map showing the exact location and driven there. That was until I met Anthony Cassidy.

We met by accident because he told me not to film him whilst I was filming. He seemed rude. However, after hearing our journey plans he warmed to us. He became the mysterious wise man of the day: a cycle-travelling photographer. He was middle aged, had thinning hair, a beard, and was missing an arm. He wore a beige sleeveless jacket with pockets for keeping camera film and accessories.

He seemed independent and worldly. He was determined and organised but a free spirit. He lacked that jaded-look from being in the daily grind for too long and had an infectious positivity and attentive look in his eye.

'It doesn't matter what else you lose, as long as you have your passport, you're okay.' He kept his passport in a purse hung around his neck and said that he always kept it there. When travelling, people always want to share their wisdom with you; their tried and tested hints and tips for life.

'When you are in Asia, it gets really hot in the summer. You lose a lot of water. My advice is drink two litres of water at the beginning of the day before you leave,' he said, with a hint of an

Irish accent in his long-since, internationally-modulated, English. I had larger-than-life, comic-book-style, imaginings of mosquito infested Asian streets, which were constructed entirely from books I'd, read or films I'd seen.

Anthony decided to help us out. He thought for a moment, as if he was going over ways to find a solution to our problem. He then climbed on his bike, and cycled with one hand whilst propping his phone up against his neck and shoulder to make a phone call. It was quite a feat to behold: cycling on the cobbled streets, with one arm.

We cycled for a short distance to a printing shop ran by 'Jan the Man', a friend of Anthony who kindly allowed us to check on the Internet for where the parcel had gone. I got the tracking number from Chain Reaction Cycles. Anthony called them to get the address.

Over Anthony's shoulder was slung a camera bag so his camera was never far from reach. He'd stop regularly to take a photo of something along the way. He was continuously observing. We passed Anne Frank's house and I paused to take a photo of a bike, which stood out amongst all the other town bikes chained to the railings. It had a huge bouquet of flowers attached to the front, which looked like they would make it equally difficult to steer as to provide an extremely effective airbag-style impact protection.

Eventually we bade farewell to Anthony, found the depot, retrieved my handlebars, and made our way out of Amsterdam.

6

The Joy of Sleeping On Boats

The wonderful thing about Holland is that there are cycle paths everywhere. The main roads always seemed to have a small road next to them, which we could use. A canal towpath took us to Utrecht. We were looking for somewhere to camp when a lady with short wavy hair, wearing a black t-shirt called to us from the deck of her boat.

'What are you guys up to?'

'We're looking for a place to camp, do you know anywhere?' said Tom.

'I don't really know anywhere near here, but you can sleep on my daughter's boat "Miranda" if you like.'

There is something about boats, which instils an instant tranquillity. Perhaps it's a feeling of safety, of being able to cut loose from the land, or gently floating on the water's surface.

We were still paranoid about leaving the bikes anywhere. It would have been a catastrophe to have them stolen at this early stage. I'd heard a tale of two Brits who were planning a big cycle tour but only made it to Cambridge because the bikes were stolen outside of the pub where they were enjoying a pint. With Amsterdam having the biggest rate of bicycle theft in the world – admittedly due to the abundance of bicycles – we weren't taking any chances.

Mark and I dismantled our bikes and trailers and carefully carried them across the thin, springy plank that connected the boat to the land. I had to concentrate just to walk across it. Tom, in a spontaneous moment of madness announced he was going to take his entire loaded bike and trailer across the plank. The tension was unbearable, but after three minutes of shuffling along, and a look of concentration that could have adorned the face of a world-champion chess-master, he made it. I wasn't sure quite why he did it: maybe to show-off, to challenge himself, for deliberate dramatic effect, laziness or just plain fun. It was an impressive feat nonetheless.

We cooked sausages and mash on deck, and then retired to the hold. I slept tremendously well, bobbing on the calm water. In the morning, the lady invited us for a coffee. She was an architect who designed parks and public spaces and her husband was a designer. She invited us to go and visit his studio, which was in the basement of a school.

He was currently working on a competition to design roundabouts, but he also had some other more unusual projects. He had a bike that you rowed, a bike made from large-diameter tubing so the light and bell were contained inside the bike frame, an upside-down boat turned into a car, and a car which when parked doubled up as seating with four seats moulded into the chassis. They were fascinating, but I got the impression that he was consumed in his work, without much monetary success, and it was causing a strain on the relationship with his wife. I think she believed in his work and wanted to support him.

Eighty kilometres south of Amsterdam, we reached a town called Hertogenbosch, which literally translates, as 'The Duke's Forest'. Confusingly it is colloquially called 'Den Bosch' by the locals.

'We want to get to Hertogenbosch!'

'Ah, Den Bosch, keep going straight on.'

On the way out of the city that evening, we took to the small city paths, and asked for some water from a friendly lady whose house was beside the river. She invited us in and we nervously pottered about being uber-polite as usual. We put the bikes round the back of the house, which had a beautiful rear courtyard and jetty onto the river. The riverside was replete with lush green reeds, and lilies scattered about in the rippling water.

Karen lived in a small but well kept redbrick cottage. She was about thirty-five years old with brown, shoulder length hair. Her husband Jake owned his own plumbing business and they had no children.

They lived in an immaculately kept house. We sat in the living room, which was decorated in white with modern furnishings. Nothing seemed out of place. I was nervous about spilling my coffee or getting dirt on the sofa, but our hosts were very laid back and Jake seemed to be inspired by our travel plans. It was a dream of his to do a big journey on his motorcycle.

We lay our sleeping bags out on the floor in the garage, between Jake's motorbikes. One of them was a KTM, which reminded me of Charley Boorman from *The Long Way Round*. It felt bizarre and exciting to be sleeping in a stranger's garage. Compared to camping, having a roof over our head, electricity, and warmth was a huge luxury.

An unexpected bonus was in store. Mark came back from the shower exclaiming 'That is the best shower I have ever had!' Jake, through having his own plumbing business, had been able to select and install the most extravagant, decadent shower I had ever seen. It was like walking into a steaming Tardis with disco lights, multiple jets, waterfalls, sprays, and sprinklers coming from all angles. Press one button and you were steamed, another, massaged. I must have spent half an hour working out how to get the water to go on my head and not everywhere else.

The weather had been sunny in England but in Holland, it was utterly unpredictable. One minute the sun appeared, raising your hopes, only to have them dashed again as the clouds accumulated and the increasingly familiar pitter-patter started. It became rather depressing, and wasn't what I had imagined which was endless sunny days of carefree pedalling with my companions.

We ate a hearty breakfast of egg, cheese, bread, and coffee. I was intrigued by Karen and Jake's lifestyle. He had a successful business, liked fishing and motorbikes: a real man's man. She was pretty and perhaps a trophy wife. I sensed she appreciated the extra company. It seemed they were both independent people but the situation seemed to be missing something.

It seemed like a typical western European set up: materialistic, striving for perfection, tidiness, organisation, nice furniture, and possessions. I asked myself why they had invited us into their home. Were they looking for inspiration, answers in their life, intrigued or amused, just interested or just plain kind and hospitable?

We made good progress the next day, which perhaps contributed to me not remembering much other than main roads and factories, interspersed with agricultural fields. I was focused on the tarmac ahead. In a village outside the city of Eindhoven, we stopped and dawdled about, wondering where to camp. Usually dawdling about was a good way to see if something would happen. I spotted a 'forestry worker' sticker in the rear window of a car, which I read as a good omen. I asked the man for water and he invited us to camp in the garden.

He lived in a big house with his family. There were solar panels on the roof, which provided hot water and had been installed with a subsidy from the Green Party. The garden was blooming and full of herbs and vegetables.

His hobby was making longbows in an impressive workshop in his basement. Amazingly, he had also built a traditional Native American-Indian dugout canoe, and rowed three hundred kilometres up the North Sea coastline of the Netherlands and Germany. I saw photos of the construction of the canoe. It was a vast dug out tree trunk, 1.8m in diameter.

I was awe-struck about how we had again managed to end up staying with such interesting hosts. I was starting to appreciate the versatility and complexity of everyday people. I could no longer stay in the mindset that everyone was miserable, working a 9-5 job, too apathetic to do anything about it. We were a living experiment to see what average people were like. We never had to wait long to find digs to sleep. However, it did take a certain calibre of person to take in three smelly cyclists.

Sitting in the kitchen we were offered a cup of tea from a selection, including liquorice, cactus, and honey. The mother, who spoke no English, spoilt us rotten. We had a main course of soup with meat, onions, peppers, potato, and herbs. We ate freshly cooked pancakes with rhubarb, ginger jam, and maple syrup. My body was crying out for nourishment to repair aching muscles so everything tasted particularly delicious.

We left in good spirits, after a good night's sleep and good food. We rejoined the LF7, which is a long cycle path into Belgium. After a while, the flat, quiet paths became mind-numbingly boring. I hadn't done much road riding before. Cycling, for me, was either about getting around the city or mountain biking for adrenalin, fitness, and technological fetishism. I wasn't sure whether miles of cycle paths was really what I wanted to be seeing.

I regularly became irritated with Tom's behaviour. At first, he had been a ball of emotions but now his actions seemed robotic and emotionless. I felt he was doing and saying whatever he felt like, with no regard as to whether it would piss Mark and me off.

The Dutch signs petered out and we crossed into Belgium. The first town was very picturesque with whitewashed buildings, old cobbled streets, and a couple of pubs. Outside the town, we asked someone in a sports centre about camping and we were offered a patch of grass next to a skip in the car park. Tents pitched, bikes locked, and valuables gathered, we retired to the bar to drink some beer. The high alcohol content and full-bodied, malty bitterness of La Chouffe and Guisbergen did not disappoint.

The alcohol heightened our spirits and we were soon horsing about. Back at the tent, slightly inebriated, I tried to prepare dinner. I hacked at a tin of sardines with my multitool, destroying the tin and gashing my hand in the process. Alcohol consumption and tin opening does not mix!

7

Volleyball Anyone?

The next day brought with it the revelation of a hill, albeit small: the product of a navigation balls-up. We climbed it, puffing and panting for a good half an hour with the locals giving us strange looks. In hindsight, these were looks of people who never see anyone but other locals, because the road was a dead end.

In the evening, we came across a large crowd gathered in the road. With further investigation, it turned out to be the bizarre concept of a 'beach volleyball' competition beside the river. Thousands of tonnes of sand had been transported by lorry from the North Sea to create a series of beaches for the teams to compete upon.

We were kindly offered free tickets and entry to the festival that went with the event. The bikes were locked up in a dusty basement of a warehouse under the dance floor. On enquiring about a wash, we were given the offer of a communal shower with the other competitors. Having not had a communal shower since I was young enough to be naked at a swimming pool without people calling the police, this was quite an experience in itself. It was too much for Mark and he opted out.

We put the tents up and gazed around amongst all the young and beautiful Belgian teenagers gathered together to get drunk and dance to pop music. I was thankful that I had brought earplugs with me.

The next day's cycling brought to a head an issue that had been bugging me. It was obvious that my bike was too small. I couldn't extend my legs properly and I was leaning too far forward. This was putting extra pressure on my knees and causing me to have numbing pains in my lower back when I lay down to sleep at night.

I kept telling myself that it was just a bike and that I was being a perfectionist. I thought of Alastair Humphrey's tales of riding his clapped-out bike for thousands of kilometres, seemingly without problem or complaint. Of course, I was sidestepping the true problem, which I would have to confront eventually. I wanted to be able to forget my bike and 'get into the zone'.

Because I was focusing on the bike, I was also focusing on the pain of pedalling and my lack of fitness. After all the planning and preparation, I'd been unable to test out the most important piece of equipment! I felt like for all the effort and impressiveness of getting loads of sponsors, and the excitement of preparation, a part of me had forgotten that the whole point was a simple bike ride into the unknown.

8

Christianity

One evening, when I knocked on someone's door to ask if they knew a place to camp, we chanced upon a man called Simon. He offered his back lawn as a campsite, which we shared with a pack of husky dogs. In the past, he was able to take them out with a sledge in the winter but recently the winters had been warmer and the dogs weren't getting the exercise they needed.

With the tents pitched, we sat talking in his kitchen, drinking hot coffee as it started to get dark and drizzle with rain outside. We were treated to a meal of bacon and cheese in breadcrumbs, and omelette cooked by Simon's wife, and we drank French beer and red wine. Simon revealed his pièce de résistance by way of a round 'Fromage de Banon' – cheese wrapped in chestnut leaves – which probably should have been buried in concrete and sunk to the bottom of the nearest ocean to prevent dangerous toxic leakage.

Creamy, smooth, sticky, and runny, with a deep, pungent smell: Fromage de Banon yields from the region around the town of the same name in South East France. The affinage, or mould-ripening process, allows the cheese to mature for two weeks before being dipped in 'Eau-de-Vie' a colourless fruit brandy and then wrapped in chestnut leaves, which have been sterilised by boiling in water and vinegar. The alcohol prevents bad mould from occurring and the aroma from the chestnut leaves is imbued into the cheese giving a subtly unique taste.

Simon was a devout Christian and insisted that we come with him to visit the bible school that he attended and where we would be able to stay. He gave us the address and we agreed to cycle and meet him there. We were happy to be heading for a place with a definite bed for the night. The day's ride to the Christian commune was about as miserable as it could get. The dark, heavy clouds emptied relentlessly, drenching us throughout the day. I rode with my army poncho on, which flapped about annoyingly in the wind and acted as a sail, either slowing me down or pushing me along depending on the wind, which seemed to gust in all directions indecisively.

We crossed the border from France into Belgium and the road surface flowed with an inch-deep river of murky water, making cycling unnerving, and slippery. Every lorry passed too-close-for-comfort and catapulted bucket after bucket load of water at us. I was saturated and only kept warm because of the continuous pedalling exercise. I felt like I'd been totally submerged in water. My boots were full and my so-called waterproof socks were saturated.

At one point, a desperate moment of refuelling occurred at the side of the road when we took turns to eat jam and Nutella directly from the jar. The experience was so absurd. I stood in the driving rain, squinting to see the others, and couldn't help but grin wildly. Together with friends, battling against the elements, soaked to the bone beside a bleak, main road in France; I felt more alive than I had in an entire year of office work.

We found the address and turned into a farm track. After a couple of hundred metres down the track, we reached a large, white farmhouse and we were ushered into the basement to store the bikes and gear.

All my belongings were drenched because my panniers were packed badly and I hadn't bothered to put stuff in the waterproof liners. I hung my diary on a hot water pipe to dry. The ink had run but, luckily, it would still be readable.

I will remember the shower that I then took as the most satisfying I have ever had. The feeling was amplified because I was freezing cold and the water was incredibly hot.

Alone in the basement, I decided to record a video diary. I had many things to say but they seemed to come out as a string of unfinished sentences. I wanted to express my emotions in words but they were too complicated. It had initially been my idea to film the entire journey. I thought it would be great to be able to pick up a camera and record exactly how I was feeling and that it would undoubtedly be very interesting to anyone who watched it. I soon realised this wasn't quite how it worked. I would have to learn how to present myself in a particular way on camera and learn how to film things properly to communicate the journey to a wider audience.

I joined the others, who were eating dinner in the main hall area. The building smelt damp and old.

It was quite unnerving that, from the outset, I felt somewhat indebted to these people. It felt like their hospitality was in exchange for my belief in their god. Maybe it was my own paranoia and over defensiveness in face of the unfamiliar situation, but I think that their collective belief in something was infectious, regardless of the subject.

We had been invited to attend a church service that evening in a nearby town. A visiting pastor from Kansas City in America was giving the service. He was a slim, clean-shaven, blond haired man, who must have been in his mid-twenties: like a young, American, Daniel O'Donnell.

He had an air of calm superiority about him that made him incredibly annoying. People buzzed around him whilst they did sound checks and he greeted various members of the congregation. On the outside, he looked perfectly nice, but something about him roused my inner sceptic.

The service started out normally, like one I attended with my parents when I was younger. Prayers were read, people kneeled to pray and hymns were sung. The guitar-playing-pastor's set started gently, by way of him playing repetitive tunes with lyrics about god.

At first people were sitting down, but after the second or third hymn a stocky man, with an unfettered mop of frizzy white hair, stood up slowly, like a charmed snake, and began waving his arms about above his head. This soon prompted others who no doubt felt released from their inhibitions by the action of the first person. They joined in rocking back and forth and swaying.

Gradually the pastor sang louder and played faster, varying the words of the mantra. The music became more elaborate and a drummer joined in pounding out a hollow bass-filled rhythm. The music became more exciting, and I could see how it was working to create the evangelical mood and euphoria amongst the congregation, who became more and more animated: crying, shouting, and praying. The rhythm grew loud, riling, and emotive. I found the music uplifting and it reminded me of being in a nightclub.

One of Simon's friends was sitting behind me. Somewhat unnervingly, he began to loudly repeat the lyrics to us just after they had been sung which added a bizarre twist of dogmatic bombardment. 'And god will let you in again. God is all around us, let him into your hearts!' he repeated with earnest in his Scottish accent. I nodded politely but I wasn't exactly 'into the experience'. I wasn't preconfigured for it.

Back at the commune, I sat in the hall writing my diary. I felt that travelling by bike connected me better with my surroundings and environment and I was learning more about the reality of people and places. Importantly, I was able to observe from a detached point of view and with a sense of perspective.

9

Team Talk

The most challenging thing so far was understanding our differing motivations for travel, and life, and maintaining independent thought whilst also working effectively as a group. Each day I was experimenting with different ways to act because I began to see myself differently through the continual interaction with others. I felt I needed to start at the beginning, with a new philosophy of simplicity. I needed to unlearn some habits in my social reality.

The next day an opportunity arose for us to discuss a system for daily duties. Tom had often cooked, leaving Mark and me with the washing up. He had taken responsibility for navigating and if he made a mistake then he carried full blame. This caused Tom to feel singled out, which was unfair. There needed to be a share of the daily duties in order to spread the responsibility. I suggested we create roles and rotate our responsibilities. The roles were Navigator, Cook and 'General Bitch'. General Bitch's job was to wash up, take psychological abuse, provide moral support and hold out drinking water and energy bars, that sort of thing.

10

La Vraie France

We got back on the road in the late afternoon and took a scenic route on a track that was like riding on a washboard. After a few kilometres through a ripe wheat field, we arrived at a little French village. A sign outside a rustic house with long window shutters read: 'vegetables for sale' (légumes à vendre). Mark ventured inside and met a jolly round-shaped man whose belly was protruding over his shorts. He had a red face, a large moustache, and thinning black hair.

With a combination of descriptive arm waving and Mark's limited French, we bought some vegetables and tried to communicate finding a place to sleep. The slightly inebriated French man, confronted by three crazed *Rosbif* on bikes, looked confused but seemed to understand us and beckoned us to follow him onto a patch of land with a barn. Here, with a big smile he pointed at the ground and gestured his hand flat against the side of his face, which was the universal sign for sleeping.

Mark was brewing up some tea when a lady from the village arrived. Jolland, who had her holiday home in the village, was a long-retired lawyer. She seemed wise and had clear memories of when she had visited England: Bournemouth, Sussex, Dawlish Warren in Devon, and Exeter in June 1987. She acted as a translator for the French man, who wanted to explain that much of his vegetable produce had been ruined by the excessive rain that had fallen that season, and therefore he had only a poor crop to sell.

The next morning we showered in Jolland's home. She lived in a cottage, whitewashed with tall, sky-blue shutters that were opened wide to let in the fresh morning breeze. It was a sunny day for a change! She had many books in a dark, wooden bookshelf in her hallway. We were invited to have a bowl of strong, French coffee: rocket fuel for pedalling.

The next evening, after a day's riding through quaint French villages, we asked a local if there was somewhere we could camp, and were directed to the village sports field. A game of football ensued with the local teenagers: England v. France. After losing badly, I cooked chorizo with tomato, courgettes, onion, garlic, and macaroni, whilst sitting in an old, stone-built *lavoire* with water trickling calmly from the spring. A lavoire usually consists of a room with a stone bath in it, which would traditionally have been used by villagers for washing clothes. There was a lavoire in every village in that area of France and they were perfect for cooling down and getting out of the sun.

We were planning to sleep in the lavoire that evening but a man came and spoke to us. 'Bonsoir!' He said. He gestured for us to follow, so we gathered our stuff together. We passed a lady, who told us, in English, that he was showing us a place to sleep. By the light of his car headlamps, we walked along a dusty road for about a kilometre to a patch of land with a small orchard. The air was heavy and beads of sweat dripped from my face. There was an old shipping container. Inside it had a sink, cupboards, and a table. The interior was dusty, grimy, and smelt bad.

I was desperate to have a wash and the other two made fun of me. There was a rainwater storage tank in the allotment. I opened the tap and bent down under it to splash some cold water on my face and body. I discovered in the morning that it probably wasn't as cleansing as it was refreshing, when I saw the abundance of worm-like larvae swimming about in it!

The night passed in a surreal haze. I lay on the dirty floor, breathing dusty air. I fell half asleep, then awoke not long after when I felt something crawl over me, and just caught sight of a large rodent disappearing out through a rusted hole in the floor of the container.

Mark was fast asleep and was making a bizarre sucking noise

when he breathed, as if he was a heavy smoker or drinking hot chocolate. I had a strange dream where I was in a fight to the death with Tom: we had cartoon weapons attached to our arms and were swinging them wildly at each other.

The morning brought an understandable sense of urgency to leave the room. The more uncomfortable the place you sleep, the more you are motivated to get going in the morning, but our head start was delayed because we were invited for a spectacular breakfast at the house of the English-speaking lady from the night before. She was a psychotherapist and her husband was a technology teacher. They lived in a tidy house with a lot of old, dark wood furniture. We had homemade loaves of bread with jam and bowls of the best coffee I had ever tasted.

On the road that morning we stopped to talk to some farmers who were harvesting wheat from the fields, thinking it was a bit early to be harvesting crops in July. I could remember the harvest festival celebrations at primary school at the end of August. It turned out that, because of the heatwave in April, the crops had been prematurely ripened. Combined with the rain, this meant they had to be harvested early to prevent them from being ruined.

We had ridden for sixty kilometres and decided to sit in a lavoire for a while to avoid getting soaked in a sudden rain shower. Whilst waiting for the rain to stop, we met Jean-Marie and Andrée, a friendly couple who took pity on us and invited us to their home for the evening.

We chatted merrily whilst pushing our bikes along the road, through a gate, onto a neatly mown patch of lawn with an orchard and a caravan. Jean-Marie opened the caravan door with a jolt and presented us with our accommodation for the evening. Andrée looked concerned as Jean-Marie busied himself to make the place more comfortable. His actions were overruled, and Andrée insisted we stayed with them in their house.

We wheeled the bikes and trailers through their little front door. The first room was a garage with a boiler at the end where we hung wet things to dry. A door went through into the kitchen. It was a humble place, but cosy and welcoming. We were given slippers to wear, which was a welcome reprieve from waterlogged boots, and we drank hot coffee.

Jean-Marie owned the local corner shop. His children had moved out and he and his wife seemed content with life. They appeared to be very much in love after many years of marriage. Jean-Marie was jolly and laid back. His eyebrows dipped and rose and his moustache twitched, perched over a hearty smile. He seemed very happy to have us join them for dinner.

Andrée had short, black hair and a preoccupied temperament. She made sure we were comfortable at every opportunity. She was very inquisitive and always pleased when she got a satisfactory answer to her simple questions about us. Mostly she was busy making dinner, which consisted of vegetable soup – a homemade recipe – and meat with cheese and bread. Jean-Marie obviously benefited from being well looked after by her.

Using our basic knowledge of French, and Tom's phrase book, we had an entertaining evening joking and drinking beer and red wine. Jean-Marie unsurprisingly said he disliked the French president, Sarkozy, and – one I'd never heard before, but perhaps quite a typical French comparison – compared Tony Blair to a toilet.

In the morning, following a breakfast of toast with jam, cake and coffee, we went on our way. The sky was a bleak white. A stubborn blanket of cloud foretold that the weather wasn't going anywhere soon. I cycled with my head down for the rest of the day, disenchanted by the weather. Legs spun round, my poncho flapped in the wind, wet tarmac passed steadily underneath. The surface water on the road made a familiar noise as my tyres rolled over it. Spray from the wheels threw specks of dirty water onto my face and put grit in my teeth but pedalling meant relative warmth and moving somewhere different. Stopping meant cold, wet feet, and the same grey sky overhead. The light barely changed throughout the day, making it difficult to know what time it was.

We rode into the town of Besançon. At the tourist information centre, Mark and I met a man called Jean-Pierre who came over to look at the bikes and trailers. He invited us to stay at his home. He was a horticulture lecturer and his wife, a landscape architect. Their garden, unsurprisingly, was in a league of its own. It contained a stunning array of plants: bamboo, palms, orange trees, passionflowers, banana trees, and many more, all neatly organised, and arranged.

The garden had a feeling of calm relaxation as I wandered around reflecting on it.

You could travel the world via the plants: from East Asia, to Kenya, to South India. We ate and drank wine with the family. After dinner, the family went to the cinema and we were left in charge of the house, having only just met them that afternoon!

Breakfast, by way of baguette and coffee, was followed by farewells, and good cycling progress was made throughout the day.

Tom started to irritate me. When we spoke, I felt like we had slipped into a way of being that reminded me of secondary school: two nerdy kids, shuffling around, being stupid, until we got bored or annoyed with each other. I wanted to say something about it but felt it would have created more tension. However, as the old adage goes: a stitch in time saves nine.

11

A Few Pesky Hills

I distinctly remember noticing the architecture change from French style houses with tall windows, shutters, and red roofs to Swiss style chalets. Cattle roamed across mountain meadows. Their cowbells sounded like wind chimes. As the light faded, we passed through an area of dense pine forest.

The sky was pink, which contrasted against the backdrop of lush green fields. A farmer allowed us to camp in one of his huge industrial barn units. There was fresh excrement sprayed up the wall. As we entered, Mark commented, 'It's going to be a smelly night.'

Tom made jam with mirabelle fruit, which we had picked earlier in the day. Jam with French bread was our regular staple breakfast and provided plenty of sugar and calories for cycling.

I didn't sleep well that night and in the morning it seemed like Tom was deliberately making as much noise as possible by clattering his kit, stomping around in his boots and rustling his tent in order to remind Mark and I that it was time to get moving. I decided to retaliate by being faster than him to pack up.

Back on the road, we descended into a beautiful, idyllic Swiss valley, terminated by a lake with chalets dotted around its coastline. We had reached the Jura Mountains and now had to climb the ridge in order to reach JP's house, which was our destination.

Hours went past slowly like the upward tick, tick, tick of a rollercoaster's conveyor mechanism as it ascends to the pinnacle. Beads of sweat formed on my forehead, trickled down my face, and I could taste the salt as it continued its descent. There was no point in trying to go faster than a steady cadence, otherwise I got out of breath. My lack of fitness meant I couldn't exercise continuously below my lactate threshold on a steep climb, so lactic acid quickly built up in my muscles.

The hill's gradient varied throughout the climb. On steeper sections, I had to work at a higher intensity, whereas on less steep inclines I would 'rest on the bike' and work at a lower intensity. In training terms, this is similar to the 'Fartlek' training routine developed by Swiss man, Gösta Holmér. It was first used officially in the 1930s to improve the performance of Swedish cross-country running teams. Fartlek translates as 'speed play'. Training alternates between high intensity effort and low intensity rest periods. The benefit is that it improves both aerobic and anaerobic respiration.

The beauty of my surroundings instilled a sense of calm as the afternoon drew on to dusk and trees turned to silhouettes against the sky. When Mark and I reached the mountain pass, I thought back to a couple of months before, when Tom and I had flown to Geneva to visit JP. It was a gratifying feeling to have cycled to a place that I had previously reached by air and it served as a tangible demonstration of what could be achieved by bike in just a short period.

The journey served to fill the geographical and cultural gaps in my mind about what lay between my home and the spot where I now stood. By air, I hadn't 'travelled' on a journey from London to Geneva, I had effectively been teleported. The only information which I had from the journey by plane was the inside of Heathrow and Geneva airport and fleeting glimpses through a small circular window of the countryside below, beyond the clouds.

I was damp from sweat and the temperature had fallen significantly, so I put on my jacket. We descended the road. I spun the pedals and shifted up through the gears until I was pedalling flat out in 24th gear.

The night was invigorating and crystal clear. My fingers numbed from the wind chill and the freezing air seared up my nostrils. It was the most exhilarating thing I had ever done in my life. I had climbed for hours in the afternoon sun to then descend half the distance again in a matter of minutes. In the distance, the lights from houses on the mountainside reflected and twinkled on Lake Geneva.

12

Meetings With Remarkable Men

I saw Tom's bike and trailer outside the chalet. Kate, JP's wife answered the door. Tom was sitting in the living room with some friends of JP. On the table were plates of barbecued meats and potatoes, and an open fire flickered at the hearth.

We tucked into dinner and chatted about the ride so far. The journey already seemed epic to us, unseasoned, travellers. Later on, JP produced a special bottle of Jura single malt whisky and we continued telling stories until my eyes could no longer be prevented from closing.

Leo Tolstoy wrote, 'Everyone thinks of changing the world, but no one thinks of changing himself', and Gandhi said, 'You must be the change you wish to see in the world'. These words rang true for me now. I knew I wanted to make a positive difference in the world but I began to realise that first I would have to change myself. By cycling and meeting people, I was broadening my experiences, and learning about others and myself, in order to form better relationships with people.

People were always interesting because every person is a demonstration of a human life lived in a unique way. The nature of the adventure seemed to encourage people to open up and talk about their problems and life philosophy.

After lunch the next day, we sat on JP's balcony, and talked about climate change and philosophy.

'As you guys cycle around the world, you have an opportunity to talk to people, particularly farmers, getting their anecdotal stories because they are the ones who see and live the changes.' JP shaped the air in front of him with his hand gestures whilst he talked. 'Farmer's live close to nature and develop a strong bond, but it's all changed in the last twenty or thirty years. Increasingly, the snows start later and end earlier.

'Farmers are planting earlier, and many of the crops are overwintering.

'The church harvest festival is usually later on in the year whereas now the harvest is brought in a month or six weeks before.'

JP continued, 'The environment is interconnected. It is the life support system of all living matter on the planet and is necessary for survival of all living things.

'The climate affects the hydrological cycle and global weather patterns, which in turn affects the ecological system and biodiversity.'

The next day was spent relaxing and enjoying the warm sun. JP's house and garden contained a number of objects from his travels to Nepal. A Buddha statue stood on the green lawn beside neat flowerbeds and shrubs. It looked serene. It had a smooth, rounded form. There was a trampoline and I had a go; each time I bounced into the air, I smiled to myself.

Mark and I went for a walk in the afternoon. He talked about how much he missed his girlfriend. He was deeply in love with her. It made me think about what love meant to me and whether I would find love on the trip.

I thought that love was a combination of physical – chemical – reactions, and experiences and memories, which came together to create an intoxicating partnership – but this felt like a flawed reductionist definition and I was conscious of how little I really understood love.

In the evening, we went to a barbecue at the home of the president of the Ramsar Convention. I was rubbing shoulders with the most influential environmentalists in the world and I felt honoured.

The next morning we packed up ready to leave but we were invited to another gathering at the house of Duncan and Siobhan: a representative for the WTO (World Trade

Organisation) and a head nurse for the UNHCR, respectively. Siobhan was Irish with long, straight, red hair tied up in a ponytail. She was wearing an apron for cooking. I felt like we'd come to see the Oracle from the Matrix. She was very animated and articulate and had wise eyes that engaged you. She was full of encouragement but she, unnervingly, compared the experience we would have to that of a hostage. A hostage is abruptly thrust into a paradigm shift and situations outside of their comfort zone. Once released from their imprisonment they feel euphoric and a sense of shock sets in. She said that they have to be detained so that they don't blather sensitive information to the press that would prevent them from living a normal life in the future.

She had framed the journey in terms of her own experience. I couldn't understand the point of everything she was saying but it did touch a nerve somehow.

She spoke of her experiences in Darfur. The longest lasting memory was the smell. She had to block up her nose up with cotton wool to mask it.

She painted a terrible picture of some people in flood stricken New Orleans who, when faced with a survival situation were subjected to such unthinkable events as domestic violence, rape, and disease spreading uncontrollably.

We told her about our route and with a certain amount of lightheartedness she warned of bandits in Turkmenistan, warlords in Mongolia, women with 'legs up to their breasts', and the Mafia in Uzbekistan.

Running her finger over the map at rural western China, she advised:

'No, not much there,

'Yes, you can get a boat to Australia.

'Iraq, Afghanistan, Sumatra are bad,

'Burma is impossible,

'The roads in north west Australia are bad, you should avoid them.'

13

Verena

The road up to Les Gets took all afternoon. It was a grey and ugly dual carriageway but the mountain scenery and fragrant pine forests did offer some respite from the hours of crawling along the tarmac.

I found Tom sitting outside a bar with three freshly poured jugs of alpine beer. 'You genius!' I exclaimed. It was just like in the beer adverts. I had never seen a beer take on such a glowing colour of gold before as I held it up to the sunlight. It was a well-earned break. I savoured the opportunity to rest my legs and enjoy the mountain scenery.

The beers sunk, we continued onwards, and made it to Tom's previous ski-chalet employer's place just before sunset. We were kindly given a room for free, with clean white sheets, comfortable beds, and hot showers.

In the morning we were up early and pedalled to the resort of Les Gets and Morzine to do some mountain biking. Tom went off alone, whilst Mark and I explored the custom-built bike trails, which wound and plaited themselves about the hillsides.

Armour-clad downhill mountain bikers would periodically emerge from the trees and launch themselves through the air overhead.

I was happy to be doing some off-road biking. I enjoyed the opportunity to play, and use the bike as a toy rather than a tool.

In the pub in the evening, we got talking to Sebastian, who was a local resident of the area. For many years, he had made trips into the mountains. He spoke of windsurfing on alpine lakes; camping at minus thirty; living off wild mushrooms, strawberries, bilberries and raspberries; and eating rodents called Marmots.

I was mesmerised by his stories and began to realise that adventure was anywhere you went looking for it, so long as you had the enthusiasm and will power to make it happen.

After pedalling down the valley, we came across the Montreaux Jazz Festival. I had the idea that we would relax and listen to some Jazz but I didn't hear one note because we spent the whole evening wandering among the festival stands asking anyone who seemed interested about somewhere we could sleep for the night.

Recently we had become obsessed with finding somewhere 'safe', with permission to camp, but we ended up sleeping in a public park anyway by the lakeside and no one bothered us. At this point I was the worst culprit for being paranoid about camping.

In the morning, we were tired and couldn't get motivated to pedal. Mark and I sat on a bench and a cyclist stopped, and spoke to us. Her name was Verena Lepre. She was a slim, athletic woman in her fifties with short, light brown hair, and deepness in her eyes. She said she had done some cycle touring in the past, and invited us for lunch at her house, whereby we discovered that she had spent eight years cycling the world with her husband. Before that, she had worked as a nurse for thirty years.

One day they decided to pack in their usual routine and go on a bicycle adventure. On September 4th 1996, they left with the initial aim of getting to Kathmandu, Nepal. After eight years on the road, they finally returned to Geneva on December 19th 2004, having travelled forty-two countries.

Verena made Spaghetti Bolognese whilst we chatted about her travels. Along her route, she had chosen to live in some places for a while. She spent six months in India and Tibet, a year in Australia and another year in the Americas.

As she continued, continents rolled off the tongue as if she was talking about two week summer holidays. I had no idea of the wealth of her experience but I thought she must be as wise as the earth.

'What were the most memorable experiences from your journey?' I asked.

'We hitched a ride on a yacht from San Diego to the Galapagos Islands.' Verena replied. 'In Arabia some locals told us that if we knock on the door of the prince it was tradition that we would be hosted for three nights. We thought, "Why not?", and were indeed showered with hospitality. We had a palatial room, wonderful food, and servants tending to our needs. Muslim hospitality was the best in the world.'

They sold postcards in Japan to help to fund their travels. Her husband, a professional photographer had taken thousands of photographs from the journey.

Her house was generously sized, but perhaps that was partly due to its noticeable lack of clutter, which many people in the West seem to accumulate through the years. It had a transient feel to it, probably because it had been rented out whilst they were travelling. There was a large garden surrounded by conifers with a dark green, Japanese-style pagoda in the centre.

In the living room was a photo blown up to A2 size. It had been taken out of the door of their tent whilst camping in Tibet, and looked out to the mountains.

There was no television and she spoke passionately of her hatred for the fear that negative news media creates in the world when, in reality, there is so much good to report.

Verena was willing to pass on some of her wisdom. I remember it as a list of useful maxims:

'You should not expect more than three nights of hospitality.

'You should treat others as you expect to be treated.

'Share and give back when you can.

'There is freedom on the road. So much freedom … Use it wisely.

'Don't plan what to do in a day. Plan what to do over six months and then take it as it comes.'

Verena's words hinted there was a 'traveller's code of conduct' for being a guest: a role to play and rules about not overstaying your welcome.

I couldn't help but feel wonder at how we managed to bump into Verena by accident. She had so much knowledge and experience to offer us. Her experience of cycle touring exceeded possibly anyone else we could meet. It was another example of serendipity. But what is serendipity?

In the context of science and technology, a prepared and open mind is required on the part of the scientist or inventor to detect the importance of information revealed accidentally. This is the reason why many accidental discoveries occur in the field of specialisation of the scientist. Albert Hofmann, the Swiss chemist who discovered LSD properties by unintentionally ingesting it at his lab, wrote about this:

'It is true that my discovery of LSD was a chance discovery, but it was the outcome of planned experiments, and these experiments took place in the framework of systematic pharmaceutical, chemical research. It could better be described as serendipity.'

The French scientist Louis Pasteur also famously said:

'In the fields of observation chance favours only the prepared mind.'

Verena told us she thought there was a plan for life and not all meetings are coincidence. When a great deal of energy is focused on a goal, it seems to become magnetic and things gravitate to it. Tom and I had prepared thoroughly for our adventure. Perhaps we had set ourselves up well for chance occurrences and meetings.

We left the next day and followed the number one and number four cycle paths, which climbed steeply up to the town of Aigle. The road ran adjacent to terraced plantations, which covered the valley sides. The vegetation buffeted in sporadic gusting winds but even with the breeze, the weather felt hot enough to cook on the tarmac. It was humid and the weather looked changeable.

We passed through an ugly concrete road tunnel where cars were queuing because of road works and the fumes made me choke. After an hour or two of more pedalling the weather abruptly turned and we sheltered by the roadside from a torrential downpour. After about fifteen minutes, the rain showed no sign of subsiding. My poncho's waterproofing capacity was exceeded; I was soaked to the skin and cold.

Rather than waiting, Mark ran out into the rain. He returned a few minutes later gesturing for us to join him. I pedalled up a stony track and saw a barn not far up on the hillside where Mark now stood. It was constructed from thick heavy sleepers and was probably still used as a cattle shed in the winter. It was dry inside and there didn't seem to be anyone about, or any occupants, so we pitched the tents and I prepared a curry for dinner.

I thought Tom was acting particularly strangely that evening. It was obvious he was doing a great deal of thinking. We were all dealing with the experience in our own way, and it was impossible to work out what the other was thinking. However, being together in a group did offer moral support. The start of the journey had been the most difficult because the change in lifestyle was so extreme compared to the comfort and routine we were used to.

14

The Rich Who Stare at Polo and Other Swiss Stories

The next day we headed to the town of Gstaad. I managed to take a wrong turn and split from Tom and Mark so I sat by the roadside in the next village to wait for them. After thirty minutes, I checked my phone. Tom and Mark had gone a different way but both routes joined later on so I decided to continue alone.

Mist shrouded the town at the pass before the descent to Château-d'Oex, fourteen kilometres away. I enjoyed the independence of being alone and the thrill of the cold air chilling me through. My sense of curiosity opened up immediately and I began to fantasise about the freedom I would have if I was travelling alone.

I reached Gstaad, which is a very swanky, exclusive place. Perfectly maintained dark wood buildings in a traditional style lined the immaculately maintained flagstone streets. It was a playground for the elite rich, where designer-clad Americans, Japanese, Germans, and Swiss, brushed shoulders. To add to the ostentatiousness, the Polo Gold Cup was soon to take place. It was advertised thus:

'Experience the beauty and speed of this equestrian sport in the Saanenland. Watch from the stands as fine horses and the world's best players compete for the Gold Cup.'

I eventually found Tom and Mark. Tom handed me a baguette with cheese for lunch whilst grinning wryly about the communication and navigation mistake. Suddenly, large drops of rain started splashing down on the recently dried tarmac. It soon intensified to a heavy downpour. Luckily, the proprietor of a small art gallery invited us in to take shelter. This may have had something to do with the vagabond cyclist (Tom) lying on the street directly under her shop window, which probably didn't look good for business.

She made us hot coffee whilst the rain cascaded down outside. My attention turned to the surreal artwork, which included a half-man-half-rabbit and a pig's head statue.

We must have looked particularly needy against the backdrop of luxurious Gtaad. We thought that the needier we looked, the more people tried to help us but in reality it was obvious we were a bunch of Westerners on a bike tour.

We left the town centre and Mark met some people who allowed us to pitch tents in their garden. Our host was the ex-editor in chief of the *Neue Züricher Zeitung* – a Swiss newspaper with two hundred journalists and wider coverage than *The Financial Times* or *Le Monde*.

He was slim figured, wore a dark blue suit jacket, shirt, and beige trousers. He had astute, intelligent eyes that peered out through round glasses. His wife was a professor of history of art and she had been in Spain for five years restoring paintings. She had blond hair, and a pair of spectacles hanging around her neck.

A friend was staying with him who was an Orthopaedic surgeon who had served in war zones in Yugoslavia, Vietnam, and the Falklands. He wore a red shirt and white trousers and had neatly cut, straight white hair and a moustache.

We sat in our host's kitchen at a table spread with an immaculate, checked yellow tablecloth. Wide grins could not be contained as we ate generous helpings of delicious homemade Spaghetti Bolognese with coleslaw and Black Forest thin cured ham. For desert, we ate slices of traditional Schwarzwälder Kirschtorte, a Swiss cake speciality comprising layers of chocolate cake soaked in Kirschwasser (a local alcohol) and topped with icing, whipped cream, and cherries. This was helped down with glasses of wine and Zamsaal: a local type of schnapps.

After dinner, we walked to the best hotel in Gstaad to listen to a famous Hungarian jazz pianist and, on the way, our host told us a little about the local history.

'Gstaad burnt down one hundred years ago and everything was rebuilt or refurbished,' he said. 'Switzerland has a solid economy and attracts many skilled doctors and engineers from Germany.

'The gap between the rich and the poor is wide and the middle class is disappearing.

'Industries such as robotics, watch making, and textile weaving are our most important.

'There are four main languages.'

'We are proud of our pragmatism and are not affected by the influx of the rich,' said his wife, speaking of those who go to Switzerland to horde their money due to the – by Western standards – low tax rates.

In World War II, plans were drawn up to invade Switzerland, but it avoided war through military deterrence, concessions, and good fortune – as other events delayed an invasion. A fundamental part of Switzerland's prosperity is due to its ability to have remained a neutral country.

We entered the plush restaurant of the hotel, with its polished marble floor, and ambient lighting, and were shown to a table. Our host offered us any drink on the menu. I had a Dora single malt whiskey. To think the night before we'd slept in a cow shed felt extremely bizarre. Our trip seemed to enable us to ignore the boundaries of class.

The next morning we continued along the cycle path. We dodged tourists, passed cascading waterfalls, emerald lakes, and alpine chalets. The place was so well preserved that everywhere I looked resembled a picture postcard.

That evening, we ceased riding and Mark knocked on the door of a chalet set back from the road. A man answered and we asked him about a place to camp. He said there was a meadow on the hillside where we could go. I asked him if he had witnessed the effects of climate change recently. He was well versed on the subject and had collected newspaper clippings about destructive hailstorms – with hailstones the size of golf balls that smashed car windows – and localised flooding and landslides caused by the melting of the permafrost. It was reassuring to find someone with a clear interest. I came away thinking that the problem is not something that the average person can solve. He can only learn to live with the effects.

With the tents pitched, I gazed over the mountains in the twilight. They looked like hibernating, prehistoric creatures, lying down side by side. The lakes looked tranquil and esoteric in the dusk light. Wispy bands of cloud hung effortlessly in the sky as the first stars emerged.

From Saatsela to Luzern, we pedalled under the continuously metamorphosing sky, passing more lakes, fields of colourful tulips, post-modern architecture, and traditional chalets. Affluent people were everywhere: clean streets, immaculate and efficient public transport systems. The poor were either non-existent or very well hidden.

Away from the built up area around Luzern, we followed the cycle path beside a railway track. After a few kilometres, Tom stopped. Lying beside the path was a freshly killed duck with blood oozing slowly from its small cranium. 'You're not ...' I said to Tom.

'Its dinner,' Tom replied bluntly, before I could finish. 'It's going to go to waste otherwise.'

Mark put it in his pannier. We had gone from five star hotel drinks at the poshest ski resort in Europe to eating train-killed duck.

The lake in Rapperswil was sided by large houses. At the rear of each house was a jetty, moored with a sail- or motor-boat. The land around the lakes was either built-up, residential land or cultivated farmland. We spent a long couple of hours searching for a suitable place to sleep. We were yet to realise that we could camp anywhere we could 'get away with' rather than obeying 'no-camping' signs. It wasn't the proper thing to do, with many paid campsites available, but we didn't believe in paying to sleep. It was one of the rules. Finally, we asked some people who were having a party at one of the houses. They showed us to a little park by the lakeside where we waited until after dark and then pitched the tents.

'I'm not wasting money eating food from our supplies when we've got this perfectly good meat,' said Tom. Making dinner from the duck was a small gesture towards being self-sufficient and living off the land.

It was my task to pluck the bird. I tore feathers from still-warm flesh, then Tom carved meat from the breast and Mark noted, 'It's just like cutting a chicken breast.' I was worried that we would get sick but at least I knew it was fresh. I told myself it would be exactly like poultry bought in a supermarket, if not better. Twenty minutes later, we were eating a spicy duck and lentil curry and it wasn't bad at all.

In the morning, the opportunity for a swim in the lake was too good to pass by. The sun shimmered enticingly over the surface. We stripped down to our Lycra shorts and took turns to launch off the jetty into the ice-cold water – 'Wahheeeyyy!'

Packing my panniers that morning, I noticed that my camera bag was rattling. I looked inside and saw that there was shattered glass everywhere. The camera filter had smashed. Now the lens was scratched and glass dust was inside. I knew I would have to send it back. I felt a wave of gut-wrenching disappointment. The camera represented a dream to become a photographer. I tried to put the disappointment out of my mind as we continued cycling; I would send it back, and it would be replaced under warranty, but I couldn't get the idea of the broken object out of my mind. I had already developed an emotional attachment to it. I had never realised it so much before that it was possible to be so disappointed over a material item. It aggravated me and I wished I had never bothered with the camera in the first place.

15

The Blacksmith

That evening Tom announced that his knee was incredibly painful and he couldn't cycle anymore. A farmer provided us with a wonderful campsite on his land and then kindly took Tom to have an x-ray at the local hospital. The doctor recommended three days' rest with no cycling, so we took the train to Salzburg; Tom's parents had already booked a visit and we were scheduled to meet them there. Just like that, we were no longer simply cycling all the way round the world.

We arrived at Salzburg in the afternoon. Liz and Richard, Tom's parents, were waiting in the square. It seemed like ages since I'd seen them at the leaving party. They were staying in a nearby hotel and we joined them for dinner before heading down the river to find a place to camp.

A few kilometres along the towpath, I saw some firelight flickering down by the riverside. Mark and Tom went to investigate. There was a party. 'It's amazing,' said Mark excitedly on his return.

We climbed down the embankment and there was a beautiful wood fire crackling, people sitting around talking and drinking, and meat was sizzling on the fire. The light from the full moon shimmered on the river's calm surface.

The party was hosted by an Austrian mountain climber called Stefan. 'Where are you heading to?'

'We are cycling round the world,' Tom replied. Those magic words seemed to evoke mystical thoughts of epic adventure in the minds of others. Stefan had done some cycle touring before and was happy for us to join them.

We sat around the fire to enjoy a welcome evening of

socialising. One of the partygoers was Richard: a twenty eight year old Englishman who had previously travelled by bike from Laos to Cambodia. He had then studied a TESOL course in Taiwan and travelled overland back from Laos. We were discovering that, as cycle tourists, we weren't such a rare breed after all.

'Cambodian hospitality is unbelievable,' said Richard. 'Our hosts had nothing, but they would always offer a meal of meat and rice, and in return I offered presents of stationary and pens,' he added.

Christine, an Austrian girl in her late twenties, had just returned from travelling in India. 'I'm interested in the role of women in religion. I lived in a Buddhist retreat in the north. During meditation, the Buddhists close their eyes for ten hours. I tried to meditate for so long, but it was very difficult. The Western World is one big head-fuck so it is difficult to clear my mind.'

She added, 'In India it is very hard for foreign women to travel alone.' On one occasion, she had been followed by a man who tried to molest her. He had claimed to have wanted to help her and had betrayed her trust. In her quest to find explanations for her being interested in certain things, one thing she had discovered was that others saw her differently to how she saw herself. This was something I could relate to. It was common for people to open up and give me an overview of their life when I met them. Maybe it was due to the transient nature of travel meetings, or the big scope of our journey.

Later on in the evening, Stefan produced his fire breathing kit. Mark and Tom took turns in holding the flammable oil in their mouthes before spraying it through a flame, the resulting fireballs temporarily illuminating the river beside us.

After the last embers of the fire had died down, the party ended and people either went to sleep or left. The moon was full and high. I got inside my sleeping bag and quickly fell asleep.

I was in a deep sleep when, as if wrenched awake by a vivid nightmare, I sat bolt upright. I felt water on my face. It was bucketing rain. For a moment, I thought the river was washing me away. In a semi-conscious frenzy of self-preservation, I strung my poncho between two of the bikes, threw my possessions underneath, threaded myself back into my sleeping bag, and, feeling satisfied with my improvised shelter, fell back to sleep. In the morning, Tom saw my creation and thought it was a work of genius.

We rejoined Tom's parents for breakfast and, after bidding farewell, we continued downriver towards the Black Forest and Germany.

The afternoon's cycle took us across an undulating landscape, dotted with houses, with dark roofs that sloped downwards to almost touch the gentle green hills surrounded by rhythmic pine forest. It seemed a perfect setting for the Hansel and Gretel fairytale. Whilst cycling through this landscape I thought I understood why it was called the Black Forest. The density of trees gave it a dark personality. These were the woods of stories and legend, like the dark wood from the Wind in the Willows. However, the hills served to wrap the countryside in a cosy sense of security. Each small hill we scaled led to another area, which looked similar to the last.

In the evening, we arrived in a small town called Buchanen. A workshop with an interesting sign made from intricately woven and sculpted metal attracted us. In the driveway were metal statues and sculptures.

Tom and I peered around the door of the workshop to see if anyone was there. A man, about our age, with long, blond hair was happy to meet us. His name was Patrick.

'You are welcome to stay at my house. Normally I am a blacksmith but today my friend and I have spent nine hours painting my car with thin white stripes.' A black hatchback sat in his workshop and was covered in a crosshatched pattern. His friend was in the process of adding the last few lines.

Patrick quickly became our hero because he had an iron-working studio with many tools and so much equipment. He promised to show us around the next day.

We followed his car down into the town. He lived in a flat next to the river. Inside his house, I noticed a long bow propped in the hallway. Seeing my interest in the weapon, Patrick beckoned us to come into the adjacent room to see it in action. The room – a clearing, dedicated to arrow firing – housed only a large wooden target fixed to the wall. He proceeded to demonstrate, pulling back the long, taut string, loading the foot-and-a-half-long arrow with heaps of potential energy. In the split-second after letting go, the arrow pinged hard into the wall at the other side of the room. I walked into the next room to make sure that no one was skewered on the other side.

The area Patrick lived is famous for its metalworking – a traditional craft, held in high regard and linked with the area's medieval history – allowing this niche business to thrive.

At seven in the morning, we went to the workshop. There were three kilns, and various tools organised neatly on the wall.

As a souvenir of our visit, Patrick handcrafted three keepsakes. He cut a small sheet of iron, heated it in the fire and then, with a few well-placed blows, hammered it into a leaf-shape. He had a tool with an embossed leaf vein print, which he used to imprint the pattern. He bent the stalk, creating a hook to hang it from a leather necklace. The object was told to give good luck to its owner for four years, after which they must give it away to another person to grant them good luck.

We left Buchanen and continued along the cycle path, passing orchards of apples, pears, and plums, which offered an excellent opportunity to snack on the energy-rich fruits. We had established an efficient daily routine and were clocking up a greater number of miles each day. I became increasingly excited about seeing the Danube River. In my mind, it was our direct route to Vienna and Eastern Europe.

16

Three Rivers

The cycle path reached the confluence of the three rivers: the Inn, Danube and the Ilz. Here stood the city of Passau, a city that seemed to consist entirely of young people. Ten thousand of Passau's fifty thousand inhabitants are students of the university.

The city's Gothic and Baroque architecture looked exotic, with colourful exteriors and unusual shaped roofs, which gave the place a unique character. The blue domes on the Cathedral caused me to dream of reaching far off places.

During the Renaissance and early modern period, Passau was one of the most prolific manufacturers of sword and bladed weapons in Germany. Passau blacksmiths stamped their blades with the Passau wolf, which was usually a simplified rendering of the wolf on the city's coat-of-arms. Superstitious warriors believed that the symbol conferred invulnerability on the blade's bearer and the swords were highly sought after.

We had planned that on reaching the Danube we'd celebrate with a beer so we sat in the square next to the Cathedral of St. Stephen to do just that. We laughed, joked, and ate kebabs beside the river. It was a scaled down English night out.

Reaching the Danube seemed to induce a sense of urgency for us to make progress to Vienna. We pedalled fast away from Passau along the river.

At this stage, showering had become a luxury and the opportunity for us to have one was sought out with great enthusiasm. Pedalling along that morning, I spotted a sign for a swimming pool so we each sneaked passed the guard to have a shower without spending money on a swim.

There were many cycle tourists riding along the Danube. A tourist industry has developed along the route, with many restaurants and places to stay. It was definitely the most cyclists we had seen on the journey so far.

We caught the ferry for free across the river from Ashach to Ufet and then made good progress, nearing our target distance of one hundred kilometres. In the afternoon sun, we went for a swim from a floating pontoon, which was ideal for horseplay: doing backflips, and throwing each other off. The riverbed was soft and silted underfoot but the water was a pleasant temperature.

That evening we cycled through the city of Linz, weaving in and out of other cyclists, roller-skaters, and skateboarders using the pathway. I saw some BMX bikers doing stunt jumping and wanted to go watch them. Speaking to them, we discovered they were sponsored professionals and they suggested we could camp there. 'If we are riding late into the night, sometimes we camp or have parties here.'

Before turning in for the night, I moved our trailers nearer to the tents. In the morning, as Tom cycled off, a bungee got tangled in the spokes and snapped an important piece of the trailer, which held the fabric taut. He was furious with me but, luckily, he managed to fix it temporarily with a stick.

In the afternoon, we saw a man floating along the river in an inflated tractor inner tube, with his possessions in a bin bag floating beside him. We shouted to him and he paddled to the side of the river to meet us.

'I can't believe what I am seeing. Where are you going? What are you doing?' Mark said in stunned amazement.

'I'm just floating down the river. I am hoping to make it in time for the Szeged Music festival in Hungary.'

'What a wonderful idea,' I thought. Not a care in the world, being leisurely carried along by the current. Suddenly, pedalling seemed like rather a lot of effort. All that energy was being expended whilst going in the same direction as a river.

Riding provided a lot of time to think. Sometimes I found myself thinking negative thoughts, and sometimes these were about the other two. These thoughts, I decided, were mainly caused by tiredness. I made a pact with myself to recognise negative thoughts and prevent myself from prematurely acting on them whenever possible. This reminded me of something that JP had said. He had explained the meaning of word 'responsibility' in the context of environmental issues, saying that responsibility was exactly that, 'the ability to respond'. If you are a responsible person, you can take action to make change. Actions start at the level of the individual – and I needed to work on my personal responsibility.

I was reading a book by the Dalai Lama, in which there was a particularly pertinent quote:

'After the initial emotion response to a situation, learn to control the reaction you have'.

Recently, I had noted that Mark had been singing to himself, repeating the same lyrics. One afternoon I asked him what he was doing.

'I'm memorising lyrics.'

He had been singing sections of 'Desolation Row', by Bob Dylan, throughout the day.

'I've just finished the first three paragraphs, do you want to listen?'

He proceeded to impressively recite the lyrics. I was amazed to hear how Mark was using his time, because it seemed impossible to know what was going on in Tom's head.

17

Vienna

My friend Nadia lived in Vienna, so we had a guaranteed place to stay. The cycle path continued alongside the Danube and into the centre of the city. Along one section of the path, the walls had been designated for street artwork and graffiti. The results were spectacular and skilful with many themes: science fiction, cartoons, and technical landscapes; bright and colourful or dark and moody.

I was relieved to reach Nadia's flat and know that I could relax in the company of a friend. Nadia has long, curly, frizzy, black hair. She is a fiery mix of Moroccan and French, a passionate communicator, and a soulful, open person. I met her first through a friend when she was working as a teacher in Austria. She got a job at the UN in Vienna and had moved there the year before.

That evening we went out to meet another friend, Carolin, who worked at a bar in the centre of the city. It had been Carolin's birthday party a couple of days before so there was beer left over which she donated to us, thirsty cyclists. The pub had a good atmosphere and the beer began to take effect. The night wove itself into a string of memories of laughter, surreal humour, and meeting new people.

We went for dinner the next day at Carolin's flat. She lived in a small flat with a couple of rooms. We sat around the table. Sunlight came in from the side window.

'Have you read *Norwegian Wood*, by Haruki Murakami? It's about existentialism,' asked Carolin.

'No, I haven't. I don't know much about existentialism but have you seen the film, *Waking Life*, by Richard Linklater?' I replied.

I hadn't really been thinking about the trip in the context of any philosophy; I was just wrapped up in the process – but our conversations over dinner awakened an interest in the philosophical themes of our trip.

Tom was reading *A Brief History of Time* by Stephen Hawking.

'Did you know that the universe is shaped like an inner-tube?' he mentioned.

'No, I didn't know that.' I said. 'That's a good analogy for bike travel though. The bike is my personal universe. It helps me to move through space and time, and events and people orbit around my course and me. However, when you travel on a plane, you see and experience very little of the countries you fly over and your experience is confined to the plane cabin and the people you choose to meet within that space, the in-flight magazine and film. Your culinary travel experience is reduced to a shrink-wrapped meal, tea, coffee, cola or miniature bottle of branded alcohol.'

I had gone from staying in one geographic location and meeting the same people to continuously moving, meeting new people, making new connections, and seeing different places each day. Life went from a repetitive pattern of the same actions and experience to many new experiences. I had made a big absurd leap into the unknown. I was following a passion and discovering myself through my meetings with others.

I felt I was more in control of my own survival, which was very rewarding. In the Western World, we are often disconnected from the responsibility for our own survival. It is passed on to public services, friends, relatives, and work colleagues. Through convenient communication mediums, some of the effort is taken out of being sociable, and private transport takes the effort out of moving from place to place. In the capitalist West, the focus for life has shifted towards earning money and materialism.

Without the distractions of computers and television vying for our attention, Tom, Mark and I would regularly discuss life, the universe, and everything.

Meanwhile, hanging about at Nadia's, stagnation kicked in, and I began to feel lethargic and restless. Tiredness lurked, thoughts drifted and surged. I day dreamed, killed time, and procrastinated. I thought about writing a blog or cleaning my bike.

Something that Verena had said came into my thoughts. 'In the West, you always have to be doing something. It is important to take time to do nothing, meditate, and let the brain unwind.'

My brain was working over-time. I wanted to clear my mind.

18

Eastern Europe: The Gateway to Freedom

The following morning we left Vienna, passed through Slovakia and the number of sexy girls in tight jeans and high heels suddenly increased tenfold.

The next day, the cycle path turned to gravel as we travelled away from the urbanised area and the people seemed to disappear. In the late afternoon sunlight, we passed a solitary man on horseback leading another horse in tow. I began to get a sense of wilderness that I hadn't felt so far on the journey. It was something I had been yearning for.

Tom was complaining about his painful knee and pedalling on slippery, energy-sapping gravel wasn't helping the issue. We needed to get off the track and at the next bridge was a border crossing into Hungary. We had reached Eastern Europe.

The difference from Austria was immediately apparent because of the former-Soviet architecture. Hungary was a significant country in the collapse of the Soviet Union in Europe. The Revolution of 1956 and the opening of its border with Austria in 1989 accelerated the collapse of other Eastern Bloc countries under Soviet control.

The first town was dusty and uninteresting. We met a German woman called Jutta who was travelling on a recumbent bicycle. She had already been on the road for seven years and she paid her way by selling handicrafts. She planned to cycle to India. She wore traditional German clothing: woollen trousers, and a blouse, which looked unbearably hot in the summer heat.

We agreed to cycle with her for a while and headed out of town, passing the first of many old Soviet factories. It had large, rusty gates and broken windows and behind the gates was a crumbling, concrete building in a state of such disrepair that it looked post-apocalyptic.

We stopped in a small village to refill our water bottles from a hand pump by the roadside. The locals assured us that it was fine to drink, despite the strong sulphurous smell. I filled my bottle and closed the lid.

A minute later, I went to take a swig and as I opened the nozzle on the top, I was greeted, rather worryingly, by a hiss of escaping gas as if I was opening a carbonated drink. However, I thought if the locals can drink it, then I'm sure it will be fine; I was probably toughened up to the challenge by now.

We stopped by the riverside for some lunch. Jutta went for a swim. I walked a little way up river, stripped down to my Lycra shorts and paddled in the cool water. I floated on my back and allowed the current to carry me downstream, which was very relaxing; then I dried myself off and walked back to Tom and Mark. Whilst walking back I sensed that something wasn't right. Mark sat with his head in his hands. He looked up; his eyes betrayed strong emotions and his reddened face was running with tears.

'What is wrong mate?' I said.

'I have to go back to my girlfriend ... Now.' Mark replied. 'I'm going to catch a train to Budapest and fly home from there.'

He had bottled up his feelings over the past days and had grown more and more worried about being away from his girlfriend. I thought I could understand, but I didn't know how to react. I knew that love was a strong thing but I didn't realise that it could make someone act like that. I naïvely thought that there must be another reason, or that he was chickening out. We tried to talk him out of it but there was no way that Mark was going to change his mind.

We caught the train from a small station with no platform. The train was an old rust bucket with weathered yellow paint, which was peeling off. It screeched to a halt and we piled the bikes into the carriage, bade farewell to Jutta, and the train slowly chugged and rattled away from the station. I sat back in my seat and watched the autumnal scenery pass by as we headed towards Budapest.

19

Shogun Assassin

The sky was cracked with veins of red above the industrial sprawl of the city's outskirts. Graffiti tags were scrawled over the walls beside the train. Faceless people moved about in the unidentified suburban district.

When the train arrived at Budapest Central Station, we pushed the bikes out into the lobby. We wanted to find somewhere to sleep the night. Mark and I approached a man who was looking at our bikes and us. 'We are looking for somewhere to stay, do you know of a hostel round here?' The man got up and made out as if he was scanning the area.

'I don't know anywhere around here. You can stay with me if you want, but my home is very small, as long as you don't mind. There isn't much space for your bikes and luggage. It's not far from here. I will give you directions and you can cycle.'

On first impressions, he seemed a little strange. I didn't have a good feeling about him. He was in his early thirties and spoke in bolts of trailing speech with a hint of desperation. He had dark hair and a world-weary face, was of medium build, and wore a blue jacket and jeans; he could have passed for Italian, I thought. He also had an unnerving twitch, which caused him to jerk his head to the side when he spoke. As if in an attempt to fix the inconvenient habit, he would fiddle with his nose and eyes.

He gave us his address and we cycled through the city streets. I felt like I was on the set of *Batman* and this was Gotham city. A white Lamborghini roared down the high street. A tall woman with skinny legs and blond hair walked past. She was wearing shiny, red, knee-length boots, a short shirt, and skimpy boob tube. She looked like a plastic doll from a Hollywood movie.

The grimy streets and buildings looked menacing but exciting. We found the address and our host lead us into an Italian style courtyard outside his home where he lived in a small bedsit. We went into the kitchen and the first thing I noticed was how messy it was. Adjoining the kitchen was a small living room with a mezzanine above it for sleeping. By the far wall of the living room was a shelf with a huge collection of DVDs and beside the shelf was a computer table with a padded chair in front of it. The chair's cover was extremely worn. The carpet in front of the seat had two foot sized imprints worn into it. It looked like the chair had never been moved. It was evident that he spent a lot of time watching television and using his computer.

He offered us dried salami and bread to eat for dinner. We sat on red sofa seats with faded, threadbare upholstery. It reminded me of a chair that my late grandfather used to sit in and fall asleep. Whilst gazing around the room I noticed some unusual objects. In the centre of the ceiling hung a light and from it hung a makeshift sculpture of empty toilet rolls, strung haphazardly together. Propped up against the wall was a Bokken (a wooden Ninjitsu training sword). Tom and I both trained in Ninjitsu and were familiar with the object. Seeing our interest, the man was eager to demonstrate. Like a child doing a fantasy role-play, he got up onto the seat and launched himself through the air. Legs flailing, he slashed wildly at the cardboard rolls and the light swung in circles around the room, turning it temporarily into a strange disco. He was odder than I had anticipated. He also had a crossbow nailed to the wall but I decided not to enquire about it.

On further investigation of the DVDs, it turned out he was a fanatic about Samurai films. He asked us if we would like to watch one and he suggested one called *Shogun Assassin*. I was tired but thought, 'Why not?'

The man turned off the light, pressed play on the DVD and we started to watch the film. Shortly after the film began, Tom said he was tired and went to sleep upstairs.

The film *Shogun Assassin* is a Samurai film, which was made for British and American markets. It is very violent. The plot consists of an honourable and good Samurai who served his Shogun master well but, as the years pass, the Shogun grows old and senile and becomes paranoid of anyone who might take his power. One day, he sends some ninjas to the Samurai's house to kill him but they fail, killing his wife instead. The Samurai then goes on a journey of vengeance. He has a toddler son to care for, whom he takes everywhere with him through forests and deserts in Japan. Along the way, he takes on mercenary work. The film ends with the final fight with the Shogun and his bodyguards who are named the 'Masters of Death'.

The film was dubbed into American English. The DVD had been recorded from a video tape and the image quality had an analogue grain to it. In the hours that followed, the storyline and soundtrack of the film would serve as an accompaniment to real life events in the flat.

I was relaxing, but I felt a little uncomfortable – probably, I thought, because I was still wearing my cycling clothes after a sweaty day. I noticed Mark was shifting around a lot in his seat, then he starting clutching his midriff and looking desperately at me. The dim reddish light in the room was accompanied only by the flickering light from the television. 'Are you okay mate? Can I get you anything?' I said.

'It's my stomach Andy.' Mark replied. Shortly after, he dashed into the toilet and vomited. I closed the door to shut out the noise but I could hear him through the thin walls.

The film continued:

'When I was little, my father was famous. He was the greatest Samurai in the empire, and he was the Shogun's decapitator.'

Another loud bout of retching came from the toilet.

'He cut off the heads of 131 lords for the Shogun. It was a bad time for the empire. The Shogun just stayed inside his castle and he never came out. People said his brain was infected by devils and that he was rotting with evil.'

I heard muffled groans coming from the mezzanine.

'The Shogun said the people were not loyal. He said he had many enemies, but he killed more people than that. It was a bad time. Everybody living in fear, but still we were happy. My father would come home to mother, and when he had seen her, he would forget about the killings. He wasn't scared of the Shogun, but the Shogun was scared of him. Maybe that was the problem. At night, mother would sing for us, while father would go into his temple and pray for peace. He'd pray for things to get better.'

The soundtrack of the film seemed to come from my own head. My consciousness started to feel heavy and I began to spin out. Something far in the distance, an evil dark army was on its way to battle me. I could feel its presence. My surroundings began to fade and my vision became blurry as if I had dust in my eyes. I blinked to clear it. Shapes and shadows began to blend into one another. My host's face was a circle in the darkness, and then it clouded out and disappeared. He became an innocent bystander observing the situation. He was immaterial and irrelevant. He was a total stranger. He was the proprietor of hell's own hotel checkout. The devil began creeping into my mind. It twisted my thoughts like a dose of a diabolical serum.

There was silence marked by a break in the film.

Only the drawing on a cigarette and exhaling of smoke could be heard. The smoke seemed to fill the room. My nose was blocked and my throat was dry with a bad taste. Was it perhaps from the salami I had eaten earlier? Perhaps it was the sulphurous village water. A couple of days before we had drunk water directly from the Danube without boiling it and then found a dead dog lying by the riverside only twenty metres away, bumping in a macabre fashion against the concrete channelized wall.

The Danube is a big river, with many cities lining it. In hindsight, it probably contained all manner of industrial chemicals, decaying matter, household waste, sewerage deposits, urban surface run-off, and oil. Whatever lived in the river – apart from the dog – had probably developed thicker skin, and a higher tolerance for whatever was in the water. We hadn't.

As our host chain-smoked and the indeterminable time passed, I realised that he was an insomniac. He watched films all night to occupy his sleepless hours.

Mark returned from the toilet and collapsed into a formless, grey blob. I knew I had it coming because my mind tormented me. I felt threatened by my surroundings. What the hell was going on?

'That was when my father left his Samurai life and became a demon. He became an assassin who walks the road of vengeance. And he took me with him. I don't remember most of this myself. I only remember the Shogun's ninja hunting us wherever we go. And the bodies falling. And the blood.'

Tom scrambled – half fell – down the ladder from the mezzanine. He flailed his arms out ahead and burst through the kitchen door. He attached himself to the toilet and began the process of ousting whatever was melting his insides.

Eventually, it hit me too. I ran to the bathroom, just missing Tom who staggered out beside me. I vomited violently into the toilet. My head vibrated and my body shivered. The toilet cistern was broken. I groped for the handle to flush the toilet, but it flushed continuously.

I had lost all sense of shame. I stripped down naked and alternated between sitting on the toilet, thrusting my head into the bowl, and washing myself in the shower. I spent the next twenty minutes with my insides flexing, contorting, and straining. Eventually the physical reaction subsided; I dried myself and returned to the living room. The film continued:

> The master of death says [his jugular fatally slashed] 'Your
> technique is magnificent.'

I lay down on the dirty sheets of the bed, up on the mezzanine.
The stink made me feel worse. Sleep was impossible. I twisted
and turned, desperate to be unconscious.

After a couple of hours, it happened again. Tom went to use
the toilet, I ran past him, and was sick right in front of him whilst
he sat there. The last remnants of the food I had eaten earlier got
pushed down between the gaps in the plughole with the palm of
my hand as I struggled to stand. I felt so weak. Tom did the
honourable thing and filmed me with the video camera.

The light of the morning began to creep into the room. I was
exhausted. Then our host, who had been up all night, said he
needed to go to work. We gathered our stuff as best we could
and shovelled it outside of the door into the fresh morning air.

Doing anything required an immense amount of effort. Usually
I would be bed-ridden by such an illness, but we were forced to
move on. I used the bike as a crutch and followed Tom down a
side street. I was like a wounded soldier staggering away from a
failed mission. The bike and luggage felt ten times heavier.

I didn't know what Tom's plan was, because there wasn't one.
He lay down on the pavement outside the entrance to a busy
supermarket. I watched from a few metres away as someone
threw a coin to him thinking he was a tramp.

We continued to push the bikes for what seemed like an
eternity and found our way to a park and a patch of grass under a
large tree. I collapsed to the floor and fell unconscious for the
best part of six hours. Occasionally I would open my eyes
halfway and the world would be turning. There were leaves on
the trees, birds in the sky, people wandering in the park around
me – but nothing seemed real.

20

The Yurt With The Monk

At some point during the afternoon, Mark picked himself up and explained he was going to find the airport. I was disappointed that Mark was leaving but there was nothing we could do to change his mind. He provided another dynamic to the group, which it was a shame to lose.

Tom and I went to an Internet cafe and had received a response from a Couchsurfer called David who lived in a village outside the centre of Budapest. We cycled the thirty kilometres having eaten only a bit of salad and a piece of watermelon during the last thirty-six hours. There was nothing left inside me but, strangely, I didn't feel hungry when I pedalled and I had enough energy. The cycle ride made me feel better.

David lived in a Mongolian Yurt in his garden. I walked past the impressive construction towards a small campfire where people were sitting. I ate a small piece of meat cooked in the fire but within thirty minutes I retired to the Yurt and collapsed into a deep sleep on the carpeted floor.

In the morning, in the daylight I discovered who the other guests were. There were some blond Norwegian girls and a group of American filmmakers who were making a film about Couchsurfing.

There was a cottage at the top of the garden with a bedroom, living room, kitchen, and a bathroom. He had built the cottage himself with the help of some previous guests. In the living room was a computer, a large bookshelf stocked with philosophy and mountaineering books and, in the corner, sat a fish tank with some turtles. His life revolved around his home and his interests in philosophy and mountaineering.

I slouched around all day, used the Internet, and ate. I spent a considerable amount of time sitting in the Yurt in meditation gazing in wonder at the circular structure, which was about sixteen feet in diameter. It had a pleasant energy to it.

A wooden trellis stretched with thick felt constituted the walls. The roof was constructed from wooden struts leaning to a point in the centre and stretched over with felt, creating a tee-pee shape. There was a hole at the top, allowing wood-smoke to exit. The floor was covered with a Middle-Eastern style, red patterned carpet. On one side there was a chest of drawers with some ornaments, a shrine to Ganesh, and a photo frame with a photo of a girl with dark brown hair.

David was tanned and well built, with shoulder length, wavy, brown hair. He wandered about all day wearing nothing but a pair of orange, cotton trousers, which certainly had an effect on the women who came to stay.

He was a very interesting character who had travelled extensively. He had hitchhiked around Asia, spent six months in India living as a Sadhu (Indian holy man), and six months in Tibet working as a Yak herder. He loved hitchhiking. 'You have to make the effort to talk and find out about the person and you have to be patient to get your next ride.'

He made a living through high-altitude climbing, doing sponsored and commercial expeditions. His current project was to climb Mount Everest without the use of supplementary oxygen. Only around ten percent of all Everest attempts are without supplementary oxygen and, at the time, David thought that only one hundred people in the world had achieved it. He had a group of friends who had always gone climbing together in Europe, the Alps, and Eastern Europe.

'Climbers either climb European mountains forever, or outgrow them and venture into Asia. But Asian mountains are a whole different ball game. Not only do you have to be a good climber; you have to live with a different culture and infrastructure.'

David was deliberately very open with his personal philosophies. At night, we sat around the campfire and drank wine. He was particularly interested in the 'Person Centred Theory' of Carl Rogers.

While Freudian psychoanalysis focuses on abnormal behaviour, tracing it back to conflict between an innately primitive inner process (or 'Id') and a socially constructed 'Superego', Rogers' theory states that people are essentially good and healthy but their behaviour through life is affected by how the 'Self' develops by interacting with others. People, having experienced 'positive regard' from others (like their parents), develop conditions of worth and the continued need to feel positive regard. This leads them to develop a selective perception of the world and to seek out similar experiences. The problem is that this selection is based on the past and not on the present, which leads to 'incongruence' between the Self and the experience of the present even to the extent that the person is not fully conscious. David called this 'concept over experience.'

Rogers also refers to something called the 'actualising tendency' which is how the organism develops in order to fulfil its potential, through having all of its drives and motivations in line with its best possible interests at that moment. David gave me *On Becoming a Person* by Carl Rogers, and the following quote is from the book:

'Experience is, for me, the highest authority. The touchstone of validity is my own experience. No other person's ideas, and none of my own ideas, are as authoritative as my experience. It is to experience that I must return again and again, to discover a closer approximation to truth as it is in the process of becoming in me. Neither the Bible nor the prophets, neither Freud nor research, neither the revelations of God nor man, can take precedence over my own direct experience. My experience is not authoritative because it is infallible. It is the basis of authority because it can always be checked in new primary ways. In this way its frequent error or fallibility is always open to correction.'

In American and Western culture, conditions exist which reinforce behaviours that are perversions of the actualising tendency. For example, an advert encourages you to be a certain way, look, dress, talk or act differently to your actual experience.

David's remedy was to practice meditation which would help to step out of the 'the control train of thought'. He called this 'hanging out with the I thought'. He gave an example:

'I would ask myself; what am I doing? I am sitting on my backside, and my backside is sore. This is my direct experience. This is me, sitting on my butt, my butt is hurting and whose butt is hurting? Mine. Self-enquiry sucks. Who is having doubt? I am having doubt.'

The actualising tendency is a process, which can take your whole life. 'You may leave the process but then find it again. You have to listen to your heart. If you ignore it, it begins to lie and you might start believing in other things, like material gains – jobs, cars, etc. – as the main purpose. But if you listen to it, it will start to open up again with persistence.'

The following day, I got a lift with David into Budapest in his red Lada. On the way, he told me a traditional Indian story about Rama, a Hindu boy-god who is asked by some religious pilgrims for a mantra to get rid of demons. Rama is told by his guru to give them a story about the Buddha, who jumps mountains without thinking about it. He does godlike things and then forgets about what he has done. Through meditation, the mind is capable of incredible things but it doesn't require rational thought to achieve them because the thinking process also works unconsciously; bypassing linguistic, objectified, rational thought. There is a great deal of untapped potential.

Nadia came to visit Budapest and we went to the Gellért thermal baths together. Since the thirteenth century, references have been made about the healing waters, which contain calcium, magnesium, hydrocarbonate, alkalis, chloride, sulphate, and fluoride, providing a variety of health benefits.

The present building was built between 1912 and 1918 in an Art Nouveau style. It was rebuilt after being damaged in World War II. Inside, it feels like you are in an ostentatious fantasy world, surrounded by Art Nouveau statues and fountains. Neo-classical columns surround the pool and support the first floor balcony. The baths are warm and relaxing, but too hot for much swimming.

I went into the Sauna and then immediately into the chilly plunge pool. Not for the faint hearted. After the baths, we visited the castle on the hillside and looked over from Buda to Pest. The majority of tourist photos are taken of this view from the castle, so the council cleans the riverside façades of the buildings. The other sides are blacked with carbon deposits from car pollution.

The following day, as planned, we left the yurt but it felt a somewhat premature farewell. After only thirty kilometres, Tom pulled over to the roadside. His knee had not healed yet. He still couldn't cycle and needed to find a doctor to get his leg looked at. After asking various people, we found ourselves on a wild goose chase that took us round a number of completely run-down medical centres where no one spoke English. We tried to contact some Couchsurfers in the city centre but none replied so we cycled back to David's. It was frustrating to return to where we had started that day, but it was necessary and I was happy to be back at his place.

David had some turtles in a fish tank in the living room and said he wanted to build a pond for them so the next day I suggested we make one. I dug a one-metre deep hole in the garden, which we lined with waterproofing membrane and filled with water. David put the turtles in and observed their reaction to the new environment. He seemed pleased but hesitated for a moment, as if to confirm his thoughts, and then got into the pond himself.

He looked very content – quite like a turtle himself – moving slowly, and floating about with his big smile and flowing hair.

It was very satisfying to make the pond and to contribute something to David's abode. That evening, we sat around the fire again. The remaining sunlight was filtered by little patches of white cloud swirling around like vortex in freeze-frame. A powerful gust of wind disrupted the conversation and blew embers from the fire all over the garden. The chimney flap on the Yurt blew open and danced around chaotically. The rain began to fall in large drops, which splashed and displaced the dirt, leaving little indents. We gathered stuff off the lawn and balcony and hurriedly moved them into the house. I watched the sky flashing white. The day's humidity had culminated in an angry storm. Electricity built up and was released in clear, violent bolts. I couldn't recall ever seeing a storm like that in England. I gazed in awe at the dramatic show. Afterwards, the air was fresh; the storm had ended, offering a clean, fresh start.

David expressed his disdain for politeness and manners because of their ability to put you into a certain state of being. For example, a 'thank you' state if someone gives you something, or a 'sorry' state if you make a mistake.

I could relate to that with the British way of politeness but it surprised me that he said that he loved certain aspects of the British way of being. It hadn't occurred to me that Britishness was such a well-known phenomenon. It was so familiar to me that it was invisible.

David mentioned he had recently been reading about Sir Francis Younghusband, who was an explorer in British India. He had been elected the youngest member of the Royal Geographical Society and received the society's gold medal for pioneering a route through the uncharted Mustagh Pass.

He was appointed the British commissioner to Tibet and led an expedition there with the official purpose of settling disputes over Sikkim-Tibet, but the true aim was to establish British Hegemony. It was essentially an invasion and resulted in a massacre of 600-700 Tibetan monks.

On the retreat from Tibet, however, Younghusband had a mystical experience, which suffused him with 'love for the whole world', lead him to regret the invasion, and drove him to set up the World Congress of Faiths. David said that this kind of strange occurrence was typically British.

21

English Girls Make the Pedals Go Round

One afternoon, we went to the Széchenyi baths in Budapest, built in 1879 in a Neo-Baroque style. The main swimming pool was surrounded by numerous other pools and spas. People chatted or floated around, enjoying the sociable atmosphere and calming warm water.

After leaving the baths, we went into the city to meet some fellow Couchsurfers. Maria and Magalie were two English girls travelling together, nineteen and twenty respectively. They attended the Brit School together: a theatre-studies sixth form college in London. Maria was English but lived in New York. She was blond, slim, and athletic with an infectious energy behind big eyes. Magalie had dark brown hair and an instantly disarming and playful personality. We went to a Turkish restaurant together and then to a rooftop bar Couchsurfing party. Soon I was talking and relaxing with a group of people from a variety of countries.

Later in the night, Maria said, 'Andy, Tom suggested we come with you tomorrow, what do you think?'

'A brilliant idea!' I replied.

We celebrated by going into the dancefloor. A disco ball cast dots against the walls. If you concentrated on the dots and not the floor, it got very disorientating, or maybe it was just the beer. David was dancing like a lunatic, swinging his arms around like a windmill, although there was something graceful about his unselfconscious movements. It looked like a cross between an Indian dance and a Tibetan shamanistic ritual. His dances seemed to match well with electro rave music from the nineties.

The girls didn't have bikes yet so we went to a scrap yard and picked up three for fifty Euros and then, the following afternoon, we left the Yurt.

The weather was drizzly and grey as we pedalled down the misty road. In the evening, we camped on a football pitch. Tom and I were used to the camping ritual but the others weren't and, to them, it was new and interesting and that made it fun.

The next day, the sun shone. We stuck to the back roads and used just the compass to navigate. The roads had degraded into a sandy track when we decided to stop for the day.

There was a farmhouse. I knocked on the door and it was answered by a middle-aged man who understood when I made the usual gestures for sleeping. He and his wife, who made a sweet couple and were obviously deeply in love, seemed excited to meet us. Their children had flown the nest and they seemed to be living on the memories of happy family life. The man appeared with a bottle of 'Pálinka', a traditional brandy made from plums that packs a punch. We were given one shot after another until I was quite drunk. We ate a wonderful spread of food and shared stories with our hosts. For Maria and Magalie, it was an eye-opening experience; it was the first time they had experienced this kind of hospitality.

The next morning we returned to the sandy track, which was almost impossible to cycle down. We strained to push the heavy bikes and the tyres slid and sunk into the sand.

After five miles, we got back to tarmac and stopped for supplies. I felt that people were reacting differently to us. Children took more notice and sometimes ran after us or shouted things. People looked poorer.

Beside the country roads were many apple trees, which we took advantage of for energy. There were thickets of cannabis plants growing and the air had a pungent, organic smell.

We would normally stop outside urban areas to camp, but this time we found ourselves in the suburb of a large Hungarian town. We ventured up a side road and at the end was a large house with a pond. The owner came out of his house and ushered us over. He introduced himself as Fahri and said we could camp in his garden.

In the morning, Tom and I were having an argument (we were now sharing a tent). Our banter was broken up by the arrival of our host's partner with a tray of Pálinka shots for breakfast. It certainly did the trick to diffuse the argument, resetting my consciousness as I grimaced at the strong tangy alcohol.

After one more day of cycling, Magalie caught the train back to France. She had enjoyed the experience so much though that she would be back again to join us later in the journey.

22

Border Troubles

'Assess the day's activities and reproach and rejoice them.
Go through what one has done and assess the ethics and
actions'
– Pythagoras verses

In the EU, you can pass between countries without hindrance so
we hadn't thought much about crossing the borders. I looked at
the map with Tom and he showed me the line between Hungary
and Romania. It was just a line on a map but it signified a new
country and a destination successfully reached.

We asked around in a small village for directions to the border.
I gestured east saying 'Romania'. In response, people seemed to
indicate that the border was there and could be reached via a
small road but then appeared to provide some additional
information, which we couldn't understand because of the
language barrier. We chose, perhaps rather foolishly, to ignore
this, and instead follow the road. At the end there was a steel
barrier painted in the national colours of Romania. Great, we had
reached another country! It was time to celebrate so Tom filmed
Maria and me crossing the border, messing about, and jumping
from one side to another.

We continued down the road into the first village and I could
immediately see a difference in the landscape. Rows of
ramshackle houses were joined by a rocky, unpaved track. A
disused tractor sat rusting in a field. Chickens squawked and
flapped around in the road and pigs nuzzled about on the
ground.

I talked to an old man, dressed in a grimy red shirt, grey

trousers stained with oil, and worn black leather shoes with a hole where his toe poked out. He comprehended nothing of my attempt to communicate through hand gestures. Maria attempted to speak Spanish, which didn't work either. Romanian is a Latin language and supposedly, it is the most similar to Spanish. However, they are not mutually comprehensible. I tried to speak to an old lady who was hobbling about outside her house but she gestured her hand in a sweeping fashion shooing me away.

There was a shop in the village and an attempt was made to communicate but to no avail. People stared at us and a group of children gathered round my bike trying to fiddle with the gears. One pulled at the trailer flag. A man with a thickly set jaw and unwelcoming look in his eye ambled up to us in an attempt to look threatening and succeeded. The weather was grey and overcast and a mysterious emptiness hung in the air. With this friendly welcome we decided to make haste as fast as possible further into the country.

It felt like we'd travelled back to another era. A solitary shepherd, ghostly looking, followed his flock alongside a rusty rail track. Dry grassland stretched to the horizon and in the far distance were haze-tinted hills. The feeling of space and wilderness was sudden and unnerving. I felt attracted to it and repelled by it in equal measure.

The next town was a soulless grey outpost. The grid of potholed streets was sided by box-like, concrete buildings with tin roofs in various states of repair or construction.

We went into a little shop, constructed from bare concrete blocks with large windowpanes and cracked glass. The shelves were stocked with just a few tins and supplies. I asked a man, who looked like a farmer, about camping and he seemed to understand and pointed up one of the side roads.

We followed the rutted, uneven track; dodging puddles, and potholes. We passed a few villagers and a group of children playing. At the end of the track an enormous pile of household rubbish, which we avoided, and found ourselves walking out onto a vast plain, dotted with only a few small barns and stray dogs. We rode aimlessly into the space. Progress was slow, since it was difficult to ride on the damp squashy grass. I tried to feel a bit cheerier. I told myself this was a great adventure and we were really getting out into the wild places. I was naïve and inexperienced.

We asked a man working by one of the cattle sheds if we could pitch the tents beside his barn to be more sheltered from the wind. I sensed something, which made me feel uneasy. The wind grew stronger. The deep dark clouds hung like giant gorillas, waiting to swing down and beat the ground with mighty hairy fists.

I got out the guide ropes to better secure the tent. Large droplets of rain began to splash down. I felt a little tired from the day's riding. Twilight descended. I began to wonder what to do about dinner. We only had food that required cooking so I figured that I should probably try to cook in the porch of the tent, but I was stopped mid-thought-process by two sets of headlight beams that swung round towards us through the rain. The cars parked beside the tents. I strained through the darkness to see our unexpected visitors. There were five men in total. One man started to speak in Romanian. He realised we didn't speak Romanian and barked 'Passport, passport!'

I thought, 'Bugger, we're going to have our identities stolen, our women raped, and tents burnt in a medieval rousting.'

I attempted to ask why but the man insisted we give him the passports with increasing urgency. I went into my tent and sifted around in the darkness, feeling increasingly frustrated. Upon passing it over, I looked at Tom. He returned a worried but stoical glance.

I asked to see some identification. They were the border police. The policeman took our passports and told us to pack up the tents and go with them. We had cycled ninety-five kilometres that day and not yet eaten. Psychologically, I had prepared myself for a relaxing evening and night's sleep in the tent and now I was going to undo everything and pack it all back onto the bike in a fast-intensifying rainstorm.

The immediacy of the moment was accentuated by a heart-stopping bolt of lightning that struck the ground and flashed like a giant camera in front of my eyes. Adrenalin kicked in. I continued to obey the police and pack.

I quickly bundled my belongings into my bags. I was worried about leaving something behind in the dark but luckily found my head torch on the grass. I thought the police were going to give us a lift but quickly realised that they wanted us to walk, somewhere, as yet, undefined.

As suddenly as they had arrived, the cars disappeared, leaving us in the pitch black with a young guard. Maria walked ahead with the guard. Lightning forked down nearby on the plain. Devoid of tall things to earth to, it seemed God was randomly selecting and exploding poor cattle into balls of sizzling, flame-grilled beef – which was a tantalising thought on an empty stomach.

I frantically scanned the ground for items left behind, grabbed my bike, and followed the others. The path was illuminated only by my head torch; scything, sideways rain sliced into me; lightning turned night to day for split seconds at a time.

The guard suddenly pointed and exclaimed something in Romanian into the darkness. In hindsight, I'd take a guess it was 'look out for the terrifying dog'. A huge, grubby-faced, grey and black mastiff – lit up by a perfectly timed flash of lightning – hurled its snarling jaws at my face. Bloodshot, wild, and rabid eyes met mine; sour spit, and bitter mucus flew this way and that. But enough about me; I jumped back. The foul smelling beast vied to take a chunk of polystyrene helmet or preferably something meatier but luckily it missed by a fraction.

My hair was waterlogged and water covered my face. I smelt the fresh rain and breathed it in. It tasted like steel and salt. It was the first shower for a few days. Ice-cold water drenched my clothes and streamed down my spine and legs and into my boots, which filled to the brink.

We walked the couple of kilometres back to the dark town,

over the muddy grass, onto the street, which was now a slippery mud bath. A police van was waiting for us. I chucked my things inside. I was sure the policemen were grinning at us.

The door slid shut and soon we were aquaplaning along a wet road at high speed. The windscreen steamed up and the policeman wiped it for the driver. I filmed a little: three drenched, pitiful, humans but still smiling. It became absurd. Having made it to the relative safety of the dry van, a sense of euphoria began to kick in. We started joking and laughing. In absurdity, there was a sense of true freedom in not knowing what was going on.

We arrived at a large concrete building at the official Hungarian-Romanian border: a town called Varsand. We were met by an angry moustached man who explained that we had crossed the border at the wrong place and that's why we had been brought here.

We sat in the lobby whilst the officials checked our papers. After a few hours, they set us free and we crossed once again from Hungary into Romania, this time with a little less celebrating but greater sense of certainty. At the duty free shop on the Romanian side, we drank a celebratory beer and then slept on the tables.

23

Romania

'All experience has a positive side and the possibility to learn attached to it'
– David

The morning brought eerie foreboding weather, as if the weather-maker had fallen ill for the day and couldn't be bothered to make proper weather. Summoning the motivation to leave the warmth of the border restaurant was difficult. I donned all of my waterproof clothes: socks, trousers, jacket, thermal Lycra dungarees, neoprene over-boots, and two of my Buff hats. I looked like a deep-sea diver rather than a cyclist. I questioned my sanity for a brief moment as I pedalled along the cold, misty road. Visibility was reduced to two bike lengths around me.

Having not eaten anything the night before, we decided to sit in the bus shelter and cook a chilli stew on the stove. Eating lifted my energy levels immensely. As we were rinsing the plates in a puddle by the road, some people turned up to wait for the bus. Unsurprisingly, we got some funny looks.

The road ploughed for miles into the plain. Romania was a shock to the senses. It was a stark change from Hungary, which had been only slightly different to Austria in terms of feeling and looking Western European.

It was difficult to understand how one side of a border could appear to be so much more wild and poor than the other. This was the first of many illustrations that countries don't gradually change as you go along; borders can have a real affect, culturally and economically, because they make people think they are separate.

I was scared of Romania at first because it looked poor and destitute. Agriculture was the mainstay of the rural economy. I saw a shepherd and contemplated his daily tasks involved in looking after the animals. It looked very boring, but then I thought that maybe he sometimes needed to fight off wolves.

A shepherd must know his plot of land and the weather incredibly well: traits that are important, in general, for an essential human synthesis with the environment. However, these faculties are perhaps being lost in the distractions of mediatised society, which values the representation of something more than the real thing.

In the villages, there seemed to be very few young people about. I passed rows of houses set back from the road with walled front gardens. Old people sat outside their homes and looked over at us. All sorts of domesticated animals roamed around: horses, hens, dogs, sheep, and geese. I thought of my grandparents on their farm in England. I imagined Romania could have been like England in the 1950s.

Having Maria about was great. She added warmth, humour, and a level-headedness that had been lacking between Tom and me. She was a mediator and brought some much needed female energy.

We passed some small farm-holdings by the roadside. I'd never seen a horse and cart used for real farm work before. A family were driving a cart loaded with manure. A man whipped the horse and grappled with the reigns to keep control.

Geographically speaking, I was still relatively close to my home in England but the industrial time-shift was very visible. 'If they managed with a horse and cart then why change?' I wondered, 'because you can take more, faster, with tractor or a truck; and because more, faster, and more money is better?'

That evening, we turned off the main road to look for somewhere to camp. I asked a guard at what looked like the grounds of a hotel, but it turned out to be a castle that was being used as a psychiatric hospital.

We decided to find a good campsite on a hillside. The sun's warming rays emerged pleasurably from between the remnants of rain clouds. The grassland was illuminated, turning from grey to a warm, glowing colour. The sun in the middle distance lit up areas of the land through gaps in the cloud. We hauled the bikes up the hill until we found a spot to camp; gorse, and thistle free. We set up the tents and enjoyed the last minutes of the afternoon sun.

It felt good to look down from the hillside over the last of the flat, Hungarian plains and know we were moving on to the next stage in the journey. It was a relief because I was bored of flat land. I could see the foothills of the Făgăraş Mountains in the other direction.

I looked over at the small village not far from the hill where our campsite was positioned. There were small, similar, basic-looking houses. Green trees were dotted amongst the houses and gardens. A few modern cars were juxtaposed against the settlement and they looked out of place against the rustic simplicity of the houses. Hay bales were stacked up outside a few of the properties. Each house had its own animals. It was different to anything I'd seen so far.

In England, villages have become luxurious places to live, containing expensive houses. Health and the natural environment have become commodities for the rich to buy. In Romania, it looked like the village hadn't changed much for hundreds of years.

I appreciated the company of Tom and Maria. I realised how important it is to really listen to people. Two people can be living similar lives but be in completely different personal universes as far as perception and experience is concerned. Nature and nurture, upbringing, and independent life experiences mean that everyone has their own unique trajectory in life.

It's easy to go through life seeing everything through your own lens and assuming that other people see things the same way, but this is not so. I think that a part of me expected Tom to see things similarly to me in most cases. Often we did see things the same way, and there were some similarities in our pasts, but the complexity of life is in the details and the present moment. It's a bit like navigating. A small change of course can mean ending up in vastly different places.

Tom was building a campfire and I was about to start preparing dinner when a man turned up on a motocross bike to check on us. It was his land, but he didn't mind us camping and was very friendly and he soon left to go back down to the village. It was nice to have his blessing. If I had permission to sleep somewhere, I tended to sleep better, because I was less worried about being disturbed in the night.

The night was clear and windless. The smoke from the fire rose straight up towards the stars. I lay back and breathed deeply – at which point I smelt a nasty smell of burning plastic. I realised I had placed my waterproof socks too close to the fire and they were melting.

The following morning we left early. On the road were tractors, horse drawn carts, and a contraption like something out of *Mad Max*. It looked like a car with only the engine and a seat, and instead of the steering wheel were wide, swept-back handlebars.

We reached the town of Deva. People were gathered in bustling crowds outside the bank cash-points to take their wages. I noticed that many people had darker skin and dark, liquid brown eyes.

I didn't want people to see me just as a rich tourist from Western Europe because I didn't identify myself as one. Instead, I hoped people would see the hard work that had gone into cycling this far. I couldn't escape from where I had started. Thinking like this frustrated me and I wished I could just forget it all and be a person on a bike and not a sportsman on a mission.

We were very conspicuous with our flash bikes and trailers and this had its positive and negative side effects. A part of me wished I looked like a dirty tramp on the oldest, most rundown bike possible so that people wouldn't take a second glance.

In a village called Descera, a local took us to an English-speaking lady in a bar. She showed us to a patch of grass, in an apple orchard behind a church, where we could camp. The church looked either half built or half destroyed. It was something I'd never seen in England. The churches in the villages near to my home were usually very old, quaint, neatly kept, and built by monks and peasants around the 14th century.

In the adjacent field, a group of children were playing football in the balmy, late-afternoon sun. The sunset was bright pink and it seemed to go on for ages.

The next morning was crisp and clear and there was dew on the grass outside my tent. We followed the road through a mountain valley, carpeted in lush grassland and dark green pine forest. A meandering stream snaked along the foot of the valley. We looked for a place to camp at a village. I asked a family in a house. An old lady tending to their garden said we could camp on the grassland down by the river. In the centre was a pagoda on a concrete foundation, usually for village events, upon which we could put the tents.

There was lots of wood washed up on the riverbank from when the river had been in flood. When building a fire, placing the wood stacked like a Jenga game is the best for warmth. The typical Tepee fire is best for cooking as it concentrates the heat to one point. I hung up clothes to dry beside the fire. It was a luxury to have dry clothes, even if they were dirty. I had got used to the smell and dirt by now anyway.

The following morning we climbed for about an hour or two out of a bowl shaped valley. It could have been 'The Shire' from *The Lord of the Rings;* simple, quaint little houses nestled between leafy green trees with a fluffy covering of mist.

A lunch of chunks of bread and bean stew was consumed in a bus stop at the peak of the hill. Rain would start pattering on the roof and then stop and then start again. The clouds danced around the sky, causing the landscape to change colour like a chameleon: some areas in sunlight, and others shrouded in a blue-grey veil of rain.

Every hill I cycled was a challenge but thankfully, each time I got to the top, I got the same feeling of relief and excitement about flying down the other side, which made the effort worth it. Down, down, down – distance with no effort and time to gaze at the landscape: green hills, woodland coppice, haystacks propped up with long branches, a church steeple rising above a sleepy village, houses with red sloping roofs, and a tethered horse grazing, tearing at tufts of grass. Patches of grey cloud permeated the sky like watercolour brush strokes threatening to run.

At the next village, there were many cars and people, and a field full of stalls and tents selling various wares. We followed our noses and found a stall selling barbecued sausages and beer. Afterwards we found a place to camp on some farmer's land and the farmer himself came, chopped wood for us, and gave us armfuls of fresh grapes.

The next evening, Maria asked some women who were standing by the roadside about a place to sleep. There was a group of children playing around them. The women, probably in their mid-twenties, looked poor, but were smiling. They giggled amongst themselves at Maria's request and then appeared to be conferring. One of the women, who was holding a baby, invited us to stay at her house.

She lived on a scruffy plot of land off a street lined with a number of similar ramshackle dwellings. The plot contained two buildings. One looked like a half-built house. It had no windows and the brickwork looked poorly finished.

The other building contained one room and we went inside. It smelt heavily of unwashed humans. On the walls hung fabric decorated with a flowery pattern. There was a bed, a sofa, a small coffee table in the centre, and a chest of drawers, on top of which was a widescreen television.

We were ushered to sit down and a large bottle of fizzy orange drink was produced. The woman put on the satellite television and switched it to a channel that showed traditional Romanian music. She turned it up until it was practically impossible to communicate over the racket. Evidently, they were proud of their television.

The entire family lived together including the ageing grandmother. She was dressed all in black and wore no shoes. Her skin was wrinkly and her hands looked weathered and leathery. The mother of the baby spent most of the time rocking the child and tending to it, whilst the other two children made nuisances of themselves, running about, screaming, and fighting.

We were brought some plates of tomato, accompanied by a small pile of salt and some pieces of rubbery pig fat. I placed a piece in my mouth and had to chew it for ages before I could swallow it. Thankfully, my cycle-induced hunger enabled me to eat anything.

I asked to use the toilet and was pointed down the garden where there was a small hut built from pieces of what looked like waste ply-board. Inside, there was a plank to sit on with a circle cut out of it.

Underneath the hut was a deep hole full of crap. It was my first experience of this type of toilet. I felt ashamed to crap into a dark hole behind the house of my host and there was a thick, earthy smell that made it difficult to breathe. Flies buzzed around my backside as I pulled my trousers up and hastily got out of there. The toilet served its purpose perfectly well.

The television continued to blare loud distracting noises. The channel was changed to a pop music video. Scantily clad women shook large rear ends and wide-boys with aviator sunglasses sported gold chains and shuffled around next to an expensive, shiny car. It was strange to sit with the poor family who seemed to have very few possessions and watch this materialistic orgy on television. However, bizarrely, they appeared thoroughly captivated by it.

As the evening progressed, I grew tired. The old women noticed my tiredness and prepared some bedding for me to lie down on the sofa. My legs hung over the end.

After some time, Maria said, 'I really don't feel well.' She staggered to the door. For the next two hours, she alternated between the bed, the toilet, and a bucket in the yard. The only running water was from a tap outside the front door of the building. She eventually recovered and was able to fall asleep.

I woke in the night and looked around me. Earlier, I had fallen asleep before the family had. I was surprised to see the entire family sleeping on the floor of the room, including, to my horror, the grandmother. I thought they would sleep in another room. I realised that they had given up their beds so we could have some comfort. It was very touching but I felt ashamed.

The following morning we were getting the bikes in order to leave and I noticed our helmets were missing. I looked around but couldn't see them. After twenty minutes of searching and a considerable fuss, they mysteriously appeared on my handlebars. The two naughty children looked very guilty.

Maria was very weak, but she managed to pedal. We were aiming to reach a town called Sebeș where we were planning to have a day off. Some of the villages we passed through looked like slums, with ramshackle buildings, dirt tracks, and not a square metre of tarmac in sight. Piles of litter were tipped by the roadside and people hung about, seemingly without purpose.

In a village called Blandiana, a man invited us in out of the rain. He ran a little bakery beside his house. We sat in the warmth and my senses were intoxicated by the delicious smell of fresh baking. The baker cooked us some hot vegetable pasties that were extremely tasty.

On the way into Sebeș, we had to follow a busy main road. Cars passed too close for comfort and eventually Tom lost it. He pulled off the road, took off his helmet, kicked it high into the air, then took the video camera and shouted 'Fuck!' into it at the top of this voice.

In Sebeș, we couldn't find anywhere to stay. We were too tired and wet to be bothered to camp.

I went to ask someone in a petrol station. A man who could have passed for Italian, in a black leather jacket, and black jeans, offered to let us stay with him. I grinned at Tom 'Something always works itself out in the end, doesn't it?'

We followed the man to the outskirts of the town along a dirt track road scattered with water-filled potholes. Each house along the street looked like it was either in a state of construction or repair. Some had big gates and walls and some were no more than shacks.

Alex's house was quite small, but it was hidden behind huge gates. There was a concrete driveway and a muddy patch of grass and steps led up into the front room. There were two rooms in the house: the kitchen and a large bedroom. The kitchen was painted a sour yellow colour. There was a sparse selection of cheap looking plastic furniture and some veneered, seventies style kitchen units.

Tom, Maria and I sat at the dining table, and drank coffee. Magalie had arrived on the train to rejoin us in the early morning.

Alex's wife, Gabbi, cooked some food at the stove. There wasn't a bathroom in the house: just a wood-shack toilet in the backyard. Maria and Magalie were offered the opportunity to take a shower at Gabbi's mother's house.

After they left, Alex prompted us to sit down at the dining table with him. He began telling a sob story whereby he indicated he had no food; he made a hand movement across his stomach to communicate hunger and said he had no money to pay for his child's schooling. He then took out a piece of paper and scribbled down some numbers, eventually settling on a figure of two hundred Euros for one night's stay.

I felt a mix of guilt and anger at this. I wondered if he had planned it from the moment he met us. Tom was furious and snatched the piece of paper. He drew a picture of an earth with a bicycle and arrow going around it and underneath he wrote '200 Euros = 56 days food.' Alex was silent.

24

To The Mountains

We packed our belongings and sat outside the front door. I didn't know what Alex's reaction to our refusal to hand over money would be. We gave him forty-five LEI – about fifteen pounds – to cover the food and coffee. Maria and Magalie arrived back, chatting buoyantly with Gabbi. We explained to the girls what had happened and swiftly left. I felt betrayed and disappointed. Also, I felt tired and I needed a good night's sleep.

I felt better when we had left Sebeş behind. We rode out towards the mountains, passing sporadic housing developments on the outskirts of the town.

We arrived in an eerie looking village. The houses looked rickety, the streets dark and unlit, and there was rubbish strewn by the roadside. However, I felt protected somehow by the mountains. Maria had become frustrated by our inability to decide on a place to sleep and was getting sick of the fruitless bickering. She asked someone about accommodation and, soon, a large crowd of locals had gathered to see what was going on. The people looked shabby, dirty and poor but they were full of energy and curiosity. Soon someone had offered us a bed for the night.

We followed our new host down a rocky track over a concrete bridge to a line of small houses on the other side of the river. It felt weird to be accepting hospitality again so soon after Sebeş and I felt paranoid that we would get into a similar situation, even though we had had only one bad experience and many good ones.

Our hosts, Ornesto and Felicha, lived in a one storey wooden building with two small rooms. The first room acted as a kitchen and bedroom. In the corner, there was a wood burning stove for heat and cooking. The second room was larger. It contained two single beds at opposite sides of the room. On the far wall hung a carpet showing a very kitsch image depicting Jesus with light beaming from his head. In front of the carpet was a small shrine with some candles and, beside that, a television. There was a dark wood cabinet containing a collection of tacky looking crockery, but in general, our hosts appeared to have very few non-essential possessions.

Felicha was a tough-looking woman. She had a squinting eye and short, jet-black hair and was always smiling. Ornesto was a well-built man with olive-coloured skin. His face had a large scar across the cheek. He wore a sleeveless vest that showed his muscular arms, one of which sported a tattoo from his days in the army. After finishing his military service, he had been unable to find work, which had made life very difficult. They both emanated a strength born of living simple lives that required daily physical exertion.

We had a cup of tea and cooked Spaghetti Bolognese. Felicha and Ornesto refused our food at first but eventually accepted a plate.

A storm broke out and lightning flashed, followed shortly by a power cut. We sat by candlelight in refuge from the storm. I was quite glad we weren't camping.

I asked if I could have some water to wash. In hindsight, this was probably rather selfish because Ornesto insisted on warming water on the stove for me, which used up firewood. Whilst the others sat and chatted in the other room, I stripped down and bathed in a small tin bath in the kitchen. Luckily I'd just finished and managed to grab my towel before the entire extended family turned up to meet us. There were cousins young and old. I didn't get everyone's name but all were friendly and curious to meet us.

I was glad to get a good night's sleep in a comfortable bed. In the morning, I awakened to the smell of mushrooms frying in breadcrumbs on the stove. Ornesto had walked into the mountains before dawn to pick them and they were the most delicious mushrooms I had ever tasted. The white, fleshy meat had a texture somewhere between an omelette and a juicy piece of steak. Accompanying this was homemade jam, bread and a spicy meat soup.

I was incredibly grateful. The negative stories I had heard of gypsy communities in the mountains were incongruent with my experience. We bade them farewell and, as we left, we saw some children playing in a homemade go-kart on the embankment beside the river. As I pushed my bike towards the bridge that we had come over the night before, a horse burst out of the forest and cantered down to the water to drink.

Seeing the wild creature doing as it pleased was particularly memorable. It exuded a strong personality and grandeur. None of the villagers seemed to bat an eyelid at the horse's dramatic entrance. The children continued to play without reacting.

Ahead of us lay the climb into the Fǎgǎraş Mountains. The weather was sunny and it awakened my spirit; my lungs scooped in the fresh air. We saw very little traffic other than an occasional logging truck.

We stopped at a rare shop to get some supplies and the only car we had seen all day, a shiny Audi saloon, pulled up. The driver gave us a note to show to the owner of a cabin in the mountain. The note read, 'Please help these nice people.' If we found the cabin then we would be guaranteed a place to sleep.

We found a great campsite and decided to spend two days there. Even in that short time, I began to develop a sense of place. I collected firewood and cleared access to the river for water. I hung our ten-litre water carrier in a tree so that it could be used to take a shower.

At the pass, I emerged to a view over a blue lake stretching ahead of me. The view was well worth the effort of the climb. We continued around the side of the lake and found a large, solitary building on the top of the embankment. We went inside and returned with the owner who, on seeing the note, gave us a room, free of charge. 'My, my, my, you have come a long way and it is very hard to ride a push bike in the mountains. There are some bikers staying here, from Scotland, but their bikes have engines!'

In the evening, we met Dougie, who was leading the group of motorcyclists. He offered us soup and cherry liqueur. He loved the mountains in Romania and had been working for the motorbike guiding company for some years.

In the morning, there was a sharp frost and I was jealous of the motorcyclists who were eating a huge fried breakfast. Tom had the inspired idea of asking if we could scavenge their leftovers. We took bags of sausages and bread and ate fried eggs and mushrooms from the table. It was lucky because we had no money and there was no shop until the next settlement: thirty-five kilometres after the next mountain pass.

The road turned to dirt track; reddish-ochre in colour, rough and rutted, strewn with small rocks. In winter, when the snow melted or when it rained, the road most likely turned into a drainage channel. We climbed for hours. I split off from the others and became lost in a trance of pedalling. It was so peaceful. I could hear nothing but the wind in the trees.

When I was a child, I used to go down to the stream at the bottom of the field behind my house and play for hours, either alone or with my friends. We would try to walk along the length of the streambed and we would have to duck under brambles and wade through sticky, smelly, thick clay-mud, avoiding the tangle of weeds. There was a tranquillity which immersed me in my own world. There was no practical application to traversing the path of the stream but I was playing for the sake of it. Being alone in the mountains, doing just as I pleased, I felt a similar sense of freedom and adventure.

The road went downhill for around 300m and I could see over a forested valley. The trailer bounced and weaved as I freewheeled down the track. Water and dirt splashed up from puddles. The tyres churned and slid through pools of mud. I held tightly onto the handlebars for control.

In the next valley, some gypsies were living in tents made from plastic sheeting pinned over some simple wooden structures. I couldn't believe people were living like that in Europe. They looked like refugees. Were they workers? I didn't know.

We got some supplies in a small shop and then pedalled until we reached another lake. I spun my legs effortlessly. We came across a sign for a hotel, which pointed down a dirt track and reached a building, which was held up by rickety, wooden scaffolding. I approached the doorway, which led into a dimly lit bar where there was a woman sweeping up.

She stopped what she was doing and walked over to me. She had frizzy, grey hair, and a cigarette hung from her pursed lips. I explained that we wanted to find somewhere to sleep. She grunted something in response, clearly annoyed that we weren't paying guests. I pushed my bike in the direction she indicated and a gargantuan, concrete tower block of Soviet-style hotel apartments came into view. Most of the windows were smashed and there were long cracks in the outer walls. It looked like a film set for a war film.

I went up to one of the buildings and peaked in. It reminded me of a school that had fallen into disrepair. There were long corridors and eerie empty rooms. Maria was exploring the upper floors and found a room covered with papers scrawled with calculations and numbers. Bizarrely, another was filled with piles of old pairs of shoes.

I didn't sleep well that night. The eeriness of the building infiltrated my dreams. I dreamt of long infinite tunnels and corridors. I endlessly trudged along them, opening random doors to reveal nothing, rubbish, or disjointed memories from my past.

I'm sure the dream represented my journey, and the meetings, occurrences, and discoveries it contained recalled pieces of information from my previous experience of life. Instead of being presented in a linear order, they were spread around; linked by the process of travel. I was trying to make sense of my experiences through past memories. Alternatively, perhaps I was seeing the reality of my former, static life, which was made up of a string of memories of images seen in the media and fragmented social meetings with no joining narrative; the product of a mind born into a western society and subjected to a stream of more or less ordered, externally conceived information, its entire life. What was real and what was fake? My brain had no way of knowing. It was near impossible to get an objective perspective from which to analyse or understand my subconscious reaction to the journey's experiences. Perhaps this was a reflection of the seeking process in general: sometimes offering a way forward and sometimes not.

To add to the strangeness of that night, I was awoken abruptly by something jumping onto the upper side of the tent. I started, and almost tore a hole in the roof. Tom didn't seem to notice as he grunted and turned over. I presumed it was the dog, but I never did find out; when I checked outside the door, there was nothing to be seen.

Early the next morning we climbed up to a mountain pass and flew down the other side. I screamed at the top of my lungs and went so fast that I couldn't breathe. Everything was fantastic until, out of the corner of my eye, I noticed Maria's bike wobbling dangerously out of control and then flipping over, sending her bumping heavily onto the ground. I skidded to a halt and ran over to her. She got up slowly and, luckily, was only grazed and in shock. The ancient tyres on her town bike were not built to deal with rough mountain roads and patches of slippery oil.

I spotted a waterfall and we stopped for a swim. After we had cleaned Maria's wounds, I stripped down to my cycling shorts and tiptoed into the water. I plunged myself joyfully under the flow. The entire volume of the river's water fell onto my back providing a pummelling massage. The clear water cascaded powerfully: cold, and refreshing.

We continued on to Voineasa, a sightseeing village on the edge of the mountains where tourists often went to start treks and climbs. There was a good selection of supplies. We bought lunch and consumed the Romanian equivalent of Chelsea buns, fruit turnovers, and beer for the cheap price of thirty pence.

Pedalling on, we passed over a hydroelectric dam. I paused on the bridge and gazed down at the sheer drop, lined by a smooth concrete wall. The others swooped down the road into the valley below.

In the evening, I called my parents. My cousin Sarah was getting married. It was also my grandparents' sixtieth wedding anniversary. I felt I was missing things that were happening with my family but I was also having my own experience, which was important.

In the next town, we wound our way up a busy, and therefore dangerous, road. Cars were overtaking two abreast on a single lane. People accelerated, blindly overtook, and then pulled in quickly at the last second to avoid being flattened by oncoming lorries. Without warning, a grey hatchback skidded uncontrollably round a tight bend. Perhaps the driver hadn't noticed me. A tonne of roaring metal and screeching tyres passed far too close for comfort. The driver was going too fast, had over-steered, and was fighting for control of the vehicle. I cursed at the top of my lungs; I couldn't believe the stupidity of some drivers.

Tom and I reached the top of the climb. I stopped at the brink of the hill and threw my arms in the air. I screamed and fell back onto the grass. The girls arrived slowly. Maria had three gears on her town bike so it was no good for hills. They had looks of determination, but brought bad news.

A pack of wild dogs had attacked them. Maria had managed to kick one of them in the jaw but Magalie had hesitated and had been bitten on the back of one of her ankles. She was quite nonchalant about it. 'I just got bitten by a dog.'

'You need to get the required medication within twenty four hours, because of rabies,' I said.

She washed the wound at a water point outside a farmhouse. Coincidently, the occupant was a veterinary surgeon. He thought it would be okay if Magalie washed it well as it wasn't long since she had been bitten. That seemed to take some of the urgency off the situation for Magalie, but I wasn't convinced. 'I will go to the doctor when I get back home,' she protested.

The weather was muggy – the kind that brings you down if you're not careful. We asked about somewhere to stay from a lady sitting by a table, selling bottles of Pálinka outside her house. She didn't know about anywhere to sleep but she gave us a bottle of brandy for free. Although in general, perhaps, drink wasn't what we needed.

The weather decided what it was going to do as we arrived in a town called Pitesti – and, unsurprisingly, it rained. It was a typical Soviet style town, with concrete tower blocks, rusty iron balconies, and grand municipal buildings. I was getting sick of being drenched to the skin. Cars sprayed water, which soaked my trousers, but whenever things started to degrade into a miserable situation, a survival mechanism was activated and my mood would get a boost. My sense of humour always kicks in and I can't help but see the funny side to things.

We were soaked to the skin and asking people for a place to stay. A number of people suggested we ask at the hospital. It seemed like a reliable place to find accommodation and my mood heightened. When we reached the hospital the guard spoke no English and decided to ignore us so, disgruntled, we carried on down the road, aiming to get away from the built up area and find a place to camp in the countryside.

There was a farm on the way. None of the workers spoke English, although they seemed to understand that we were looking for a place to stay. We continued. Eventually a man stopped us 'Where are you going?' he said.

'We are going into the countryside.'

'You can't go down there; it's getting dark,' the man protested, 'there are gypsies and thieves and it's dangerous.'

The man insisted we go back and ask at the farm, and he came with us to translate, which brought some success. We put our bikes into a barn. Many workers, ages ranging from young to middle-aged, gathered to watch us. As we were led into the building, I wondered what we had got ourselves into. I walked down a bare corridor and arrived into a dormitory packed with dirty and scruffy looking families. Everyone crowded around us. I felt very uneasy. I didn't know if I could trust the people and I was worried about our things being stolen.

I didn't get the chance to find out because the owners of the farm arrived and invited us into their house. I felt relieved about not staying in the farm with the workers but I felt guilty for distrusting the people and I was disappointed not to learn more about them.

We arrived at the farmer's apartment in the nearby town. It was small with a few rooms. We were invited to sit at the dining table, which was laid with a plate of smoked meat and cheese which we washed down with shots of cherry brandy.

Maria spoke in Spanish with the farmer's wife. They got on very well. It looked like Maria had found a long lost aunt. Her name was also Maria – a popular name in Romania. She worked as a hairdresser and offered to organise a hair cut for us, which was irresistible considering the state we were in. Her son's name was Marian and he was studying in college hoping to get a job in Western Europe. Her daughter arrived at the flat and sat with us at the table. She worked as a financial advisor and her husband worked for the mayor of Bucharest.

'There is still a lot of corruption in the government,' she said. 'He gets only two hundred Euros a month salary, which is frustrating when he sees money wasted on inefficient bureaucracy.'

His job was stressful and he was often expected to travel away from his family. The incentive was the abstract notion that after fifteen years of work they would receive an apartment. The father said that he thought things would get better since Romania joined the EU.

The following morning, we bade farewell to the family. I wanted to get to Bucharest quickly and see how fast I could go. I had heard that some other cycle tourists were doing one hundred miles a day, but we had been doing on average only fifty kilometres per day.

I imagined myself in a race. My knees and thigh muscles strained and my heart pumped strongly in my chest. The pain opened up my consciousness. I moved like a ghost; people didn't have time to react when they saw me. I managed fifty kilometres in a couple of hours but I was so much 'in the zone' that I could barely remember seeing anything other than the handlebars and tarmac ahead of me. The speed and concentration had destroyed my lateral vision.

The road was dull and got wider and busier as we approached the city. Magalie was scheduled to fly in the evening so we had to get to the airport. We were on the correct side of the city and had only to follow part of the ring road through a green belt development of globalised brand department stores and 4x4 car sales showrooms to get to the airport. Only a couple of hours earlier, I had passed people riding horses and carts and selling bags of vegetables and potatoes at the roadside in order to make a meagre living.

At the airport, we were eyed with considerable suspicion. We propped the bikes up by the front entrance but were immediately told to move them by the security guards. We wondered where we would sleep and still make Magalie's flight. We got a trolley, took apart the bikes and made it look like we were flying out the following day.

I cooked dinner on the stove sitting on the pavement next to the bikes. After dinner, I pushed the trolley past the security guard who eyed me suspiciously. We found a place in the terminal with some floor space and slept in our sleeping bags.

I had felt myself grow closer to Magalie and we had become good friends. I was sad to see her go. She was a friend, disappearing away into departures, which was something that I would have to get used to.

25

Electric City

We cycled to the office of the WWF in Bucharest. Bucharest was first mentioned in documents as early as 1459. Since then, it has gone through a variety of changes, becoming the state capital of Romania in 1862 and steadily consolidating its position as the centre of the Romanian mass media, culture, and arts. In the period between the two World Wars, the city's elegant architecture and the sophistication of its elite earned Bucharest the nickname of the 'Little Paris of the East' (Micul Paris).

As I rolled down long, Soviet-style boulevards, I looked around at the architecture. The high-density tower blocks looked ominous and inhumane, designed to stack as many humans as possible into one physical space. The grand Stalinist architecture looked like an idea of the future conceived decades before. Now it just looked imposing and dystopian. It reminded me that each epoch has seen grand ideologies imposed over the people but never have any of them allowed the people to fully realise their potential. Average people just had to 'make do' with whatever was available to them under the current system.

In 1977, there was an earthquake of 7.4 on the Richter scale, which claimed 1,500 lives and destroyed many old buildings. Then, Nicolae Ceausescu's leadership (1965-1989) saw a program of systematisation where a historic part of the city was destroyed and replaced with Soviet-style buildings. The best example of this is the Centrul Civic (the Civic Centre), including the Palace of the Parliament, where an entire historic quarter was razed to make way for Ceausescu's megalomaniac constructions.

At the office of the WWF, we spoke to a lady about the deforestation we had seen in the mountains. She said that they had been working to try to stop unregulated logging but it wasn't easy to get the government to pay attention to environment issues because of the more popular issue of economic growth.

We met a Couchsurfer named Rado and followed him through the city centre traffic. We passed the train station and I saw one of the ominous looking 'security teams' that patrolled the streets. Blue, armoured vehicles and men dressed in urban combat fatigues were hired to protect businesses from the Mafia because the police were corrupt.

We carried the bikes and luggage up four flights of stairs. Rado lived in a small but well kept flat with his mother. 'I am an environment student from Bucharest University. I work on an organic farm in the countryside. My girlfriend is in England and I miss her.'

We had arrived in the city at an opportune moment on 'the foundation of Bucharest day' (it was founded 559 years ago). There was an electronica festival happening in the city centre and art was to be projected onto the side of the Bucharest parliament.

As we drove into the centre, I watched the world pivoting around the tin can which enclosed me. The streets were mostly shrouded in darkness, but for a few lamps emitting a dull glow. Bucharest at night looked a little like the city from *Blade Runner*; neon lights were fixed atop tall tower blocks. People walked about in the shadows. The atmosphere was electric.

We followed the flow of people. They were all moving to the main square. The epic building's façade looked like sixteen Soviet tower blocks stacked together like gigantic Lego bricks. It was a monstrosity, a physical manifestation of the human ego way out of control and a gargantuan waste of building materials. It was fitting that chaotic and colourful, sometimes ghastly, weird and alien images were projected onto the building's face. It was a finger poked in the eye of the former system. Absurdity and the carnivalesque situation unfolded. Visions ranged from yellow, blob-shaped alien-beings to collages of renaissance artwork. Plumes of fire rose from a huge iron dragon sculpture upon a float, whilst acrobats performed upon it.

Some works particularly caught my imagination. One was an image of two doves in flight, which overlapped together on a dark blue background. Another piece looked like an explosion of white paint. The composition seemed to leave the building and the light continued over the crowd. Loud electronic music boomed out, but it struggled to maintain clarity, and reverberated and echoed in the open space, which dampened its final effect.

Another evening we were invited to go to the flat of a friend of Rado, called Mihai, and Tom offered to cook a curry. Whilst we were picking up ingredients and supplies for the evening, Mihai commented on why there were so many roadworks in the city. 'It's because the mayor owns his own construction company. He contracts them to dig up the roads and then fill them in even if no work is needed.' He said that there was also a problem with stray dogs in the city and often he needed to fight them off with sticks and stones. It was not something you would expect to hear about a European city.

Mihai lived in a refurbished apartment. From the outside, it looked like another crumbling concrete tower block. I realised that although externally the building looked like an image of a dystopian city, internally every unit was different and a pocket of expression. When one extreme is created, so the other is created. During the Soviet years there were many underground rebel movements of anti-institution art and culture, but this was capitalism. The flat was decorated with stylish furnishings. It had grey, leather seats; a glass, minimalist coffee table; a marble-topped work-surface in the kitchen; and smoked glass, translucent doors with chrome, cylindrical handles. It looked like it could have been a showroom for Hi-Fi equipment or an advert for Ikea. It looked like the ideal city bachelor pad, and that kind of living arrangement occupied a space in my desire because I knew that, in another life, I would have probably been in a similar situation; however, it felt too close for comfort and I was glad to be on the move. Scratching the surface, the situation was an insular private space to escape to and entertain with dinner parties. We danced, ate curry, drank Polish vodka, and watched films on a cinema projector.

Tom had sent out a few mails on Couchsurfing.com about further accommodation. Without it, we would never have been able to afford to hang out in Bucharest for so long. Alex Tomescu replied and gave us his address. It turned out that he lived in the same building as Rado and we had only to take our luggage up in the elevator to the top floor to arrive at our new host's home.

Alex was smartly presented and in his late twenties. He had short hair and wore stylish sunglasses and designer clothes: jeans and shirts in simple colours. He was a successful solo violinist who had won a coveted Stradivarius violin; he was a pioneer and an expert in his field. His life was devoted to playing the violin and he was always under pressure to be the very best.

He was a relaxed individual and thrilled to be involved with people. He was always thinking and pondering people's characters and relationships. I got the feeling that he was a dreamer at heart, thinking about adventure and possibility. He had discovered how to make life open up to him and was surfing on that wave. He was kind, generous, and liked to have fun but remained in control of himself.

As we arrived in his posh apartment, I was worried about making a mess. It was clean, with a white modern interior, open plan kitchen, dining and living room. On his bookshelves was Romanian literature and art. Some colourful expressionist and surrealist paintings hung on the wall. The artwork was Soviet in style, with geometric shapes. The living room led out onto a balcony with a view over the canopy of the trees in the adjacent park.

We watched *Seven Years in Tibet* but I was so tired that I fell asleep half way through with thoughts of eastern places in my mind.

Alex's ex-girlfriend was Korean and he loved Korean food and culture and had learnt the language. He had a 'dealer' who got him the best food. At dinner we ate spicy slices of pork in hot and sour sauce, squares of dark green seaweed, red hot chilli chutney, and kimchi – pickled cabbage with chilli and sesame oil – the Korean national dish.

I felt good about the general experience of our journey at that time. I was excited about the possibilities available and opened myself up to the experience. I stopped worrying that maybe I wasn't achieving some abstract, preconceived, emotional goal and realised that the experience I was having was exactly what I wanted. It was thrilling and none of it mattered anyway because it was all just life, and fundamentally that, at the time, is what I thought I wanted: a life before I was dead.

Alex was a connoisseur of honey. He opened a cupboard in the kitchen where he kept about fifteen different jars. A couple of them were more buckets than jars. He produced a box full of small rectangular biscuits, which were a throwback to the Soviet era when you could only get one type of biscuit. He was hoarding a box of them because they were the very best biscuit to eat with honey: not crunchy, not very sweet, inoffensive in colour, and sizable enough for multiple scoops of honey.

He explained that some of the honey was good for health, some for memory and some particularly full of energy. Each honey's taste depended on the flower from which the bees were getting pollen. For example, the Acacia honey had a certain taste; it was a little bit flowery and slightly fruity, with a mild sweetness and a colour like dark ale. It was quite runny and syrupy in consistency.

Alex was eager to go cycling with us at some point, so after dinner a group of us cycled around Bucharest at three in the morning. The streets were quiet, apart from some boy racers who tore down the high street in their souped-up cars. We passed a large government building and a pot-holed, tree-lined pavement and joined a path that circled around the artificial lake Cismigiu – built by German architect Carl F.W. Meyer.

The lake was famous for the writers and poets who had come there to relax. It felt like we were on a night stealth mission to follow Alex Tomescu wherever he wanted to go. I liked the energy of Bucharest. There are so many shades to the place. It didn't lose its personality during the Soviet era and, indeed, this boosted its will to maintain a strong sense of its identity.

26

A Concert in the Mountains

The following morning we drove to Sinesa. Alex had invited us to a private concert in the mountains, and a friend of his, Adia, came along too.

It was interesting to travel by car: our first time for ages. Places and people rushed past. My brain had got used to taking in my surroundings at the speed of a bicycle, moving slowly enough for you to consider everything you see. If you want to reach out and speak to someone, you can stop and meet them. Travelling quickly, the world goes by in a series of images like a television montage.

We donned our smart shirts for the occasion. At least one piece of clothing that passes for smart is essential when travelling, because you never know when you might need it. We arrived through the hillside forest at the house of George Enescu, the famous Romanian musician, where Alex was scheduled to give a small, private concert to a group of officials for an IMF (International Monetary Fund) meeting about financial assistance for Romania. The idea was that Alex could coerce them with his sumptuous violin playing.

To watch Alex play was an astonishing experience. He exuded a kind of confidence that I would associate with a child who had been practising every day for a school concert and knew what they were doing so well they could play it backwards, forwards, left, right, and standing on their headteacher. He played a note like a ninja throwing a punch. His smile was so powerful, his joy so infectious, that it looked like it ran far deeper than his face conveyed; it was almost as though he was tapering his expression for fear of revealing himself as privy to some funny secret, or the key to the meaning of life, and being ousted from society in response. Yet, this exuberance swelled within him as he played.

When he was playing, the violin could have been invisible. His stance was strong and confident as if he was conducting his own orchestra with vigorous and precise movements. His body moved up and down with each movement, as if flowing on the waves of the music. The tension appeared to build up in every cell of his body and was subsequently released at the end of each section. Like water, flowing towards a cascade, the notes took him wherever they led. He could be strong and violent and then sweet and smooth, and changed between the two masterfully.

His face and mouth made it look as if he was blowing the notes onto the strings. His nostrils flared like a predator picking up the scent of its prey. His upper lip quivered and his eyebrows moved up and down as a teacher alternately frowning and being pleasantly surprised at the work of a student. His facial expressions belied a range of strong emotions, particularly joy and pride.

His fingers ran across the strings like a manic spider. I was lulled into a sense of security in a calm section of the music and then shaken out of it with an attack of notes and a breakdown, like a cat pouncing or a bird of prey swooping in for the kill. The level of skill needed to pull that off made me feel like I just saw someone walk a thread strung across the Grand Canyon in a split second and I was left wanting to see it again.

After the concert, we went to a luxury hotel restaurant with grand, crystal chandeliers and tables set with silver service. We sat at the table with Alex, his pianist Horai, and Horai's wife. The meal was sumptuous, accompanied by champagne and brandy.

We had a free hotel room for the night, with a balcony overlooking the mountains. We decided to have a party. When I regained consciousness in the morning Alex was asleep on the bare struts of the bed, which had been dismantled. I had my arms around Adia, and Tom was lying beside Maria in a huge pile of towels and bathrobes. The room looked like a bomb had hit it.

We sheepishly and self-consciously tidied the room and then drove to Braşov, where we stayed with one more Couchsurfer called Alina. She fed us delicious traditional Romanian food of polenta (boiled cornmeal porridge – nicer than it sounds), sausages, and pickled cabbage with more Pálinka.

An urge to leave the city was creeping up on me. I didn't regret our slow progress, but Alastair Humphreys – a British cyclist – had crossed Europe in five weeks while we had taken four months to get to Bucharest.

There was one last thing to do before leaving. One of our video cameras had broken, so we made the risky decision to spend a significant portion of our travel budget on new ones; as we were set on making a quality film, it was deemed necessary.

Leaving Bucharest was a shock to the system. We had been stationary there for two weeks. We cycled through the rush hour traffic and the – at first – relaxing morning light, gradually turned to scorching sun. Alex cycled with us out of the city in order to show us the way. I had become familiar with the city centre and now we were back to unfamiliar surroundings, which felt unnerving.

We followed a big dual carriageway past more high-density housing blocks into the suburbs. Tom stopped by the roadside. 'I've lost my wallet!' he exclaimed. Alex and Tom went back to Alina's to look for the wallet. After an hour or so, he returned and he hadn't found it. 'It's either been stolen or I left it in the post office this morning when I sent the parcel.'

Tom would go without his wallet from then on and rely on his back up funds.

Inspired by Bucharest

Alarms echo into the night
Dogs roam the streets
A gypsy family labours laying concrete
A tuned car accelerates like in a computer game
Stalinist buildings hold memories of revolution

People stride with confidence, purpose, and energy
Chattering in a language with Latin roots,
Crows flock chaotically in the dusk-reddened sky
Romanians: expressive, opinionated
Their country has a strong spirit

27

Frontier Psychiatry

It was one day's ride to the Bulgarian border. The landscape was increasingly deserted. We passed concrete behemoths of Soviet agricultural fallout and rusting machinery. These systems were designed with a great Soviet future in mind and intensive farming that would support burgeoning populations and development. Now they stood frozen in time and deserted like a stray guard dog, which was once proud and useful.

We passed through the lesser-used, secondary border town of Olteniţa, which appeared to survive from border trade alone. We missed the last boat to cross the river at five and take us into Bulgaria, so we sat on the bench outside the police station. We considered sleeping there, but there were many mosquitoes buzzing around because of the water. I went to ask the police where we could sleep but they were unhelpful. However, the ferry owner, Nicco, said we could sleep in a room on his other boat, which was moored by the waterside, in exchange for a two-litre bottle of coke and our attention to view his family photos. The room was cosy with a comfortable carpet. The boat moved gently on the lapping water. We sat on the boat in the afternoon sun and cooked some lentils on the stove.

We took the early boat to the border at Tutankea. The wind was refreshing and helped to wake me up as the boat churned through the water. We seemed to be the only passengers. We were directed to a stuffy little office, with closed shutters, on the first floor of a building. The man there checked my passport but was confused by the chip mechanism. He spent a good half an hour ringing various people up, holding it up to the light, turning it upside down, and generally looking confused. Eventually he gave up and gave it back to me.

Maria rode slowly and was quiet throughout the morning. The road wound its way through vast agricultural fields. The hills were frustratingly medium sized. They weren't large enough to get a sense of satisfaction after climbing them or a thrill going down the other side. We ate banana, mayonnaise, honey, and peanut butter sandwiches for lunch. The road became very boring. Lone trees sprouted from vast, ploughed fields. The villages were small, similar, and monotonous.

Late in the afternoon, as I was pedalling along, the rear wheel of my bike made a loud cracking noise. I stopped to look at it but couldn't see a problem. We ventured down a side track, into a coppice of trees with a spring next to a stream, and camped beside the track.

28

It's My Birthday, But Time Has Stopped

It was my 25th birthday the next day. It sounded old. I had an impending feeling that perhaps I should be doing something a lot more sensible than cycling. However, it wasn't a desperate feeling and I ultimately felt good – which seemed the right way to feel. Most days I felt like I had learnt more about life than I ever did in the average day before I left. In the morning, I was pleased that Maria and Tom remembered my birthday.

I could sense a mutual desire to make faster progress into more interesting surroundings. Cycling along, I heard another cracking noise and inspected the frame at its most susceptible points near the headtube, weld, and by the bottom bracket, but the frame was solid. I spun the front wheel, no problem, and then the back wheel. I did a double take. There was a six-inch-long crack in the rim. It looked as though the spokes had been too tight; causing the metal to part ways in a horrible gash that displayed the rim innards. 'What a lovely birthday surprise,' I thought.

We had known this was going to happen and it happened right on cue. Every other adventure cyclist who had used that particular Mavic rim had cracked it after six months of travel. We had to change our plans. We decided to ride for a while and then hitchhike into the next town to find a replacement wheel. The rim seemed to hold at first but it gradually deformed and bowed outwards. I wrapped gaffer tape around the rim to keep it together.

Impressively, the wheel was still in one piece when we reached Varna, on the coast of the Black Sea, about two hundred kilometres away. It was a sprawling place, geared up for tourism in the summer, but now all the seasoned businesses were closing up for the winter.

The road descended to the coast through sprawling, out of town industrial and commercial developments. We bought some supplies from a supermarket for lunch. I rode through a deserted industrial estate. An impatient person in a silver car had to wait briefly for us to pass at a junction. The driver jumped out of his car and shouted, 'You stupid cyclists, you think you own the road, fuck you, fuck you, fuck you!' He shook his fists, waved his arms in the air, and walked aggressively toward me so we promptly left.

We sat and waited in the centre for a reply from Couchsurfer Vlado. He came to meet us and we followed him across town in the darkness and drizzling rain. He drove slowly with his hazard lights on whilst we followed him over a poorly lit road bridge. A car screeched its tyres and skidded, narrowly avoiding crashing into him, so we agreed to meet him on the other side of the bridge. My legs screamed with pain, my vision was blurred with tiredness, and sweat was running into my eyes. I gritted my teeth and dug deep. I didn't want to be cycling on dark roads in the rain. Then, frustratingly, my shoelace got caught in the chainring and started to wrap around the bottom bracket and I fell off into the steel railings. I felt anger born of tiredness and frustration. I disentangled myself and was incredibly glad to reach Vlado's and rest after that episode.

The next day, Tom orchestrated a masterpiece of spicy Chinese cooking: soup, sweet and sour chicken and rice; a sensational experience for the taste buds compared to the basic lentils, and cheese and tomato sandwiches, we had been eating on the road.

29

Goodbye Maria

Maria's mood had evidently shifted over the past few days. She was complaining of a sore bum, knees, and hands, and she appeared more thoughtful and withdrawn than usual. She announced that she was going to leave us and hitchhike alone to Istanbul. We would see her again in a couple of weeks. We said our farewells and wished her luck.

At the back of my mind, I was worried about leaving her alone but that was the way it had to be. Tom and I cycled away from Varna along the coast, managing seventy-two kilometres on hilly roads, which was good progress. We stopped to eat chocolate spread and bread in a small town where people were milling about and appeared to be doing very little. They were sitting in groups, playing cards. We passed through a forested area and there were prostitutes, dressed in skimpy outfits, strutting sordidly by the roadside.

I put music on and got into the zone. I crawled up the hills and raced down the other side, maintaining momentum for the next hill or flat section. We turned off a quiet stretch of road down to the beach and there was an abandoned shelter, which looked like it had been prepared for our arrival. There was a quarter-full bottle of whisky, a pile of firewood, and a large container of water.

There wasn't a soul in sight other than a building with a light on at the far end of the beach, which ran north to a cove, and then south as far as you could see.

We collected firewood to create a warming fire to sleep next to. Tom cooked some dinner and we went to sleep as the light faded away. It felt good to be cycling with just Tom. I was interested to see how it would go.

The Black Sea is so called for a number of reasons. One theory is that Herodotus used it and the Red Sea interchangeably for north and south. Another is that the water is of poorer visibility; it is further north than the Mediterranean Sea and much less saline so the microalgae concentration is much richer, causing the dark colour. In naval science, the Black Sea is thought to have received its name because of its hydrogen sulphide layer that begins about two hundred metres below the surface, and supports a unique microbial population, which produces black sediments due to anaerobic methane oxidation. If a meteor were to land in the sea, there is a possibility that residents on the coastline would be engulfed in a cloud of toxic gas.

We cycled through pine forest and the sun sparkled, enticingly, on the normally dull looking sea. In contrast, we passed the most ugly seaside resort I had ever seen. It was a concrete monster called 'Sunny Beach'. I wondered how this place could ever be someone's idea of a holiday, with its tacky bars and restaurants with neon signs, a population of transient season workers and cement lorries on their way to deliver to another quick-buck development. I was sure that the resort had been hastily erected on coastal marshland: Nature's sea defence and a fragile ecosystem in itself. It was just another environmental oversight in the name of quick money. With just an increase in awareness, the developments could be built with the environment in mind.

Tom and I continued cycling for a few more hours. We didn't say much to each other. Our aim was to cover some distance. We had the goal of Istanbul in our sights.

There was no sign of Maria. We expected her to be well on the way to the Turkish border. My rear wheel was flexing badly, causing the tyre to rub on the frame whenever I pedalled, so we decided to stop and hitchhike. We had been standing on the roadside for only a few minutes when a blue estate car pulled over and out jumped Maria. She ran towards us, sobbing. It was the driver of the truck; he had tried it on with her, which had been a horrible ordeal. I felt we could have prevented such a thing from happening, had we not left her alone.

We decided to hitchhike together. I took off the rear wheel and wrapped more gaffer tape around the rim. A truck turned up and offered us a lift. The driver took us twenty-five kilometres to the next town and dropped us off. I packed all my luggage back onto the bike and into the trailer but noticed, to my horror, that I had left the trailer fork at the roadside where we caught the lift, which meant I couldn't attach the trailer and that I would have to carry all of the trailer luggage weight on the broken wheel rim. This seemed impossible. It would depend on the strength of the gaffer tape. However, considering the gaffer tape layer was now about half a centimetre thick, the rim was probably stronger than it was when it was new.

We reached a petrol station, which looked like a good place to hitchhike from. Tom and I got a lift in a white van. Maria insisted that she was fine to hitchhike alone again from there.

The white van pelted along the road. It had a Jesus air-freshener hanging from the rear view mirror. The driver lit a cigarette and we sat in silence. I looked at the map and realised that we were hitchhiking in the wrong direction. We were meant to be heading South East towards the border but we were going directly East, towards the coast.

The van dropped us off before we went any further.

'Why can't anything be simple?' shouted Tom. The unpredictability of the day's events triggered our sense of humour. We decided to forget about our problems and drink beer. There was a small town called Cosonov with a delicatessen shop where we ate plates of roasted vegetables in oil and köfte with Bulgar wheat.

Unpredictable things happily broke up the linearity of the adventure and made it more interesting. I yearned to meet people and party with them. This was hopefully on the cards with Istanbul in our sights.

We camped on a beach and then made good progress into the Rodolp Mountains, near the Turkish border. The next morning, we were out of money and food and there was no shop in sight so we cycled for four hours, with two thousand feet of climbing, having eaten nothing. Every cell in my body called out for me to eat something. I scoured the roadside hedgerows for berries and resorted to eating spoonfuls of sugar. The last village before the border was Malco Tansevo: where we ate a huge breakfast of pastry whirls, cheese, jam and biscuits.

30

Young Turks

Turkey felt exotic. I remembered Tom saying, when we were looking at a world map before we left England, 'Look at the size of Turkey. I have no idea what the hell is there.' I knew nothing about the place. My only knowledge of Turkey was that people went there on beach holidays and ate it for Christmas dinner, but there is something satisfying about seeing the reality of the world first hand. Perhaps it satisfies a hunter-gatherer instinct to discover new places and assess their food potential.

There was a chill in the air as we rode through a misty forest, passing bright red signs signifying a Turkish military base. A minaret from a mosque, the first I'd seen in my life, looked like a space rocket or missile from *Thunderbirds*. The land looked noticeably drier. It was epic with dry, sweeping, scrub-covered hills.

The sunset cast a warm, reddish light, quite unlike any we had seen. I imagined it was because we were heading to Asia. It was the light you see on postcards of Asian sunsets. I was comparing the representation with the reality. I already had an image in my mind of that kind of sunset but, in reality, it was much more satisfying.

'What is my goal now I'm in a new country?' I thought to myself. We weren't sure of our route yet. Would we go via Georgia and Armenia and suffer a Caucasian winter, or south into Iran, Iraq or Syria?

Three Alsatian guard dogs outside a cement factory attacked Tom. They barked, snarled, and snapped at his ankles, but totally ignored me. We reached the top of the hill and the dogs gave chase. The faster we cycled, the faster they ran, until they were bounding like greyhounds across the fields behind us. I shouted and teased – in a stupid voice, like Jim Carrey in *The Mask* – 'Come on, is that the best you can do?!'

After a few miles, we had outrun them.

The dry grassland was prime camping territory but the wind was blowing a gale over the hills with nothing to obstruct it. My tent blew around like a windsock as I struggled to push pegs into the dry ground. The grass was buffeted by the wind and it felt like I was pinning the tent onto a giant hairy beast, but it was comfortable with all the cushioning. I welcomed the familiar, slightly damp smell of the tent.

We reached the first town and I observed the Turkish men. The taxi drivers were well dressed, wearing smart shirts, black trousers and polished black pointy shoes. A couple of men greeted each other and kissed. A group of young men walked together. They looked like they were joking and having fun. A kebab shop owner greeted some customers, warmly, like old friends. Men without helmets drove old-fashioned motorbikes.

The call to prayer began. It was the first time I had heard it. 'Allah Akbar ...' wailed and meandered through the air.

A young boy walked past. He held his shoulders back, his head high, and had a cigarette in his hand. He tried his best to look grown up. 'It's a man's world, in Turkey,' I thought.

I went into an Internet café full of children playing computer games. An overweight, stubbly-faced, twenty-something smoked a cigarette and sat behind a desk looking bored. While I used the Internet, a kid pulled himself up over the cubicle door to look at me. When I looked up he dropped down and I heard chortling coming from him and his friends.

We left the town and cycled along a main road across a flat plain. I could see for miles in every direction. There was a sense of open space that I hadn't experienced before, which made me feel physically small. The air became heavy and I looked back to see ferocious dark cloud hanging over a village. A thunderstorm brewed. A lightning bolt shot to the ground.

I imagined a giant monster with lightning bolts for legs: a huge spider chasing me across the plains, burning everything in its path, scorching trees, and exploding cars for fun. It had lightning bolts for a smile, its eyes flickered, and parts of it appeared and disappeared as it ran. I'd seen too many Hollywood films.

Having left the storm behind we had halted for lunch when a car stopped on the road, backed up, and drove down the forest track towards us. Six guys, about our age, emerged.

'Hello, where are you from?' asked Rolly: a skinny, friendly-faced man in his early twenties. 'We are students from the University of Istanbul.'

They offered us Efes beer and lit a barbecue to cook köfte and chicken. We talked about football and the Turkish clubs and then the subject moved to politics. Alper said, 'No one likes the prime minster of Turkey but we trust the military. In Turkey, the military have the power. The government are just puppets.'

31

Turkish Hospitality

In the evening, there was nowhere to camp that would be sheltered from the relentless wind. There was a lone farmhouse on a distant hill, so I went to ask for shelter. The door was answered by a short man in a dinner suit who had jet-black hair. He greeted us with a big smile. He was accompanied by three giggling teenage girls, two brothers and the rest of the extended family.

One of the brothers was a tall, skinny boy with a slim face and dark eyes, who wore jeans and a t-shirt. He could have been the Turkish version of Rodney from *Only Fools and Horses*. The other was in his mid twenties with a wide face and thick build, and didn't say much. He seemed more wary of us. There was a middle-aged man, who turned out to be their uncle, who incidentally looked a bit like Boycie. Shortly after, the father came to the door.

We were shown a patch of land behind the house where we could pitch the tent, and then we were ushered back to the house for dinner. It was a bungalow with two living rooms, a bathroom (with Turkish style toilet), a kitchen and three bedrooms. We sat at a small table in the kitchen whilst the family gathered around and watched our reaction as we were brought different plates of traditional food.

For each dish, we were taught how to say the name in Turkish. We had çorba (soup) for a starter, and köfte (Turkish meatballs) with salad for the main course. The food was prepared by the mother and grandmother who were strong-looking matriarchal women, but the mother of the family never sat with us to eat. For desert, we ate traditional, syrup-filled, Turkish pastry called baklava.

After dinner, we learnt more of the Turkish language. I pointed to something and was told how to say it in Turkish: a pencil (kalem), a tree (agaç), lamp (lamba). We sat with the family, chatted, and looked at photos. I learnt more about the differing personalities of the brothers. The tall skinny one seemed the most intelligent. He was studying at university. Sinon was more of a man's man and he was in the army. He was quieter, but more sure-headed. The third boy was working in the nearby factory. He was married and had plans to start a business. At times he seemed sure-headed, egotistical and attention seeking and at others he went quiet and seemed either confused or amazed by us. He made it clear that he was honoured to have us as guests. 'We are Turkish, hospitality is in our blood.'

The history of Turkish hospitality dates back to the Turks' nomadic origins. If a traveller turned up, it would pay to treat them well in case you needed the favour returning in the future. In addition, the traveller might have something useful to trade. In any case, it was a good idea to be nice so visitors didn't attack your family. It was after midnight when Tom and I retired to the tents. It had been a fascinating but exhausting evening.

The next day, we found out why all the family members were together. It was the important Sugar festival to celebrate the end of Ramadan. Sinon had come all the way from Mount Ararat, where he was stationed in the army.

Sinon – the initially wary looking one – turned out to be very friendly. He offered to take us to the nearby town to witness the festivities and celebrations. We hitchhiked with a couple of Turkish men in leather jackets who looked like Mafiosi and drove very fast.

When we got there, all the residents of the town were walking the streets. There were children playing and women looking after them. There were men in groups walking with linked arms. Older men sat together on benches, observing and chatting. Boy racers hung around their cars, and drove up and down with Turkish pop music blaring.

Sinon took us to meet an English teacher called Ardesh. We strolled along with him chatting and then got into car and drove up onto the hillside. A few minutes later, another car pulled up and a couple of boys got out with some beer. 'You can't drink the beer in the town because it is not allowed'. Drinking in private seemed like the normal thing to do. We returned to Sinon's home and he showed us around. The house had a small farmstead attached to it where they kept cows and chickens. In Turkey, the animals were something to be proud of. They were a symbol of status and wealth.

Sinon showed us his sound system, which consisted of the largest fake Sony speakers I'd ever seen (about one metre high) and a huge amplifier. He played some Turkish dance music and turned it up until the windows vibrated.

Staying with the family was first-hand experience of Turkish family life, which was, to an extent, conservative and traditional. At different times through the day, the family would stop what they were doing to pray. There were fixed roles within the family. The mother cooked and looked after the children. The father was the breadwinner. The children helped with day-to-day tasks. The unmarried girls were blooming and would probably marry quite young. They talked of their dreams for life and marriage. I wondered whether the girls were weighing us up as husbands. One of them was definitely more traditional, but another seemed more of a freethinker. She was more interested in who we were and reasons for doing our journey. She seemed content to sit and observe quietly whereas the other girls initiated questions, giggled, and showed us their dancing.

Men and women had equal importance but they had well defined roles and there was strong social pressure to stick to them. The origin of the social status of women in Islam dates back to Arabia in the seventh century AD. Men could have many wives, kill women, and bury newborn girls if they felt like it. When Islam made marriage laws and put a limit on the number of wives allowed, it was accepted as the first system anywhere to give women some economic rights by saving them from the sole sovereignty of their husbands.

In Turkey, following the declaration of the Republic in 1923, one of the most significant elements in the social revolution planned and advocated by Ataturk – the 'father of the Turks' – was the partial emancipation of Turkish women, based on the principle that the new Turkey was to be a secular state.

In 1926, a new code of Turkish civil law was adopted, which suddenly changed the family structure. Polygamy was abolished, along with religious marriages and divorce, and child custody became the right of both men and women.

With the secularisation of the education system, women gained fairer rights with men in the field of education. They no longer had to wear the veils and long garments required by the old religious beliefs. Women's right to vote was granted at the municipal level in 1930 and nationwide in 1934.

Theoretically, Turkish women were far ahead of many of their Western sisters at that time. For instance, in France, women only gained the right to vote in 1944. The charter of the International Labour Organisation, adopted in 1951 and ratified by Turkey in 1966, declared equal wages for both sexes for equal work.

Although all the new regulations brought the status of women to an improved level, the actual status of women within the family institution did not provide for proper equality between men and women. Today the husband is still the head of the family. The woman does the housework, and if a woman needs to work outside the home, she has to get the approval of her husband.

When it came to leaving, I told the mother 'Hersey için tesekkür ederim,' which meant 'thanks for everything'. We were so warmly welcomed, that it set me up with a very positive first impression of Turkey.

There are many things to be learnt from my experience with the Turkish family: notably the open mindedness to strangers and willingness to learn, be friendly and exist together regardless of country or religion. The strong family unit, and well-established home space with garden and life-stock, provided security and self-sufficiency, which meant they could exist without external support and interference. However, it was clear that they were strongly connected with the local community and had a strong national identity.

We left their home and got back on the road. The landscape was mundane as hell. It looked like all the natural vegetation had been uprooted and replaced by cultivated farmland. We cycled through a newly developed town. It was ugly, with concrete tower blocks that stood clumsily in the air. The design was visually rudimentary. They were cheap, quickly erected structures. Building material detritus was strewn about the base of the buildings.

I cycled over a river bridge. The river water was an oily mixture of blue and green gunge with a layer of foam over the top. There were steaming piles of rubbish, tipped into the river without thought and dotted around the developments. It looked like something out of *Mad Max*. I felt depressed and I began to see an idealised vision of tidy England in my imagination. Children played amongst the rubble. They pointed and waved as we went past.

The roadside developments grew in size: row after row of auto repair outlets, electrical repair shops, Internet cafés, kebab houses, seedy hotels, and offices to rent. The Marmara Sea came into view on the horizon. We sneaked passed an unmanned security kiosk into a residential area next to the sea. We pedalled down to the waterside and carried the bikes down some steep steps onto a jetty. There was a roofed area, which, in the summer, would have been a little restaurant.

There were stacks of tables and chairs. I took a table and laid out my sleeping bag on it. It was starting to get cold at night. I wore clothes inside my sleeping bag and used the bivvy bag for extra warmth. I cooked a basic lentil curry. The stove coughed and spluttered because it was clogged up with black gunge from using poor quality Romanian diesel, which I was sure was made of 40% fuel, 40% water, and 20% wood chip.

I watched one of the most impressive sunsets I had ever seen. The calm water of the sea rippled under the clear sky. A wisp of cloud floated over the horizon. I felt the temperature drop, degree by degree, as the sun edged down. How many times in your life do you sit and watch the sunset? It was life affirming because it reminded me of my mortality. Once the sun has fallen, that's another day of your life, ended. It made me think. Did I have a full day? Did I achieve what I wanted? Is my life going in the right direction? I realised that none of these questions mattered, because that moment felt like pure liquid perfection.

I awoke in the morning and I saw the sun emerge. I think that is the only time I had ever watched the sun set and watched it emerge in the morning. I felt hope. We got up quickly to cycle before the traffic got busy.

32

How Does a City Like Istanbul Start?

How does a city like Istanbul start?

I pulled into a petrol station and asked an attendant how far the city was. He said, 'Thirty-five kilometres but you are already in the city.' I couldn't believe him. I felt a mixture of relief at arriving and depression that we were about to embark on cycling along one of the most notoriously cycle unfriendly roads in the world. The road into Istanbul is the main route from Europe into Asia.

The road's hard shoulder disappeared and we were forced to tussle with the endless traffic. At one point, the traffic bottlenecked into a single lane because of roadworks. The adrenalin caused me to concentrate intensely and I focused hard. My brain felt like a car's engine at maximum revs.

If I thought about anything other than avoiding being killed then the chance of it happening seemed as if it would exponentially increase. Unnervingly, my luggage kept scraping on the road barrier as I tried to keep as close in as possible, away from the passing vehicles. My bike was loaded up with my luggage over the back panniers and was therefore completely unbalanced. Knocking the barrier caused the rear wheel to wobble and the subsequent feedback caused the handlebars to vibrate.

The road widened to six lanes. We passed through endless reams of suburbia and industrial estates. There was one section of road where the hard shoulder was non-existent and a barrier meant we had to cycle on the road and fight for space with the other traffic. Drivers had to slow right down and indicate to pull out around us. A careless driver in a BMX X5 4x4 skirted round

Tom and then pulled straight across him, almost flattening him right there and then.

It was rush hour and end of school time. Buses appeared left right and centre. They were pulling out into the road all the time. I cycled on the pavement and swerved around school-kids getting the bus. Tom filmed me cycling down a drainage channel at the roadside in order to avoid the road. It was madness. What a way to find challenge and adventure. It was like a real-life obstacle course. However, people would often shout encouragement, which boosted the spirits.

We entered the edge of the central urbanised area as the sun was setting. I saw signs that read 'Istanbul Buyukesi' – big district of Istanbul. We had no accommodation arranged, but hoped we could find Maria sometime that evening. The prospect of entering Istanbul was scintillating. It's renowned as one of the greatest cities in the world.

We passed through an arch in an ancient fortress wall. We hadn't eaten anything for hours. Hunger was howling in my belly. We found the nearest kebab shop to treat ourselves. The kebab was a sausage-shaped piece of marinated mincemeat, which came with onion, salad, and sauce, and was wrapped in pide bread.

Afterwards, I couldn't help but think that the kebab did not match up to the kebab from my local restaurant in Kettering. A large Kettering kebab would be stuffed full of slices of grilled lamb – strange-textured, but moreish – and plastered with dollops of fatty mayonnaise and lashings of gum-burning chilli sauce. It usually contained enough day-old salad to keep a field of rabbit families fed for a year. If you paid an extra pound, it would be rammed to the rafters with greasy chips. Somewhere, lost in the depths of this delightful mulch, you would find a pitiful pide, which you know you should discard like the piece of soggy cardboard that it is, but you don't, and eat it anyway. There were probably some addictive chemicals added to the meat and sauce.

The Turkish kebab was an entirely different beast altogether. It was real food and had distinct, subtle, and pleasurable flavours. A kebab? Real food? I must be in Turkey.

My brain said, 'OK, that's enough now, time to sleep. I might forgive today's foolishness if you fall asleep right here, right now.' However, we were nowhere near finished yet, and I had to haul myself up out of the kebab shop seat and focus my mind. It took a while to find the motivation to continue.

Tempers started to fray. I followed Tom down the street and then he turned around and came back the same way. 'Why don't you ask someone,' I said.

Tom stopped and got off his bike, 'Why don't you do something to help?'

I could, but I was worried that Tom would take it as an insult to his navigating. We decided that it was a good time to part ways and figure things out alone. It was stressful to constantly monitor the whereabouts of the other person; at an opportune moment, Tom would cross a busy roundabout with multiple lanes of traffic. If I didn't go at the same time, I would have to wait for my chance and Tom would have to wait for me. We always tried to stay together if possible but sometimes it became counter-productive.

I shook Tom's hand and off he went. I stood for a few minutes. I wondered how to find my way to Maria's. I got paranoid because I thought a tramp was looking at me funny. He grinned slightly. He seemed to be able to read my mind, however, if he could, he wouldn't have found much there.

I considered different options, but decided to set upon the method of asking people for directions and checking I was on the right track at every opportunity. First, I asked a taxi driver who gave me a series of directions. I pedalled into a world of concrete overpasses, cross-city traffic, high street shops, and crowds of people. I stopped regularly to ask people, 'Can you tell me how to get to Ortaköy?'

To my surprise, my legs continued to supply power and I felt no pain. I just moved, slowly but surely. 'Go left; go up the hill and take the second right at Taksim square.' I said to myself.

As I passed through Taksim Square, I sensed an incredible

energy. I continued on my way and crossed a bridge over the water. The cold air from the water's surface hit my nostrils. I could see the lights and mosques on the bank. I got a mind-blowing rush of happiness, excitement, and independence. I was in Istanbul, alone, on a bicycle. At that moment, nothing else existed or mattered. I was present in the moment.

I had arranged to meet Maria at the ferry stand in Ortaköy. As I waited for her to arrive, I watched people boarding the ferries that bobbed in the water.

Istanbul is so diverse, exciting, and pulsating with energy. The culture and history is ancient, the mosques are impressive and exotic. A friend who is an architect once said to me that the best cities must have a river. Istanbul has the Bosphorus: a waterway that divides two continents and connects two seas. It has a wonderful magnetic appeal. You look out over the water that has seen so much history and your imagination is inspired.

Maria arrived on her bike and I gave her a long hug. I followed her through Beşiktaş, along tree-lined streets with colourful banners above the road.

I felt euphoric – and then, to add to my happiness, three fellow cyclists sped past. One was talking into a walkie-talkie and had a GPS attached to the front of his bike. They were playing a GPS 'Geocaching' game in the city.

Maria was staying in a flat on a narrow street in an old part of Ortaköy. I met Tugberk, our host, very briefly before collapsing exhausted in the bedroom. Tom arrived later.

33

Landing in Constantinople

The next day we chilled out in Tugberk's flat. My mind was whirling and I couldn't relax. My thighs ached from yesterday's ride. In the evening, we went to a Couchsurfing meeting in a bar. I threw all my energy into socialising with people, but towards the end of the night, Tom and I were literally falling asleep at the table. We arranged to stay with a girl called Nihan who lived in Mecidiyeköy, on the European side.

We picked up the bikes from Tugberk's and pedalled up the hill, past students leaving the nearby university, into the area of Mecidiyeköy. We arrived at Nihan's. Her flat was on the top floor and had fantastic views over the Levent cityscape.

She lived with Serdar (Turkish), Auli (Finnish), and a guy called Atte (Finnish) was also staying. He was studying to be an architect and lived in Amsterdam. He had short black hair and a thin face and wore designer, square-rimmed glasses; drainpipe, black jeans; and a green t-shirt with a red print showing George Bush with devil horns. To celebrate our meeting we were invited to a hat-themed party. We wore our colourful Buff hats to a roof bar in nearby Galatasaray, famous for its football club. The bar was stylish and chic and there were many attractive women dancing to European and Turkish dance music. A terrace in the back overlooked the Bosporus. It was good to be at a party but I wasn't quite sure, logically, if – after having spent months living as a tramp – I fitted in any longer.

A few days later, we went to see if my new wheels and bankcard had arrived at the WWF office where they had been sent. We met Maria beside the Ottoman Palace and pedalled to Eminönü, crossing the bridge at the Golden Triangle. The WWF office was tucked down a busy cobbled street. My camera lens had been delivered, but there was no sign of my wheels. I called the sponsor. They said they had sent them so we just had to wait for them to turn up.

I felt like I needed some time alone. Being in a group of three was getting on my nerves, but I wasn't sure about going solo yet either; I still wanted to travel with my companions.

It's often what you think isn't happening that bugs you, rather than what is happening. In hindsight, I think that both Tom and I got frustrated with the discrepancy between our idealised visions of what would happen on the trip and what actually did happen. We were being far too idealistic. Luckily, the reality of events is always much more interesting because it has the fuel of an unpredictable world, and the complexity of the interlinked networks of human beings, behind it.

Sometimes, due to tiredness, I just wished I could have a rest and unplug for a few days. Luckily, Istanbul promised the rest I needed.

'Kebab sir, very cheap,' said a couple of kebab sellers in stereo as we walked between two kebab stalls on opposite sides of the road. Tom walked up to one and offered one Turkish lira. 'No my friend, the price is one lira fifty.' Tom shrugged and walked to the other one and presented one Turkish lira. 'Okay because you are my friend,' said the man with the big shiny kebab slicer, giving a little grin.

Everywhere you turn, Istanbul is a visual, auditory, and olfactory feast. The waft of grilled meat, fragrant flavoured tobacco smoke, and the smell of roasting chestnuts tickled my nostrils. Children running and shouting; sellers touting their wares; men sitting, drinking tea, and chain-smoking, could all be seen on the streets and market scenes which we encountered.

We wheeled the bikes through a market. There were brightly coloured glass lamps in a plethora of colours: red, rose, ultramarine, ochre, and emerald green. Patterned fabrics were checked, mosaic, or embroidered with passages from the Qur'an. A woman wearing a shawl stood in attendance.

Sacks of spice emitted a thick aroma. I breathed deeply and the smell filled my nose and lungs. Local people and tourists pottered along, perusing the goods at each stand. There were stalls of tacky tourist items like clothes and miniature Turkish flags. There were stacked boxes of tea and powdery Turkish delight. Trays were piled high with pastel coloured spices – turmeric, pepper, cumin, paprika, chilli and mint – in neat, perfectly formed heaps. A strong gust of wind would have caused a disaster.

The store attendants were eager to sell me things.

'You like this sir? It is best quality. Where are you from?'

Rows of water pipes stood with the tubes wrapped around. The tobacco looked like blocks of coloured dates, pungently smelling of one hundred different flavours: chocolate, apple, lemon, cinnamon, mint and more. I wrinkled my nose up or crooned with pleasure at each one. Who came up with these flavours and aromas?

At the marketplace, we met another cyclist; a Canadian guy called Simon. He had straggly, short hair and wore a green racing-style cycling cap, black quarter length trousers, a t-shirt, and a sweat wristband. His skater-style shoes were completely worn out from being ripped apart on the pedal studs. He had an old racing bike with panniers front and rear. He was looking for a place to stay, so we called Nihan and he was able to stay with us.

The shops were shutting as we walked together through the fish- and meat-markets and the streets laden with rubbish. Chunks of meat hung from hooks and people grabbed some last minute bargains.

We often cooked for Couchsurfers and, to celebrate meeting Simon, we cooked chilli con carne with salad and fresh bread. Afterwards, Tom and Simon played chess while Simon talked to me about the cycling scene in Alberta, Canada where he was a regular 'cycle polo' player. The sport is the same as equestrian polo, but on bikes. Often, fixed wheel bikes are used – which means your legs go as fast as the pedals go. To brake, you stop pedalling and fix your legs so that the wheel skids. This type of bike is useful for polo because the fixed wheel allows for excellent control at low speed, and tricks such as pedalling backwards or highly-controlled track stands (balancing whilst stationary).

Atte asked if we wanted to go and smoke a waterpipe in Taksim. On the way, we met Maria and Tugberk outside a death metal, rock music bar. That area had a lively atmosphere. The waterpipe bar had mirrors, photographs, and paintings on the walls. It felt like we had walked into someone's front room. We ordered lemon, mint, and chocolate flavoured waterpipes. Each one had a fabric tube with a smooth wooden mouthpiece. Fragrant tobacco glowed on the tinfoil gauze. When I sucked on the tube, the smoke went down through the water and was cooled, giving a smoother, less harsh flavour. The act of smoking the water pipe was charged with excitement as if we were performing a luxurious ancient ritual. It was intimate to watch the others breathe in the smoke and pass the mouthpiece around. Everyone had his or her own subtle way of smoking. I don't smoke, and I hate the habit of smoking cigarettes, but smoking a waterpipe in Istanbul was worthwhile. Afterwards, we ran through the streets in a rainstorm to another bar. The rain was refreshing after the smoke.

Our friend Ben Gray from the film company came out the following Saturday. He wanted to do some filming because Istanbul was an important milestone in our journey. A party was organised to celebrate his arrival. We cooked a curry, had drinks, played backgammon and then headed over to Nihan's friends – Birsu and Esel – and then to Taksim. Birsu was tall, with long strawberry blond hair and liquid green eyes. She was quiet but exuded confidence. Esel had black hair, dark eyes, and a warm personality.

Tom, Ben and I hired a motorbike, did some filming in the city, and afterwards went to a waterpipe cafe. We were messing about and joking, blowing smoke rings, when there was a series of bangs like mortar fire. Thankfully, it wasn't an invasion, but fireworks – to celebrate Ataturk day. Ataturk was known as 'the Father of the Turks' and led the revolution against the Ottoman Empire.

Grand fireworks launched into the air and showered the sky with kaleidoscopic splashes of sparkling colours. It felt like Tom and I had always turned up at the perfect moments to join in. Our trip celebrated being alive. Fun happens when you have friends, an interesting place, new and shared experiences, and life takes its course around you. Life is full of conversation, interaction, colour, dance and music when it is lived in the moment. All these things come together in an intoxicating mix. Everyone strives to find these feelings of freedom. It's like the excitement of a child; for each person, there is a particular recipe to achieve that 'present' state of mind that makes life more exciting and satisfying.

We caught the ferry at Uluköy to Kurilada Island and Ben filmed some interviews on a beach. The island was deserted and felt completely different to the cosmopolitan buzz of the city. On the boat on the way back, we watched the sun setting over the mosques on the Bosphorus. Ben filmed, and Tom and I took photos. The sea turned orange. Birds dotted about the sky and rose and fell on the breeze. The fishing boats, like ghost ships, were cloaked in a veil of haze, like waterpipe smoke rising from the chop and swell.

The boat chugged along with its passengers but the three of us stood alone. We were making our own epic story. The future was a huge, bound book, but that book was yet to be written.

Ben left to go back to England and went to stay with a friend of Esel's. We cycled to the Sisli mosque where we met with Pinar and Pedro, our new hosts. They lived in a grand old flat with high ceilings.

'I'm sick of Istanbul now. I can't wait to leave this place. I hate being stuck in a city.' Tom said. A part of me agreed, but another part was falling in love with the place and our friends.

In the evening, Pedro prepared a waterpipe and we smoked. Some of their friends came round, including a tall cyclist with a beard and long hair, and an architect with a moustache and 60's style hair cut. Birsu and Esel came round. Birsu looked beautiful. She barely spoke a word of English but I was deeply intrigued by her and attracted to her. The air smelt of mint smoke. The evening was a melting pot of people. I barely said anything. I was smoldering with thoughts of Birsu on my mind. I kept looking over to her, but she didn't look at me. I knew that she was playing a game. People gradually went home and I noticed Birsu go out onto the balcony. I decided to follow, and went out to her. She was smoking a cigarette, her long legs bunched up under her. She kept shivering, saying she was cold. I passed her my jacket and she smiled at me. We made eye contact for longer than usual. Then we had crossed the line. She leaned forward and looked closer at me. I hadn't planned to kiss her but I did.

34

Moving to Asia

The next afternoon, Tom and I spent time researching visas and routes on the Internet. The likely route was Turkey, Armenia, Iran, Turkmenistan, Uzbekistan, Kyrgyzstan, China, Tibet, Nepal, and India.

I went to Tugberk's to fetch the video camera from Maria who had taken it to film video diaries. On the way back, I passed the Beşiktaş football fans in black and white stripes walking through the streets. The match of the day was against arch-rivals Fenerbahçe. I went closer to investigate and get some close up shots.

Someone smashed a bottle. A weary police presence eyed us from the near distance. I rode further down the road towards the Beşiktaş Palace. Police with automatic rifles stood outside the building. Shiny black cars pulled in and out of the gates. There was a conference on Iraq for the ministers of surrounding nations.

The police eyed me as I cycled past. I wondered whether they thought I could be a terrorist, with my beard and backpack, but then I thought, 'It's obvious that I'm a tourist, isn't it?'

Tom and I moved to Kadiköy to stay with a Couchsurfer called Emrah. He had long, straight hair and looked vaguely like an American Indian. He was studying History of Art at Fenerbahçe University. We played poker with him and his friends and watched Fenerbahçe vs. PSV Eindhoven on television. You could see the Fenerbahçe stadium from his roof. I looked out of the window of his flat and watched crowds of Fenerbahçe fans marching down the streets, some of them firing pistols into the air – I pulled my head inside when I saw that.

Emrah was a deep thinker. We continued to play poker until 4.30 am. Emrah said, 'Tom had a good poker face, it's impossible to tell what he is thinking, whereas it is easy to tell what you are thinking.' Perhaps it was part of the poker strategy. He was quite drunk and he said to me, 'You need to can your ego. What are your motives for travel? What did you enjoy as a child? Are you sure your motives are your own?' Although Emrah didn't know me so his words were based on first impressions, they still touched a nerve. I wondered what being 'myself' meant since the tour.

We moved from Emrah's place to stay with Katie Shields. She lived on the fifth floor of an old apartment block with oodles of character, which was close to Kadiköy market. The building had wooden stairs covered in worn, dark red paint. There were indents on the steps from years of footsteps. Over the years, layer after layer of paint had been applied to the walls, fixtures and fittings and it looked at least half a centimetre thick.

Katie was not at home, so her roommate, Ingo, welcomed us. The flat had high ceilings and there were wonderful views out of tall windows over buildings and nearby mosques. Ingo was a German photographer who specialised in taking staged photographs. He had a commission from a German art institution to live in Istanbul and take photos. He showed us one composition with a woman standing near to a cliff edge. She was holding onto a tent, which was blowing in the wind. He said his photos were inspired by life and simple observations of naturally occurring patterns. He gave the example of a plastic bag, caught in a bush, flapping in the wind, which had inspired the tent photo. He took something ugly and turned it into something beautiful.

35

Two Tramps in Istanbul

The following day we had to find somewhere else to sleep because Katie's parents were staying at her place and we couldn't be bothered to organise another Couchsurfer and move our stuff. It seemed like a good opportunity to see what would happen if we went off into the city with our sleeping and bivvy bags and, for one night, became real tramps. We wandered about for a while. It was a strange feeling to be carrying my bed with me. Did people know that I was a tramp intending to sleep rough?

We passed a few possible places but noticed other tramps were already occupying the spaces. It was getting late. When we had stayed with Emrah, he had shown us the roof of his building and its view over Kadiköy and I wondered if perhaps it would be possible to get back onto the roof so we could sleep there. We stood outside his apartment block until someone came out and opened the door. I caught it before it closed again.

We quietly went up the spiral stairs to the top floor and found the roof door open. I set out my bivvy bag. Tom crawled under a table and I strung my poncho up as a shelter from the rain. The night was dry but the air was thick and heavy.

It was simplicity itself, nothing between the sky and me but a couple of layers of waterproof fabric and my sleeping bag.

I woke with a start at an unearthly hour. There is a tenth of a second where dream and reality merge and, at that moment, I thought I had ended up in the sea. In my dream, I saw the apartment block from the side. I was on top and the entire building turned to water, began to collapse, and I began to fall through it. Consciousness kicked in and I was lying in a couple of inches of water. The rain was coming down like a waterfall off the side of the poncho. We left the building and walked through the rain in the streets. However, I couldn't help a big smile rising across my face.

It was those times – where all structure is taken away and one freefalls in the face of the unpredictability of life and the weather – when I found it all so funny. I would get a huge burst of energy and gladness for being alive. Time would seem to drain away and lose its meaning. I was only bothered about living, not thinking about dying, and not bothering myself with everyday concerns.

The next day there was still no word about my wheels arriving. We decided to make it the day's goal to see where they had got to. They still hadn't arrived at the WWF office. We asked at the post office and got an address to a depot outside of the centre. Inside, we were shuttled between different departments until we discovered that the wheels had indeed arrived and had been waiting there for some time, so we picked them up and decided to leave Istanbul. We said goodbye to our friends. I was considering staying in Istanbul with them but I decided it was too early to stop. My instincts told me to continue.

Istanbul had been brilliant. We had made so many friends who had collectively generated an unforgettable experience of freedom, fun, and togetherness. I've met other travellers who have said they didn't like Istanbul, after spending a few days there in a tourist area. They said it was too expensive or too busy, focusing on one bad thing that happened to them – like a taxi driver ripping them off – that ended up as their defining experience of the city. But outside of the package holiday experience of travel, there is a wealth of complexity and experience to be explored.

36

Part II: The Black Sea Coastline

Kadiköy looked grey and unforgiving under a cloudy sky. My bike felt heavy and I was self-conscious. I felt low after leaving our friends behind. It grew dark and began to rain heavily. We planned to cycle next to the Bosphorus and head towards the coastline.

We stopped in an ekmek (bread) shop, which was warm, and we dried out for a few minutes. How pitiful we looked can be gauged by the fact that the owner of the bakery donated ten lire to us so we could eat something. I felt nihilistic cycling off into the wet night away from the comfort of recent weeks.

Later, we asked at a petrol station about a place to sleep. One of the attendants jumped on his motorbike. 'Follow me,' he said. He accelerated and we pedalled like fury, only for him to slow down and speed up as a joke. It was funny. This guy, in his mundane job as a pump attendant, became a joker and a superhero for the brief time that he was given free rein to help us.

He took us to the local mosque but we couldn't sleep there, so he took us to the second hub of the Turkish community; the chay shop. He bought us chay and pastries and we played backgammon. After a few hours, I was starting to get really tired and the chay shop closed.

There was a man at another table who kept looking over at us. I was a little wary of him because he looked unshaven and dirty – ironic, considering my own appearance. The man approached us and talked with our friend.

He said he knew a place where we could camp, so we went with him and he showed us round the back of the chay shop. I stumbled over a load of stacked furniture and wood in the pitch black whilst he lit the way by the light of his mobile phone screen. A circle of hazy, orange light illuminated a blue tarpaulin, which he pulled back, and out jumped a cat. Underneath were a dirty old sofa and a couple of blankets. He gestured proudly towards it to indicate that we could sleep here. I didn't really fancy it, to be honest, but I smiled and we thanked the man and he left. It was a grim place but it was a space where we were safe from being disturbed by random night wanderers.

Water was dripping everywhere. The atmosphere was cold and damp and my breath condensed in the air. Tom lay down his bivvy bag on the floor inside a small shelter and went to sleep. There were picnic tables and chairs stacked up so I did a bit of rearranging and made a bed on a table.

In the morning, I felt like I'd woken up in B&Q's garden furniture section after a drunken night out in Kettering. Tom said that there had been rats running around him in the night. When we saw where we had slept in daylight we were both keen to get moving.

At lunch, we sat outside a mosque. Locals came and went. Old men sat fingering prayer beads – a set of 108 beads, each one representing a prayer.

I was in high spirits. The road snaked through a few villages beside the wintry sea and a battered beach strewn with flotsam and jetsam. The cityscape changed to hills. The landscape was autumnal with maroons and mottled ochre. It reminded me of Leicestershire, with its undulating hills, ploughed fields, and small winding roads. Smoke rose from chimneys in the villages and I heard someone chopping wood.

Some of the oldest cottages were built from wood and some from red brick, with red and grey tiled roofs. Some of the buildings looked uneven, warped, and fragile.

In every village we passed through, people shouted to us to come and drink chay. Before entering a settlement, I would decide either to say, 'No, thank you, Tesekkürler!' and ride by

161

quickly, or to accept. If we accepted, it would usually involve a lot of politeness, manly grunts, and hand shaking with perennially situated old men, who I imagined held a wealth of worldly wisdom beyond their crinkly foreheads.

37

A Lot of Rain

Near Kaynarca, a storm broke out and we took shelter in a petrol station. The attendant was smartly dressed with a white shirt, pointy shoes and neatly pressed black trousers. He seemed proud of his petrol station. Cars are still a symbol of manliness and economic progress in Turkey. In England, the job of petrol attendant is a low class, low paid job, usually the realm of spotty teenage school-leavers who are probably a bit thick and who don't make eye contact with you as they take your money.

We soon found out that the chay houses were a good place to get warm and dry and somewhere to ask about sleeping. We sat in one that evening. I looked around at the bare wooden shell of a building, which was painted in a faded blue. There was a basic till, a desk, and framed pictures of the ubiquitous Ataturk along with a map of the Karadeniz – the Turkish name for the Black Sea coast.

A man in the chay shop invited us to his house for dinner. His house was spacious and stood on a generous plot of land with a plentiful garden. We sat in his living room, and his wife brought plates of olives, pickled chillies, cheese and bread. The wife didn't sit or eat with us although she accepted our repeated thanks.

We went back to the chay shop and a group of boys came and sat with us. One boy, called Yarsi, had just finished his military service. He was going to 'Arabistan' to work in the construction trade. We spent the evening chatting and joking with the boys. Many of the old men came over to us and shook our hands as if it was a matter of course.

Yarsi invited us to sleep at his house. He lived in a big place and said he used to have a large family with five brothers. I was impressed by the size of the dwelling and inside it felt homely and cosy. The house was empty now because everyone had moved away to work.

Only his grandmother and his ailing grandfather lived with him. His grandfather lay in a bed in the kitchen so that his wife could look after him all the time. He looked grey and pale, said nothing, groaned, and breathed heavily. Occasionally he tried to move, which appeared to cause great pain, so he would quickly give up. I felt sorry for the grandmother who was obviously committed to looking after her ailing husband; he didn't look like he would hold out for long.

The grandmother had such a wrinkly face that the wrinkles covered every inch like a topographical map. Her small, twinkling eyes were set deeply into the craters of her eye sockets. Her skin and feet were dried out and she had no teeth. She spoke Turkish in an almost poetic way. She seemed completely oblivious to the fact we spoke none. Her words flowed like a sad stream and seemed to appeal for help. Yarsi and his grandmother cooked us a plate of fried tomatoes and onions, which we ate with bread.

We had been in Turkey for over a month already but, so far, we had spent most of our time in Istanbul. Now we were in a place of such contrast. The divide between the villages and the city was growing. However, family and village life were still very important. Anyone who went to work or lived in the city would still visit their village quite regularly, donate money and sometimes go back to live there later on in life.

Tom and I talked very little. We had spent so much time together that we didn't have much to say. We cycled down a deserted road, which snaked beside the coastline. It was very hilly and progress was slow. As it grew dark, we came across a restaurant and the owner turned up and gave us the keys to one of his holiday bungalows. It had a hot shower, bunk beds, an oven, and a table, which was a huge luxury.

I went down to look at the beach to go for a walk alone. From the cliff, I looked over a small cove. The waves broke over black rocks, which protruded from the headland, creating fluffy white water that swilled about. The salty sea breeze blew and when I took a deep breath of fresh air, I could taste the salt on my tongue.

As I stood there, a large old-fashioned Cadillac-style car pulled off the road. It tore down the dirt track, bouncing and skidding over ruts and long grass. It slid round the corner, splashing through a puddle of water, and bumped its way down towards a house at the end of the track.

I felt like I was on the set of a seventies horror movie. The Black Sea coast has a certain wilderness feel. It's not popular with tourists. The first section of the Black Sea coastline in the north west of Turkey is particularly rural and is a glimpse of a bygone farming and fishing lifestyle. Men work long hours, smoke, and come home to eat meals cooked by their wives who have also been working hard all day.

38

A Typical Turkish Town

The coastline and terrain became progressively hillier and impressive. The road became more built up at Akçakoca near Alapli and the road flattened and was busier. Signs of different sizes, and at different angles, dotted the roadside verge chaotically: 'Inan otogaz', 'Erciyes mobilya', 'bülbüller grup', 'keskin', 'tansas'. They advertised businesses in the next big town of Eregli.

At lunch, we were cycling along and a baker gestured us to stop at his bakery. We sat and watched him making bread. He strung out and plaited a lump of dough, and then placed it into the big cavern-like clay oven on a tray with a long handle. Soon we were salivating at the aroma of freshly baked bread. It was slightly crispy on the outside, with a soft and fluffy inside. It was delicious: better than French bread.

We cycled past a shipyard into the ugly town of Eregli, as it was getting dark. I gazed in awe at the size of the huge ships being built. Men hung from ropes and welded sheets of iron onto the skeletal frame, sending sparks into the air.

The town was really ugly with tower blocks, traffic, fumes, and row after row of the same shops: mostly auto-repair workshops. Perhaps it seemed uglier because we had spent so long in the countryside. Compared to the calm of the rolling hills, fields, and the coastal roads, the town looked like an angular patchwork of poorly thought-out architecture and pollution: a product of the human logical mind.

Some people stopped to watch us passing and smiled, waved or shouted. Schoolchildren walked home. Wood smoke rose from houses on the surrounding hills. The moon appeared large and the temperature dropped. I was worried about finding somewhere to sleep. We'd been spoilt the last few nights, which had the disagreeable effect of making me worry about whether we would find somewhere similarly comfortable.

The worrying was unfounded because we were invited to sleep in a petrol station when we cycled past. Our hosts bought us pide bread filled with juicy slivers of grilled meat, yoghurt sauce and salad. We ate them whilst sitting in front of a warm heater. For a hungry and cold cyclist, it was a treat from my wildest desires. One facet of cycle touring is the satisfaction you get from putting in a huge effort and being exhausted at the end of the day. Food tastes amazing and you are guaranteed the best night's sleep.

In modern Western life, with its convenience food and huge emphasis on comfort and indulgence, this kind of satisfaction is in danger of being lost, with the side effect that the human body atrophies and deteriorates.

Sometimes Tom and I argued, but the positive side of this was that I was learning to deal with conflict. By burning away my ego, I let other people into my headspace. I created the conditions for myself to be more present and have better contact with Tom, who was unknowingly helping me understand that he saw the world through the lens of his own unique perspective.

It is a long path to enlightenment, which starts out with basic, but fundamental and humbling realisations about oneself and the wider lessons of life. The great traveller travels as a humble student who wishes to learn as much as possible about his or her surroundings. You throw yourself into the world as you are, the world responds, and from these responses, you begin to learn about yourself.

39

A Cold Night

A farmer was standing outside his house almost as if he was waiting for our arrival. We made the usual 'camping' hand gestures and snoring noises. He gave us a spot in the field behind his house, next to a small river. It looked like an ideal campsite: grassy hills sprinkled with autumnal red- and orange-tinted shrubs.

The farmer stood around for a while watching us pitch the tents. He mimed coldness by rubbing his arms but I made negative noises, shook my head, pointed to my sleeping bag, and put my thumbs up to convince him that I would be warm. When the sun went down the temperature dropped considerably which was a shock to the system. I had to run on the spot and do star jumps to keep warm. Thick steam rose from the stew Tom was cooking.

The sky was beautifully clear. The moon illuminated everything with a subtle iridescence. It was soul-soothingly quiet once the farmer's dog had got bored of barking at us. I wore three Buffs and all my upper body layers and slept in my clothes, but I still felt the cold.

In the morning, I saw it had been cold enough to freeze my breath into an impressive crust of ice on the opening of the sleeping bag and it was quite a challenge to motivate myself to emerge into the freezing air. The inside of the tent was crusted with ice. Tom filmed me emerging from the tent, which created a cloud of powdered frost as I brushed past it.

Everywhere was white and gripped by a thick layer of frozen dew. I jumped up and down on the spot and patted myself to get the blood flowing. The poncho covering the bikes was frozen solid. In hindsight, I realised that the campsite was in the bottom of a valley next to a river and was a sink for cold air.

Tom's rear hub was making a grinding noise and had to be fixed at the first opportunity. We stopped at a chay shop for lunch. I chatted in German to a man who had worked in Belgium. He bought us a chay and then concluded the conversation with a decisive, 'Ich fähre Stadt,' and got on the next bus. Many Turkish people spoke basic German because there were many migrant workers who went to Germany to work and then came back to Turkey.

Tom and I argued about the most improbable things sometimes. The bread that I bought from the small shop was smaller than the bread that Tom had bought the day before for lunch, so he said I should buy more because he was still hungry.

We had maintained a 'food-master' system since France. If the other person was still hungry or there was excess food then it was blamed on the food-master, and so food was sometimes a cause of disagreement and didn't always work out well. It didn't make any sense to have a system that meant we didn't eat more if we were hungry, in order to save money. It was concept taking priority over experience.

The light was failing as we began to descend the other side of the mountain pass towards the town of Devrek. An epic reddish-grey valley stretched all around. A derelict house showed potential for sleeping. Tom investigated, but there were signs of other vagrants living there.

Devrek is in the inner zone of the West Black Sea region in Turkey. It is surrounded by the Gölda, Akçasu and Yenice mountains. We arrived in the town in the dark. We passed a couple of high-density housing blocks. There was a sports hall, and I remembered that Verena Lepre had mentioned that sports halls were good places to ask about sleeping.

I knocked on the door and went in. A friendly looking chap was sitting behind an office desk. He had big ears, crew cut hair, bags under his eyes, and a couple of scars on his face that made him look like he might have been a boxer at one time in his life.

He wore light blue jeans and a green, woollen jumper with a waistcoat over the top.

There were a few other younger boys sitting around who were waiting to play in a football match. We were invited to sit and we were brought cups of Nescafé – the universal name for instant coffee. A mime – pedalling with my hands in front of me – and a quick peek at the bikes was all that was needed for everyone to accept us as fellow sportsmen. There were big smiles all around and I felt instantly at ease.

The other boys there included Murat, who may have been of Mongolian ancestry. He had short, straight dark hair, brown eyes, and a calm character. There was Suleiman. He was a joker, with slicked back, black hair, bright sparkling eyes, and I noticed he had a bruise under his left eye. There were two other boys. One had an unshaven face and smoked cigarettes and the other was a smart, good-looking, thickly built boy who wore a jacket with the text 'European Tour Air', 'club', and 'Stone Urban' on the back.

Murat spoke a little English. 'Where are you from? What is your city like? I want to go to England.' We ate kebabs and watched the football in the hall, but it was too cold to sit there for long.

At the end of the evening, we were allowed to sleep in the office. A few hours ago, we had been complete strangers and now we had been entrusted with the entire building!

We were given breakfast of simit – a savoury, sesame seed coated, bread-donut – and jam, and then cycled into the town centre. I sat on the pavement whilst Tom bought some video tapes. I talked to an old man with a flat cap, who was playing backgammon with his friend. He invited me to drink a chay. Then a man in a blue suit and dark coloured jacket came over. He was a journalist from the local newspaper. Soon we had a crowd of people around us. The journalist was interested in our story for the local paper. He took photos and filmed us cycling along.

He asked us if we'd seen the famous 'stick shop of Devrek'. We found out that Devrek is famous for one thing, and that is handcrafted walking sticks. Prince Charles is an owner of note, and he even visited the shop. It takes over a year to finish some of the most intricate sticks and some of them fetch prices up to 1900 YTL: about €750.

40

From a Hotel to a Bus Shelter

We asked the journalist about somewhere to stay for the night and were given a free room in a hotel where we ate fish and drank beer in the restaurant. Then we were shown the special 'hunting' room. There was a huge, carved image of a deer on the wall and photos of hunting trips to shoot wild boar. The area was popular for hunting.

The next night we had a challenge to find somewhere to sleep. After the town of Bartin, we turned off the main road and headed towards the coast. I asked at a farmhouse about sleeping. A woman appeared on the balcony of the top floor of the house and shook her head at me. Meanwhile her dogs barked and chased me back down the drive, so we continued in the dark with the hope of reaching the coast and camping on the beach, although we didn't know how far it was.

I was already shattered and very hungry. It was a gruelling challenge. The next village had a chay shop. Each chay shop seemed to have a different social dynamic. In this one, no one took any notice of us at all. No one asked if we needed help. There didn't seem any possibility of finding a warm place to sleep. I started to feel frustrated. Outside it was freezing cold and wet. I wanted to avoid sleeping outdoors because of the cold night and my inadequate sleeping bag, which had become an ongoing annoyance.

We went into a little store in the village and were given a hot coffee. Two men in their mid twenties appeared to be living out their days together running a small convenience store in the village. They were dressed, like most young Turkish men, in a variant of 'Turkish fashion playboy' style. One had European features, and the other, Central Asian.

The Central Asian looking one was wearing an identical 'European Air Tour' jacket to the boy in Devrek. They were surrounded by lollipops, lighters, pens, chocolate, bags of sugar, and cartons of chemically enhanced juices neatly stacked on the shelves.

I think it was quite exciting for them to meet us, but, since we often sat down with groups of Turks and felt like we were old friends, we were more laid back. It was a surreal experience to turn up in a little convenience shop at that time of night – in such backcountry part of Turkey – and then have your photo taken.

Having finally run out of options to find lodgings, we ended up sleeping in a bus shelter. I lay out my thin polystyrene mat on the cold concrete and got into my sleeping bag.

The night passed in semi-sleep. I woke regularly, rolled, and shuffled about. The morning came after what felt like an endless amount of time. I was really cold. I peered out from my sleeping bag. The bikes were covered in snow. The road was thick with icy slush. My instinctive reaction was to get up straight away and jump around to get warm.

Tom sat up and looked around slowly. He didn't say a word and was extremely grumpy. Although I was energised, I noticed that my temper had become short. We couldn't help but bicker and moan at each other, although I started to wonder whether this served a purpose to have something to talk about and get the communication going.

The landscape was covered with a thirty-centimetre blanket of snow and the wind chill made it feel a lot colder. The cheap gloves I had bought in the market in Istanbul were of little use, so my fingers were numb. I got feeling into them by opening and closing my hands one hundred times, which was an ongoing exercise.

The landscape was stunning with patches of blue sky, which allowed sunbeams to emerge from the thick, grey-and-white clouds, which were heavy with snow. Mountain peaks were hidden in the cloud. Snow balanced on the barbed wire fence beside the road.

We headed towards the small but historic town of Amasra. The red roofed buildings were packed in along the peninsula, next to a little sandy beach lined with fishing and sailing boats. The town has an antiquated history. The original city, Sesamus, was mentioned in Homer's Illiad. The Rus, in the first Russo-Byzantine War sacked it around 830. The Genoese domination ended in 1460, when the Ottoman Sultan Mehmed II conquered the whole Anatolian Black Sea Coast.

In the Roman period, Amastris (now Amasra) extended inland into the valley behind the bay and lower hills. Roman buildings can be traced for one and a half kilometres inland, but now the town occupies the peninsula.

We bought breakfast and sat in a wonderful fresh-baked-dough-smelling pide shop to warm up. The ancient Roman walls were impressive. Boats bobbed on the choppy water in the bay.

The sun came out. To feel its rays was deeply satisfying and the feeling was accentuated by the contrast with the cold weather we had woken up to. We sat for a while in a chay shop before Tom tore me away. I probably would have stayed there all day otherwise.

It was a long climb out of Amasra, amongst dramatic and wild landscape. The road was rough and unmaintained. The biting cold kept us moving onwards. We ate lunch in a chay shop in Caypile next to the zorber – a traditional Turkish wood-burning stove. The chay shop offered the same benefits as the English pub; it enabled the man to get away from his wife.

One typical old Turkish man was wearing a slate-grey flat cap, matching smart jacket, black woollen body warmer and a grey polo neck sweater. His olive-skinned face was cleanly shaven. He had sagging jowls and his jaw hung loosely with his mouth slightly open. He flicked prayer beads slowly through his fingers.

He had a gold watch on his wrist, and his other hand rested heavily on the table. His eyes betrayed nothing. His attention focused on any small occurrence outside on the road as if he was watching television.

It's unsurprising we spent so much time in teashops because they were like black holes in terms of time. It was very easy to sit down and gaze at the world for hours in a nice comfortable and warm atmosphere, drinking glasses of dark tea, and eating cube after cube of sugar.

41

Hamsi

The next evening we camped in a small fishing village, which looked to me like it had been frozen in time. There were little boats moored up in the bay and rugged looking fishermen wandering about. I walked over to check out a local chay shop and, on the way, came across a hamsi seller.

Hamsi are small minnow-like fish and, when cooked properly, usually fried in breadcrumbs, a very tasty delicacy. I decided to buy some. However, I could only buy a kilo because it was the smallest amount the seller was willing to give me. It was too much, but I thought that we would easily eat it up with our cyclists' appetites.

I valiantly attempted to cook the slimy little things on the stove but the result looked thoroughly disgusting. The fish disintegrated, exposing their spiky backbones. The culinary experience was like eating fish mush and pins.

I felt the cold more than Tom and I moaned at him about being cold at night. We were both getting frustrated with the wet weather and the routine of fishing villages and chay shops. In addition, it felt like we should be making better progress. Our average daily distance had dropped right down and we were only covering between thirty and fifty kilometres.

In the town of Cide, the owner of the bike shop let us in to the changing rooms of the football field so we could sleep. It was a typical school changing room. There were slatted benches, clothes hooks, and clumps of mud and grass on the floor. It stank of sweat and smelly football socks. I cooked the rest of the hamsi and attempted to make a fish soup. However, the result was worse than before: a silvery grey coloured gruel. It was horrible and Tom complained bitterly.

The changing room was warm and I slept really well. I discovered that I was much warmer if I wore my cotton layers rather than sleeping in my synthetic cycling clothes. Sweat does not make for a good night's sleep, as you wake up in the early morning when your body temperature is lowest and find yourself cold and damp.

The next morning, we followed a cliff-side road. I looked out across the sea and saw the weather approaching in the form of dark grey, swirling clouds, which looked like they were sucking water up into the sky to form a barrier. We were about to be caught in a deluge, so we pedalled like crazy in an attempt to escape the imminent torrent. It soon caught us, and I was soaked to the bone in minutes.

Water dripped off my helmet, into my mouth. My trousers stuck to my legs. The wind chill penetrated my wet layers, and my fingers were cold. An irrefutably wise decision was made to enter a chay shop and find a warm refuge out of the storm. We stopped at a convenience store and the owner invited us into a side room, which had a zorber stove. We hung up our wet clothes and passed some hours reading. The clothes took a long time to dry. Steam rose from our mouldy, smelling socks; it was the first time they had seen water since Istanbul.

A couple of days later we slept in a small abandoned building on the hillside. I awoke early the next morning and the sunrise was impressive. I climbed up to the top of a hill to get a better view. Fishing boats bobbed on the surface of the water, their fishing nets were stretched out behind them. It felt like I was watching Turkish coastal life, unchanged for years. Pink, red, rose, and orange merged in the landscape between the sea and the clouds, which looked like smudged pastel. The colours shifted, melted, and metamorphosed.

Dogalyurt had a population of nineteen hundred people. Every town had a sign, which detailed the population of the settlement. It was possible to judge what resources would be available in the town based on a hierarchy of population, from the smallest village to the largest settlements.

Most sizes of settlement had ekmek bread shops and most had chay shops where we could buy soup and simits. Slightly larger settlements had photography shops, which sold DV video tapes, Internet cafes, and 'BIM' supermarkets, which were excellent for buying cheap food supplies. Usually only in the cities and larger settlements would we find Couchsurfers, although it was sometime surprising where we found members.

We pedalled down the hill towards the sea in order to get breakfast in a chay shop, and a van with some Turkish men passed by. One man leaned out and shouted 'chay, chay, chay!' gesturing for us to follow him. We pedalled after the van in the hope of getting a free chay – it had become a Pavlovian effect – but it pulled away around the corner and then disappeared down a side street. I concluded this was the Turkish version of cherry knocking for cycle tourists.

As the sun rose over the harbour, we ate freshly baked loaves of bread, hot and floury to the touch. I tore off great chunks and chewed away contentedly, whilst flour got into my now bushy beard.

The wooden building had dusty black and white historical photos hanging on the wall. A television in the corner was showing a Spanish soap opera dubbed into Turkish. A voluptuous woman with long black hair stood in a kitchen arguing with a smartly dressed, silver-haired man. His arms, palms and fingers were outstretched expressively. This reminded me of women. I'd spoken to perhaps three since I left Istanbul.

The next section of coast was rugged cliffs. I stopped to take a photo of a beach, accessible only by swimming, boat or a suicidal fall onto virgin sand. In a small village, old women tended to gardens and men chopped wood. Children shouted, 'Where are you from?' and, 'hello, what is your name?'

I stopped by the roadside after the town of Inebolu. There was a gaping void missing from the cliff. Piles of rubbish were tipped into the area, presumably in the absence of an official landfill site.

Tyres, plastic bottles, packaging and paper smouldered. Packs of stray dogs roamed amidst the detritus foraging for food. A lorry went past and scattered a pack of the mangy creatures to the verge. The road surface had a layer of flattened dog remains from previous road-kill. It was repulsive. We cycled with our heads down, disgusted at what we had seen. Someone had decided that it was better to avoid a problem than to confront it directly, which had lead to this disaster.

It was miles to pedal between villages. Forested valleys slunk away from the coast. The only dwellings were occasional single houses or farm smallholdings. Dirt tracks led off away from the main road and wound into the hills.

42

Observing but Not Participating

The light was beginning to fail. We looked for places to camp. We reached Gemicilier, and asked some Jaundarma about a place to camp. They pointed out a beach on the other side of the harbour so we pedalled over to a hut and a concrete platform.

It was very quiet. The wind rustled the trees. Water lapped the shingle beach. It was immediately relaxing. I imagined people playing, meeting, and enjoying the spot in the summer. The hut was full of tables, chairs and advertising signboards for use in the summer season. A couple of tables and a disintegrated sofa sat on a concrete platform outside. We lay out our sleeping bags on top of a couple of tables. Tom went off for a walk alone with his camera whilst I collected driftwood from the beach for a fire.

It was weird being there in the winter. I had a preconception of a beach being a place where people played and sunbathed. In the winter, it was just the place where the land met the sea and it seemed to lose its novelty after a while. Where had this idyllic summer image of a beach, that I held in my mind, come from? Was it from childhood memories or was it from Hollywood movies and package holiday brochures? I guessed it was a combination of all three.

I decided to make a 'hobo stove'. I found an old oil can and punctured the side with some holes to allow air to feed the fire. I laid out the firewood in piles according to size. There was plenty of wood that had washed up on the rocks. There were pieces of timber, which had been eroded and had smooth curved edges as if they had been sanded down on a machine. A long cylindrical piece of wood looked like it could have been a boat's mast, which had been torn off in a shipwreck.

The temperature was fine until the sun set and then it turned bitterly cold. The sweat in my clothes chilled me. I busied myself in order to keep the blood circulating and keep warm. I shivered whilst hurriedly building the fire. I arranged a tepee of small twigs above a handful of dry grass and newspaper tinder. Once the first sticks were burning, I added bigger lumps of wood. Within minutes, it was a blazing inferno, sucking in air, and spewing flames out of the lid. I sat next to it and warmed myself. The fire crackled, spat, and whined and sent little glowing pieces of ash skyward.

We'd already been in Turkey for almost two months. I yearned for a change but every day still intrigued me. I was a little worried about what might be simmering under the surface of the silence in Tom. I couldn't tell how Tom felt because he didn't say much or show much emotion.

We sat beside the roaring stove like pyromaniac little boys. The wok rested on top with stuffed meat pasta cooking inside, which made a luxurious change from lentils. We ate and I put the last log on the fire. Hopefully it would provide some ambient heat during the night.

In the darkness, my vision adjusted to the light from the moon and the stars. The beach was bathed in dim light. I could smell wood-smoke on my clothes. The smell reminded me of lighting barbecues at home. I thought of my family. My stomach was comfortingly lined with hot food.

I tried to wrap the sleeping bag around me as best I could, but I didn't sleep well. I drifted in and out of dreams, and the night was long, but it was life affirming to wake up outside. Life is there all around and there is no option or desire for a lie in. A bedroom makes it too easy to stay in bed and sleep all day in warmth, comfort and darkness. In fact, to wake up early and to sleep for only the amount of time your body needs to function healthily is the most efficient way of being, and yields the fullest experience.

When you go to sleep, normally there is a period of very

ineffective sleep before you drop into deep REM sleep when you have the most dreams. If you are more tired, you fall more quickly into REM sleep, and spend less time in the inefficient phase.

The road flattened out as we approached the town of Abana, after which we tackled some huge hills before being rewarded by a picturesque downhill into Çatalzeytin. It was a town that seemed geared up for tourists but I never saw any as I passed the chandlery, fishing shops, a boat works, and tourist shops closed for the winter.

The sea front was flat, with a long walkway. Tom bought food and we sat in the town square. An old man, who wore a grey, flat cap with the press-stud button undone so that the cap could be pulled down over his forehead for warmth, came over and spoke to me. He shook my hand and smiled in a welcoming way. I noticed his thick, cracked skin like aged leather. He wore a brown jacket, light blue shirt, black slacks, and unpolished black boots. The local old men were often friendly and I had a feeling that they were from an age where they saw bearded travellers like me as real adventurers, and were doing their bit for international relations by making the effort to meet me.

After food, I went beside the sea on the walkway and many children shouted, 'Hello, what is your name?' A smartly suited man was being interviewed for television.

Once the reporter finished, he turned to me. He spoke to me entirely in Turkish but I was able to say 'Ingiltere'den Türkiye'ye bisikletle geldim, bes ay' which means 'England to Turkey by bike, five months.'

A group of children giggled at me shouting and asking questions. One child seemed particularly intelligent. His friends egged him on to say things like, 'What are your mother and father's names and jobs?' Another boy tried to say something, but he couldn't get the words out well enough for me to understand and he received a beating from his friends for his efforts.

43

Filming For Fun

In a smoky Internet café, we got an email from James at String Films saying they were going to stop producing the podcast due to lack of finances. Although we had received sponsorship from Optical Express, this money had been spent on a specialist PR officer and full-time editor. The most important thing was that String Films didn't go under as a company. They were our friends and mentors. We had learnt a great deal from them.

It was never going to be easy to create a filming project of an open-ended adventure. Hopefully the end product would be worth it. They were still up for creating a feature length documentary, which meant filming less, and thinking more critically, about what we were filming.

We cycled along the road away from the town, passing a beach shack in disrepair and a shepherd with his flock of sheep. We reached the town of Turkeli by the evening and cycled into the central square. We met a teacher from the local school who said we could stay in the teacher's residency – for teachers that travelled between schools. Then, in the morning, we were asked to come to the students' lesson. I listened to the sounds in the school corridor, which reminded me of my secondary school; shouting and chatter reverberated down the corridors and busy staircases. The walls were blue with scrape marks from children dragging their bags and the carpet was worn and scuffed.

We were asked questions like, 'What is your name?', 'What is your age?', and, 'What is your favourite sport?' Tom showed the route that we were planning on the world map. We had talked with Nihan in Istanbul about what Turkish people thought of joining the EU, so we asked the schoolchildren. I was surprised that they were quite outspoken in their opinions. They had mixed feelings: partly a fear of losing cultural identity but, on the other hand, an attraction to economic gain.

We stayed with a teacher called Harun. He cooked a spectacular lunch of çorba (soup), yogurt (dogal yogurt), sausage (sosis), egg (yumurta), chillies, tomato, bread, kushpomo (a type of jam), and borek (börek). In the evening, we attended an English lesson taught by Harun at a local community centre. The students self-consciously practised their language and giggled when Harun announced there were two Englishmen visiting the lesson.

After we went back to Harun's place, two of his friends came round and introduced us to Turkish roasted sesame seeds. You can often see people eating handfuls of them, deftly de-shelling the seed with a swift pinch of thumb and forefinger, which comes a close third to drinking chay and smoking in the hierarchy of Turkish pastimes. We said very little to each other. Our attention was fully focused on amassing neat piles of seed shells on the coffee table.

Before leaving in the morning, Harun cooked us a hearty breakfast of egg, sausage, and omelette with tomato, cucumber, cheese and bread; the closest thing we had had to an English breakfast for a long time. The road headed inland, traversing many hills. We stopped for lunch at Ayacin.

In the evening, we turned off the road onto a beach where there was a fast food restaurant, closed up for the winter. It had a covered seating area, which was ideal for camping. I collected pieces of driftwood and root from the surrounding marshland area. We walked down to the beach. There were a couple of weather-beaten shacks wrapped in tatty tarpaulins and a wooden hut. Stormy waves crashed onto the beach. It was moody and deserted. We returned to the restaurant and started a fire in the barbecue to cook some dinner.

Just as we were about to go to sleep for the night, a torch light shined through the trees. A dog rustled, then bounded past somewhere close by. Through the darkness, a man appeared. He said, 'No … Not possible,' and waved his arms, gesturing that we couldn't sleep there but to go with him. We didn't have much choice other than to follow him through the darkness.

The man led us to a wooden hut on the beach, the window now illuminated with a yellow light. Inside, there was another man with a weather-beaten face whose expression never changed. His chin was covered in thick stubble and he wore a blue, woolly hat. The men said very little, smoked, and played cards at a small table under a single dim lamp. It was fascinating to watch them. They looked cinematographic. Outside, the wind howled, and the rain battered the glass windowpane.

In the morning, we saw news of the Turkey–Iraq war on the television. The Turkish were fighting the PKK in Northern Iraq because the PKK had killed some civilians around the border region. Turkey responded with typical military might. The coverage in the media was astonishing. I often saw exaggerated news reports, which used 3D graphics to glamorise them.

I watched a shot from a helicopter's radar camera, which showed a bomb hitting an unidentifiable target. The news program repeated the clip eight times in succession. It looked like the sort of thing you see on American wrestling shows. The shot was repeated from as many angles as possible to heighten the excitement of something that was highly staged and not particularly interesting anyway. It seemed that the novelty of television is as big in Turkey as anywhere else.

I pushed my bike out of the wooden lodge into the torrential rain. Cycling was very unappealing. We made the decision to return to the restaurant shack and wait for the rain to recede, but it showed no signs of doing so. The shepherd we had seen on arrival turned up. His name was Ibrahim. He lit a cigarette, and must have decided we needed his help, so he collected some choice pieces of dry wood, and broke up some twigs to make a fire in the stove. Soon it was blazing and providing plenty of warmth. I let my mind wander and thought of home and Christmas coming up, an open fire in the living room, close friends, and my grandparents.

Tom had been reading Plato's Republic and he lent the book to me. I read about the design of a community and the different classes of people suggested, such as the soldier classes. I liked the sensible, logical style. We lived within a system that owed great deal to Greek Philosophy. The thoughts of Plato have inspired thinkers, throughout the ages, who have designed the systems we live in today. However, this system has created some problems too, like ecological catastrophe, and it is not dealing well with solving them.

Once the weather cleared, we were eager to get out of there so we belted along the first ten kilometres of hills before breakfast, to warm up. By the time we reached the first shop, I was incredibly hungry so I ate tahin (a sesame seed based sweet) and drank chay. The shop had black tables and white walls and reminded me of an English pub. I asked for börek, but the lady didn't have any freshly made; she brought me half of one, left over from what I think might have been her breakfast.

44

Sinop

Tom wanted to go and see Sinop, which had been a target for us to reach, but I had got into a routine of pedalling and wanted to continue. However, I understood that it was important to refocus on the present rather than the next destination – and, besides, Sinop turned out to be very interesting.

We started the process of looking for somewhere to stay for the night. I felt like playing with the process, and it was something to do as much as anything. We asked at a fancy hotel with leather sofas and wood panelling. I went up to the reception and tried to ask in an earnest way about getting a hotel room for free, but I couldn't take it seriously and burst out laughing. It had become absurd because I wasn't actually in need anymore. I didn't need the comfort that the hotel provided in order to feel content, so it no longer controlled my actions. I expect this is something that professional tramps feel. However, the glowing little idyllic image of comfort still hung there in my mind, so we continued to ask at different places, but it was more out of boredom than anything else.

We also asked at a pension, where they wanted forty lira per night. We said 'para yok': no money. Finally, as it was getting dark, we gave up and started walking to see if we could find a beach to camp on. On the way, I went to the toilet and Tom went to sit in a chay shop and met a group of fishermen, one of which was the Turkish National Skin Diving Coach. He was a tall, thickset man with a round, friendly face and a moustache. He decided we could sleep on his fishing boat. He had a small but sturdy looking boat, about twenty feet long, with a white cabin and an orange sign with the name 'Mert Tugay 2'. We heaved the bikes and kit onto the boat and the man said he would be back in the morning to get us breakfast.

Since we had a place to leave the bikes, we decided to have a look around and we met a smartly dressed chap with a white shirt. He invited us for a beer in a nightclub, which was like a fisherman's workingmen's club with disco lights. We tried to make conversation over the top of ear-bleedingly loud europop music, but gave up and, instead, our friend invited us to eat pizza. At first, I'd been dubious of him because he came across as the 'wideboy' of the town, but it turned out he was just incredibly kind and wanted to help us.

In the morning, having slept cramped on a bench in the cabin under a smelly duvet cover, it was difficult to stretch out my legs. I felt groggy. I expected us to get going quickly in the morning but Tom was bent double and could barely move. He had developed a stomach illness and he wasn't going to cycle anywhere that day, which seemed a shame because it was a glorious day with a clear blue sky. Colourful boats were reflected on the water. Fishermen sat on their boats and untangled nets in preparation for the day's fishing.

I went to look around the shops and found a fishing chandlery with crates of floats, ropes, sturdy waterproof overcoats, gloves, fishing lines, hooks, chains, and all sorts of fishing paraphernalia.

Back at the boat, the owner arrived and took us for breakfast and we ate hot 'khembe' soup, which was a speciality tripe soup and supposedly good for Tom's stomach – although Tom protested otherwise. For dessert, we had baklava topped with pistachios. It was fantastic to be able to eat well and eat many sugary desserts to boost energy supplies and improve my mood.

The man told us about the skin diving competitions he competed in. Skin diving involves going deep down into the water – up to sixty metres – with no supplementary oxygen, and attempting to spear the biggest fish possible. He showed us how he would breathe in order to be able to do it. First, he would relax completely. Then he would fill his lungs from his stomach and diaphragm. He took us to the jetty where he used to dive as a child. 'The shifting shadows in the water indicate big fish deep down. This is a good spot, or there, and there is a big fish.' We walked to look at a big hamsi boat, which was full of the tiny little fish. The fisherman handed bags up to a small queue of people who had come to buy.

We met an eighty-year-old fisherman who had been the local arm-wrestling champion when he was a younger man. He was very happy to tell us he had beaten all nationalities – including British – and insisted we test his arm and leg muscles, which were as solid as concrete. He tested our leg muscles too and he seemed impressed, considering we were 'young'uns'.

He was quite a character and had a wrinkled, weather-worn face with deep-set twinkling eyes. He jabbered away in English with a respectable accent. However, he spoke so fast it was difficult to tell what he was saying. He began to talk about the weather in the area and how it had changed over his lifetime. Sinop is on a peninsula, and on each side is a bay. He could remember playing in the snow as a boy. In the last twenty-five years, it had been warmer and it only snowed a little bit on the colder, less sheltered side of the peninsula.

That night, in the early morning, Tom sat bolt upright, emerged from the heavy, salt encrusted duvet, and let out a burp, which lasted for thirty seconds and changed note eight times. I was scared witless. It was completely unexpected: either an impulsive reaction or a muscular contraction and it smelt like a sewage works. I lurched forward, knocked open the cabin door, and thrust myself into the cold, crisp, sea air – which happened in bullet time slow motion. Perhaps Tom had been consumed by the blackness of the Black Sea itself and now hopefully he had exorcised the demon.

In the morning, we cycled very slowly up the hill out of Sinop. The lack of conversational exchange with Tom meant that my mind wandered in search for stimulation. I thought of things like how a battery works and charges up. I couldn't remember from GCSE electronics. I wanted to relearn the fundamental things I'd taken for granted at school.

In the late afternoon, Tom said he could no longer cycle. He had no energy and felt awful. I hoped his condition would improve soon; otherwise, he would have to go to a doctor. We walked along the road for a while but it was painstakingly slow and felt futile. A chay shop owner offered us a room to sleep but a young Jaundarma soldier with a big ego turned up, demanded our passports, and wouldn't let us stay. I was angry. I tried explaining to the boy but he spoke no English: 'Otel, thirty kilometres,' he said. However, we only had to cycle a short distance before meeting a farmer who invited us into his home and said we could stay with the farm workers.

We had dinner sitting round a simple table, watching television. Although I was hungry, I felt a little ashamed to eat the farm worker's food. They looked like they had worked hard for it. I wondered whether the workers worked for money or food. Maybe it wasn't even a farm at all. I never learnt because of the language barrier.

We were shown the sleeping quarters; a pile of dirty boots sat at the entrance. In the room were bunk beds and, in the centre, was a huge zorber stove made from an oil barrel with a roaring fire inside it. The stove was so hot that I had to give it a good berth for fear of my clothes melting.

By this point, we hadn't had a shower for around two weeks. My clothes hadn't been properly washed since Istanbul. The bacteria had thrived and long since died. All that was left was a sort of earthy smell, which I was content with. My socks, however, were the worst. They were rock solid, like cardboard.

Tom wore a long sleeved dark thermal vest and navy blue workman's trousers. His muted and groggy demeanour made him look like a mental patient on the loose, or a sailor lost inland: especially with his beard and incredibly greasy hair. About a month ago, he had told me, proudly, that he was going to stop using shampoo because it made his hair dry out.

It was 144km to Samsun. We had a Couchsurfer to stay with and the prospect of clean clothes and a much-needed rest. The road flattened out and passed through smoky little villages and agricultural land. I put on a drum 'n' bass mix and belted along the road. Fast beats flowed over deep bass-lines, rattling along faster than my heartbeat, and I felt the adrenalin pumping. The syncopated rhythms rolled in and out of time with elements of my surroundings as I observed objects pass me by.

45

My Bike is a Space Ship Burning Towards the Horizon

I felt strange because I'd had too little human contact and conversation in English, and my sanity was waning. Luckily, over the next few days, Tom's health improved and he perked up so I became happier too; it was starting to get desperate dealing with his mood.

Going through an ugly industrial town called Bafra, I wondered what the point of the settlement was, other than to produce and sell material products. Lines of auto show rooms, timber mills, garages, sales showrooms, furniture shops, tool shops, one after another, smoke, and concrete. The visual environment implied that the people who lived in the town had no other purpose than to work in its manufacturing industries. I had always believed that life was worth more than that. Smartly dressed men walked around with a sense of importance. Some gazed at us in disbelief, making jokes and pointing.

On the way into Samsun, we had to cycle through miles of sprawling suburbia in the pitch dark, which was a strange experience. My vision only stretched to a couple of metres around me and my senses heightened. I pedalled fast, the traffic passed close by me. I hoped that everyone was paying attention to their driving. I completely lost track of time and it felt almost as if I wasn't moving anymore.

46

The Friendly Vampire

We met Volkan in the centre of Samsun. He had slicked back hair and, in my memory, he has been visualised as a kind of friendly vampire. He was studying a PhD in Linguistics at Samsun University. He was a bit of a dark horse but he was evidently very intelligent and sociable. He seemed to size me up, not in a bad or competitive way but rather as a connoisseur of people.

On the way to his house, a Cockney accent called out. A leather-jacket-clad Turkish man asked, 'Are you from London?' He was visiting his family in Turkey but had been living in East London for fifteen years. It made me feel that we were still not that far from home. We squeezed the bikes into the lift up to Volkan's flat and then ate and went to sleep early.

The next day, Tom and I discussed the route. We considered going via Georgia because of the situation in South East Turkey, with violent skirmishes against the PKK in Kurdistan. I looked at the website of Corax, an adventure cyclist. I read his journey accounts with awe and wonder. He talked of doing two hundred and fifty kilometres in one day 'just to get it done.' However, I got a poor impression of Georgia. He described it as a country with 'a lot of drunken people lying about.'

I wondered if we could achieve similar distances to Corax. Was it worth it? Our longest distance so far was just over one hundred kilometres. I felt a little scared at the prospect of the Caucasus and Central Asia in the winter. We could expect temperatures as low as minus thirty degrees and unforgiving mountain passes in countries I knew nothing about. I hadn't even heard of Georgia before I started this journey.

Having some time to let the experiences sink in, I found myself feeling nihilistic. What had I achieved in my life up to now? Was I on the right course? Was there even a course?

I wrote out the schema of my life so far: I was born. I was living in Stoke Albany and attending school between five and twelve years old, then I went to Bishop Stopford School up to the age of eighteen. I spent three years living in York whilst I studied Environment, Economics and Ecology, then I worked for two years; five months on the island of Korcula in Croatia and fifteen months travelling five days a week to the same office in Market Harborough, a town five miles from my home, for no other reason than abstract monetary gain.

In June 2007, I travelled 6000km through Europe and Turkey and slept in a different place every night. My life had gone from a linear existence to something else – which opened me up to the free-associating, chaotic system of everything by travelling a line across the earth.

How can anyone claim to have ownership over their own life if they spend their entire life living in systems created by the ideas and dreams of others? It's unavoidable to an extent, but these systems are clichés, not rules. Now that I actually had some life experience, to coin a cliché, my horizons were broadened. I glimpsed the possibilities. This was only the beginning.

I pondered what might happen in the next three years. Maybe I would cycle across Central Asia into Tibet and China and take a ferry to Japan. Maybe I would cycle through South East Asia to Australia and get a boat to New Zealand. Money, family, friends, girlfriends, and careers? Did any of that stuff really matter? What would happen? What might get in the way? What did I want? What was I looking for, if anything?

In the evening, our self-imposed vegetarianism was broken, because we went to a restaurant and ate a huge Iskender kebab: pide bread, piled with slices of tender meat, accompanied by lashings of tomato sauce and fried butter. Volkan and I played football – Turkey versus England – on his Playstation. He was a linguist with extremely nimble thumbs. I managed to continue

England's track record of international football successfully.

I talked to Volkan about the difficulty of the past few weeks, personified in the stormy friendship between Tom and me, but he made light of it. He made me realise that it was up to me how I approached problems, and that I shouldn't take things too seriously. It was good to talk to someone else and get a more objective point of view. We left the next morning and bade farewell to Volkan. Trabzon was within reach, and then another country: Georgia. I hoped we would get there before Christmas.

47

Darkness

Kilometres clicked past slowly. In an attempt to make more distance, and try something different, we decided to cycle into the night. I followed the small white dot from my headtorch, which bobbed around in front of me.

Cycling, rather than stopping for the end of the day, didn't feel as strange as I thought. Physically it was the same, but mentally it was different. The reference point of objects in the world around me was taken away but I was still moving. I was travelling in a dark bubble, passing shady roadside industrial units under night's cloak. There was no destination other than the next day.

There were many campsites and beachside restaurants beside the road but all were closed for the winter, so we decided it would be fine to camp in one, with no one about. Someone must have seen us because the owner turned up and said the campsite wasn't open. We told him we were from England and on a world tour and, shortly after, he left in his car.

We decided to sleep in the porch of one of the beach huts anyway, as we didn't expect him to come back. However, after about fifteen minutes some headlights appeared in the darkness. The owner got out of the car, accompanied by another shady figure. The adrenalin began to kick in. I braced myself as the pair walked slowly towards us. 'Oh my god,' I thought, when I saw that the owner was brandishing a huge … fried chicken and a tray of battered hamsi and beer. He let us have a free room in one of the huts!

Over the next few days, day and night seemed to merge. Cycling was our occupation and it became the point of our conscious hours. Visual stimulus was low, as there wasn't much left that we hadn't already seen. I listened to a techno mix. What the heck was I doing there? I was thousands of miles away from friends, cycling in the dark, with faceless cars zooming past. Pedal, pedal, pedal. I felt cloaked. Strangely, I began to enjoy the darkness. I enjoyed the simplicity. No flashing signs or adverts for Efes beers or bakeries. There was nothing for my mind to associate memories and thoughts with. There was just a dark road. It felt cleansing, if nothing else.

At the town of Girisun, a car stopped ahead of us and we asked them about a place to sleep. Their names were Ahmed and Ibraham. 'Follow us; we know a place you can sleep.'

We followed them to a building site where they worked. We wheeled our bikes up a wooden ramp, into the gap for the front door, and into a maze of unfinished corridors and rooms. It was dry and sheltered from the wind. They returned twenty minutes later with Lahmacun and ayran (a traditional Turkish yogurt drink) for dinner.

The following morning, it was raining hard but we didn't really care and ploughed onward regardless. Cycling kept me warm. On a road bridge, Tom clipped the camera onto the railing and filmed a travelling shot. We pedalled against the backdrop of the town and continued onward for a couple of minutes before a white van pulled over. Three men piled out and surrounded Tom.

They were plain-clothes police officers and looked like they were from a seventies American police drama with Burt Reynolds because they were wore leather-jackets and tight trousers. A couple of minutes later, a shiny black saloon car turned up with a Turkish flag on the bonnet. Out stepped a very smart man with a long, black coat and a red tie, who spoke very good English. They thought we were spies and had wondered what we were filming from the bridge.

I feigned stupidity and horsed around but the man cottoned on quickly and dismissed the other policeman, who seemed disappointed they didn't get to have a shoot-out with us.

In the next town of Tirebolu, a long process ensued to find a place to sleep. I asked the Jaundarma, who then asked the police, who were unhelpful. We asked in a petrol station and another guy turned up. He was either a policeman or the owner of the petrol station. He took us to a hotel and paid for a room for us. The hotel owner looked less than convinced about the foreigners in his hotel with no money. He screwed his face up and tutted.

In the morning, the opportunity for an epic breakfast was not going to pass me by. I piled my plate with eggs, bread, jam, olives, tomatoes, and cucumber, and we left a considerable pile of detritus afterwards. MTV was on the television. Women in bikinis writhed about on screen. It seemed so misplaced in conservative, rural Turkey.

The next day Tom seemed to have gone crazy and pedalled along like a demon. Something had changed in his thoughts and he seemed desperate to get somewhere else. The Black Sea sloshed against the rocky sea defences. Grey sky was a permanent fixture above snow-laced mountaintops. Recently I had seen many vans go by, crammed with people, with the words Allah Korusun – 'god willing' – on the back. Cheap minibus transport in clapped out transit vans.

I pedalled with my head down. Icy waterfalls from snowmelt dripped from the rocky road embankment. Seagulls circled over a small fishing harbour beside the road.

We slogged on to Trabzon. The city loomed into view, perched on the hillside. Tall, concrete city buildings merged with the swirling clouds. Smoke rose against a pink sunset. Cars streamed down the main road. I felt excited. It was the first big city since Istanbul. We pedalled into the centre and waited for Heyrettin, our contact from the WWF, to turn up so we could interview him and pick up a box of cold weather kit that Tom had arranged to be sent from England.

It was cold and began snowing. A child turned up, about ten years old. He broke up some wood and kindly built a fire for us to warm ourselves, and an old man with a big white beard bought us a chay from a chay seller who was carrying a silver barrel over his shoulder.

After the interview, we got a hotel room and proceeded to spread the contents of our panniers over every surface. I used a spare chain, hung from the tripod, to hang the pan over the stove and cook a stew. There was a moment when Tom and I looked at each other, briefly surveyed the room and then burst out laughing. Where did this instinct to unpack and surround the enclosed space with familiar objects come from?

The lobby of the hotel had windows with the names of the occupants written on them – like the private detective in *Who Framed Roger Rabbit*. Men sat behind dark wood desks and didn't appear to be doing much. The proprietor of the hotel was an elderly man. His ledger looked like the Doomsday book and he had an old wooden abacus to count with. His hair looked like he had skinned a bright, white rabbit and glued the fur to his head. He looked like Scrooge out of *A Christmas Carol*. His two assistants sat beside him. One was smoking a cigarette in a long, old-fashioned holder. They were gangster lookalikes.

Whilst Tom went to use the Internet, I waited outside and watched people walking by. A simit seller checked his phone and watched girls walk by. He looked bored. A pair of smartly dressed twenty-somethings met and chatted animatedly in front of me. A kid stared at me as his parent dragged him by the hand. An old man pottered past. He looked frail. He noticed me and, with a laboured movement, turned his head to look at me – but he said nothing, turned his head back and continued on, as if to say, 'I don't care about the weirdness of the world anymore, I just want to make it ten metres.' A family passed, consisting of what looked like the mother with her two daughters. I saw a pretty girl and then a dustbin lorry pulled in front of me and the curtains closed on my short film.

Tom returned. He had the phone number of a Couchsurfer called Edgem who we met. She was beautiful and had long brown hair. She invited us to her flat for a cup of tea. Her home was very posh, with an open plan living room, kitchen, and sitting room that was as long as a cricket pitch. We were given cups of tea in fine, china cups with saucers, instead of the normal

Turkish glasses, and sat in Parisian-style chairs with ornately carved, curved arms.

She was a Fine Art masters student and her thesis was on Rothko. Her family's riches were from a tea plantation and kebab restaurant. She had four sisters. I so dearly wished we could have hung around. However, she knew of a church in which we could sleep. It didn't occur to me at the time that it was weird that there was a Christian church in Turkey. It was hidden behind walls and a huge gate like some kind of police or military compound, barely recognisable as a church.

It was predominantly a Muslim area and so the Christians had been pushed into an underground community. It felt like arriving in a great castle after travelling a long distance. We were greeted by our host and walked into the silent and pretty church. It was very peaceful. There were rows of pews and the altar was lit by candlelight. The side door from the nave led into another building with long corridors and many rooms. There were pictures of Jesus and dusty old books stacked on shelves. The place felt steeped in history.

48

Bayram

The next morning, I felt like staying in the church all day because it was so peaceful but we went to see the annual Bayram festival instead, where people slaughter rams in the streets. We hoped to meet families cooking chunks of ram and expected it to be a highly public, carnivalesque affair, but the streets were very quiet. We met a shepherd who was hoping to sell his sheep. I made hand gestures to indicate sheep death (use your imagination). He indicated that we should head further up into the suburbs of the city. On the way, we met a young man called Alper at a fruit-stand. We explained what we were looking for and he was a bit 'hush hush' about it, but he agreed to indulge our curiosity and help us to find somewhere to see the Bayram rituals carried out. We walked and then peered over a fence towards the back of a residential tower block.

A group of men were chopping ram into piles of meat. Blood ran over the concrete ground. I was disappointed that there was no barbecue. It was like 'butcher's day'. A day when people are reminded where their meat comes from and to practice slaughtering. It was a quiet, calm, and private affair.

On the way back down the hill, we were lucky to be able to see the process close up. I watched the animal. One minute it was calm, healthy, alive and trusting of the humans around it; the next minute it was kicking its feet wildly. For a tenth of a second there was a pause, as its muscles tensed for the last time, and then it was nothing but a chunk of meat and a pool of blood. The blood pumped from the jugular, viscous, like chocolate sauce, and it steamed like a hot tap in the cold air.

In the evening, we ate a delicious roast lamb dinner cooked by our host at the church, which made up for the lack of barbeques.

We didn't leave Trabzon until twilight the next day. The day was lost in organising luggage and trying to contact ExtremeUK again. It felt good to leave the city and the church. Two nights was enough. I think it would have been possible to sink into my own head and never leave the place. It was too comfortable and peaceful for its own good.

We rejoined the big road, which followed the coast. The sky had a now familiar pink haze, as the light retreated to darkness. In the dark, the concept of gradient is lost. Distance is twisted. We passed dark buildings with artificial lights and saw a few fishing boats' lights out to sea. Vehicles drove past. It all merged into one big murky gloop.

We were pedalling quite slowly and I overtook Tom to warm up. Tom shouted, 'You are aware you are the only one with a rear light?'

I replied, 'Of course I am. I've been cycling behind you for that reason.'

Patience was wearing thin. After hours of riding in the dark, we pulled over in front of a row of commercial shops and a shelter beside the road for the taxi drivers.

We went over and said hello. They weren't very friendly or sure why we were there. A subway under the motorway provided an unlikely place to bed down for the night. It seemed easier to sleep where we stopped instead of wasting time asking people. However, this was a reflection of our mood at the time rather than the rule.

I woke in the morning to see a puddle of water creeping towards me. I looked at the circle of light at the end of the subway and heard the patter of rain.

Things seemed different between Tom and me. I had the feeling that he no longer cared about anything. In the evening, we pedalled through some nasty tunnels in almost pitch darkness. It wasn't clever to cycle through them without good lights but each one provided a challenge, which was a break from the boredom.

We pedalled under a full moon along a quiet and eerie road. A friendly man allowed us to put our bikes in his huge luxury restaurant and gave us a room to sleep in. The man said hello, briefly heard our story and then went into the next room, where a television could be heard and its light seen flickering through the gap in the door. It was a small and cosy sitting room with a sofa and a wood burner. The man had many hunting parties in his lodge and there was a bear and a wolf skin pinned on the wall beside a picture of Ataturk.

Tom set about lighting the stove. The man returned with satsumas and hot coffee. I wondered about Tom and whether all our little arguments had stacked up into something larger, rather than just fading away. However, all real relationships have arguments and temporary fractions. We were alive and in one piece – which was all that mattered.

49

Not Clever

Mountain peaks could be seen in the distance, topped with snow. I had visions of cycling along mountain roads amongst such scenery and I felt thrilled at the prospect.

We reached a dark tunnel with no lights. A steady stream of Turkish articulated lorries roared through. I was able to cycle through, as there was enough light to see if I went slowly. However, after reaching the other side, Tom emerged and shouted, 'Are you going to wait for me next time? You are the only one with a head-torch!'

At the next tunnel, as a joke, I cycled straight past Tom a short way into the tunnel and he was livid. He exploded into a tantrum, jumped up and down, flapped his arms, then sat down on the pavement, and was silent.

He eventually cycled into the tunnel to me, I gave him the head-torch and he cycled off. I said, 'Aren't you going to wait for me?' He turned and threw the head-torch onto the concrete, dislodging the batteries, and then cycled at a suicidal pace into the dark tunnel.

I continued along into the tunnel very slowly. The tunnel's path seemed to be in worse condition than previous ones. I expected to see Tom at the far exit, a silhouette in the circle of light, but I couldn't see him. He should have been there by now. It was as if he had disappeared into the darkness.

As I continued edging towards the light, I noticed something. It was a dark shape of bike and luggage ahead of me, but no standing figure. I thought Tom might have been waiting but I reached him and he said, 'Call me an ambulance.'

Adrenalin pulsated into my bloodstream as if I'd just free-fallen from the top of a block of flats. 'Can you walk?' I asked. Tom got up and staggered to the light at the exit. I ran back to the bikes and luggage, which had fallen into the road. I crouched down to pick up Tom's bar bag and hesitated as I saw blood splattered over the concrete.

Tom's face was streaming with blood. I cut my towel in half, gave it to him, and washed his face with water and antiseptic wipes. His eyebrow had been cut deeply.

I ran back to get the bike and, as if pre-planned, a police car arrived in the tunnel. I said 'Arkadaş' (friend) and indicated my face to tell them that an accident had happened. I pointed to the exit.

The police flagged down a lorry to take the bikes to the hospital and Tom was stretchered into the back of an ambulance.

I felt sad because I was involved, but I couldn't blame the whole thing on myself, no matter how easy that would have been. It would have been an oversimplification of the situation. To have blamed it entirely on myself would have been to wallow in a state of 'feeling sorry'.

I arrived at the hospital in the back of the police van, feeling very apprehensive. What was I going to find waiting for me? Things had taken another turn. Would Tom have to stay in this place? Would we ever leave Turkey? When I found Tom, he was lying in a bed flanked by two nurses, smiling as they stitched him up.

The police were friendly and they took us to a hotel. However, the evening wasn't all smiles and get well soon cards. It was grim. Tom lay in his bed, moaning in pain, and couldn't sleep.

I only had four pounds on me and my last ten lira note was ripped in half, so I decided to go and spend it on beer, since that's the best thing for a man to do in such a grievous situation, I thought.

I bought some Efes beer from the shop over the road. I think it must be looked down upon to drink at the end of Bayram, because the guy in the shop sold the beer to me as if he was doing a shady drug deal. He ushered me round the back of the shop and handed me the beers in an opaque black plastic bag, and then shooed me out. The beer took the edge off my senses and I went to sleep.

I woke up bleary eyed and feeling rotten. I showered and went to the police station to get the bikes and to tell them that Tom wanted to see a doctor about changing the bandage and stitches. A boy from the hotel came with me to help me explain.

We returned from the doctor and arrived back at the hotel lobby. As we were standing, waiting at the lift, I heard a distant wailing and crying. I ran up the stairs. Tom lay soaking wet in his boxer shorts, next to the door of the lift. He mumbled, 'Can somebody please help me?' He had crawled along the corridor. The bandage on his head was stained with clotted blood and soaking wet.

We picked him up and helped him back to the room, where he slumped down on the bed. The shower fitting was broken clean off the wall and the room was flooding with water. Tom had blacked out and pulled it off on his way down.

Tom wasn't going to cycle anywhere. The doctor said we should wait at least three days, but we decided to leave anyway. There were no buses until the afternoon, so we hauled the bikes over to the highway to hitchhike. After a few attempts, an old man stopped who was already taking two kids down the road to school in his pick up.

50

Sakartvelo

The last ten kilometres of Turkey was in a car. The border crossing at Sarpi was easy. We showed our passports three times and got them stamped. The two friendly girls in the tourist information gave us maps for Batumi. We decided to cycle. It was maybe a little foolish but there was no practical reason why Tom couldn't cycle slowly.

It was a new country and we were there for Christmas! We cycled through the first settlements. I was amazed by how abruptly everything had changed. The Christian cross was placed over the border and directly lined up with the Turkish mosque on the other side, as if it was a competition for the best religion: an absurd abstraction of separation.

We passed a beach, with shacks with cola advertising boards, and a village with large houses with shiny, silver roofs and huge gardens. Satsuma trees brimmed with fruit. Tall silver birch trees lined the road. The sun was setting over an extensive area of wetland, dotted with some ruined concrete buildings.

On the way into Batumi, a man carrying a shotgun on a motorbike stopped next to us. He handed us a big bag of satsumas and said something incomprehensible in Georgian. I started to wonder whether it was such a good idea to have crossed into a new country for Christmas. We weren't familiar with the new currency and I knew nothing of the language. However, I had become confident with my basic, functional Turkish language skills.

We went into a store to buy some dinner. Whereas the Turkish ones were organised with shelves and contained European products, this shop had a much more basic range of items for sale. There were Russian sausages, and tins of tuna, but it was a lot cheaper than Turkey.

The poorly lit tower blocks reminded me of Bucharest. I started to wonder, was Georgia a former Communist country? I hadn't bothered to do any research on the place.

I went to urinate beside some grand looking gates, which were completely overgrown with weeds and shrubs. It looked like a patch of wasteland, but then a policeman walked passed me and gave me a 'do I look bothered?' look. I realised I was relieving myself in the front yard of a police station.

We pushed the bike along the main streets. I saw uneven kerbs, hotchpotch fences, and boarded up building sites. Groups of teenagers wandered about chatting and joking, and buxom women dressed in black, furry coats passed carrying shopping bags.

There were more than a few beaten and battered, drunk-looking men. 'I can deal with this,' I thought to myself, 'It just isn't familiar.'

We went down a side street, empty and quiet, but then we met a group of men, one of whom spoke English. We were invited to sleep in a family home and were shown up a staircase into a cramped little room with five people. They only wanted seven dollars; however, the idea of exchanging money seemed to sour things. Maybe we should have stayed with them but I pleaded we had no cash.

Instead, we were given an empty, run down room in the ground floor of their house. It was bare and the wallpaper was peeling off. There was no glass in the windows. There were two beds with wire, spring-mesh mattresses. The family brought us delicious, spicy, herb-filled meat soup, pickled beetroot, fresh wine and sweet jam, which made a very respectable Christmas Eve feast.

On Christmas morning, I was depressed. I was sure this was a bad dream that I would wake up from. However, the morning sun beamed through the window with the promise of a new day, and new sights, to lift the mood.

I changed twenty dollars into Georgian Lari at a money exchange place in the back room of a corner-shop. A strongly perfumed woman sat in a kiosk. Beside her was a coffee machine, a packet of cigarettes, and her handbag. She seemed enthusiastic to change the dollars as if the Lari was going out of fashion.

I bought two loaves of bread, similar to the Turkish pide from a bakery, and then went to another small convenience shop to buy jam. I spoke no Russian, or Georgian, and was presented with a 360-degree panorama of precariously stacked tins and jars. I made a spreading motion in the air with my hand, but all I got was giggles, and blank looks. I tried English as a last resort, 'You know, err, jam, you sort of, err ... eat it with bread.' I held up the bread and did the spreading motion again. Suddenly a light bulb appeared above the head of one of the women, who picked out a jar of fig jam. I looked at the label and it appeared to be only one year past its sell-by-date.

In contrast to the grey streets and walls were the beautiful faces of the girls who had pale skin, blushing red cheeks, red lips, dark eyes and long dark brown hair.

We walked to the seafront and ate breakfast whilst watching people go by. A couple walked arm-in-arm. A girl went by on roller-skates. A woman pushed a pram. There was a park next to the sea. It looked like a grand plan that either was in progress or had ran out of money. Beach shacks and restaurants stood half-built. Building materials were stacked in piles. However, it was peaceful and we were free to wander around and discover the place. On every third bench, there was a canoodling couple, kissing and hugging, away from the prying eyes of parents, not caring what anyone else thought. It felt like I was in Italy or France.

I wandered about in the park and came across a huge eagle perched on a branch inside a cage. It eyed me with disdain. It seemed to say, 'Yes, it's crappy in here, can you let me out now? I'm sick of looking at kids and trying to peck their eyes out. One of these days I'll make the hole I started in the wire up here big enough to escape, and then I'll be gone.'

51

Sylvester

I bought a phone card from the post office to call my parents. Some of the phone boxes looked like they were designed to take machine gun fire: a sturdy metal box with an old-fashioned dial. I couldn't work out how to use the phone, even thought I had tried various combinations of the available numbers and buttons.

I noticed a man wearing a fluorescent yellow cycling jacket and I put the phone down to speak to him. I was probably overly friendly. I was happy to meet another person who spoke reasonable English, other than Tom the pirate tramp. His name was Sylvester and he was Polish. He was short and stocky and his long blond hair was tied back into a ponytail. He was wearing a sort of utility seat-belt with enough pockets to carry ammunition for a role in the film *Predator*.

We went to a restaurant together. It had a simple interior with exposed beams and a nice atmosphere. Sylvester spoke Russian because he was Polish and had learnt it at school. He seemed keen to let us know how much he had in common with the Georgian people. His claim to fame was that he had previously done a 22,000km bike ride from Poland to South East Asia and back again.

The food was a revelation. We had plates of spicy meat soup, called khacho. It was tomato based with coriander and pieces of tender beef. We drank beer in flagons. There were long loaves of bread called puri, which were fresh, warm and doughy. The most astonishing dish was a pizza with lashings of soul-massaging melted cheese. I ate until I was stuffed.

We decided to stay another night in Batumi and then cycle with Sylvester towards Tbilisi. It would be good to cycle with someone else because Tom and I were sick of each other. It would be interesting to see how another cyclist went about their daily routine.

We walked with him to his hotel, which was imaginatively called Hotel Lux. It had a neon sign outside and a bouncer who Sylvester seemed to be friends with. It looked like one of the most modern and well-presented buildings on the street and yet it was undoubtedly dodgy. It was thirty dollars per night and the proprietor mentioned that girls were optional.

I watched ski jumping on the Discovery Channel, football, and *Lassie* on television. You could watch *Lassie*, dubbed into German, with your optional girl. I had to settle for Tom, who, with his eye-patch, resembled a post-fight football hooligan. Tom and I filmed ourselves singing 'We Wish You a Merry Christmas' whilst tucked up in bed. It's a lovely Christmas image, I'm sure you will agree.

The next morning, outside the hotel, a group of middle-aged women with too much make-up on shuffled about and smoked cigarettes whilst we prepared the bikes to leave. We had breakfast in a café and then cycled through Batumi port and out of the city towards the hills. Georgia is a country with different biomes within its small geographical area. The area beside the Black Sea coast, running from Batumi up to Abkhazia, is semi-tropical jungle, and tea plantations cover the hills.

My breath condensed in the cold air. It was a cold, sunny day. Black Mercedes cars burned along the road as if they were in a race. They revved their engines and accelerated fast. The road was in poor condition. I began to miss the wide, well-surfaced hard shoulder on Turkish roads.

We passed Soviet buildings akin to the ones in Romania. The ones here looked even more dilapidated but at some point, they had been grand. There was evidence of a proud past, waiting for something to resurrect it.

Sylvester stopped his bike and jabbered away in Russian to a group of men. He had the gift of the gab. He accepted a cigarette from one of the men. It made me think that I was missing out by not knowing more of the language.

As we cycled, the road became flat. Lorries chugged past. A rusty train rattled past at a snail's pace. The Georgian houses with their big gardens reminded me of houses in Hungary.

Men wore berets, fur hats, and black leather jackets, as if they were from an old Russian film. A scruffy looking man wearing a woollen hat stood by the roadside, holding up a string with fish attached trying to sell them to passersby.

Sylvester had planned to visit the brother of the security guard from the Batumi hotel. I didn't realise this until we were about to arrive. Group communication wasn't his strong point. We went through a gate into a front garden where there were fruit trees growing. The house was large, built from concrete, and rusty iron poles held up the second floor over the porch. A big man gave each of us in turn a stubbly-faced kiss. He was friendly, even though he looked as if he could knock my head off if he felt like it.

We sat round a table that looked as if it had been discovered in a bric-a-brac sale. Many other buys from the sale had been used to decorate the room. It was like a setting for a low budget film or a training scene from *The Matrix*.

A dark brown glass cabinet looked like it had been bought from the Soviet version of Argos thirty years ago. Inside was a set of gaudy pink china. A 1960s television sat in the corner. The picture was fuzzy and flickered. There was a galvanised steel zorber stove in the corner of the room. It belted out heat and doubled up as the cooker. We were brought various bowls of steaming food including stew, sausages and pickled cabbage salad.

We had our inauguration into the Georgian drinking tradition. Our host sitting at the table was probably in his fifties but he could have been younger. Other than his sideburns, he was completely bald. He had a wrinkled face and his skin was greyish-blue; it looked like he'd been sitting in a fridge and had only just recently thawed out. He was extremely jovial and adamant that we should drink the entirety of a hollowed-out, wine-filled horn.

The man demonstrated how to drink from the horn. His eyes brightened as he pulled the vessel to his lips and tipped it backwards, filling his stomach. He began to look exceptionally pickled and lost control of his facial expressions – although he did look very jolly and satisfied.

Sylvester went next. He said some stuff in Russian, downed the wine and then gave an unconvincing 'everything's going to be a-okay' smile as his cheeks went bright purple.

I followed, thinking back to days of drinking competitions at university. I realised now that the purpose had been to help me hold my own in a bout of drinking at a traditional Georgian table. The wine wasn't that strong and was tasty.

52

Cheers to a New Country

Georgia made me question whether alcohol was beneficial to one's life. Did abstinence make much of a difference in terms of happiness? I set myself the goal of finding out. Ever since the age of fifteen I'd drank. I was English, and drinking was part of the culture. During university I would have qualified as an alcoholic – and I drank in moderation compared to most people I knew.

Tom slurped the last drop of his wine. The host's brother, who had been bringing the food, decided to fetch his shotgun for dessert. A lead filmed crème brûlée perhaps? It was a double-barrelled job for shooting wild boar. I held the gun whilst Tom filmed. I didn't feel scared as long as I was holding it, which says a lot about guns in general.

We decided to take a walk. On first impressions of the town, I could see only deprivation and poverty. The infrastructure was in serious disrepair.

We went into a café. Inside, it looked as if it hadn't been redecorated since the 1950s. There was an old-fashioned fridge with a clamp so that children could lock themselves inside.

We ate cheap chocolate éclairs and Neapolitan cake. I was busy transcending into chocolate heaven, when suddenly I was brought quickly back down to earth by a skull-shakingly loud bang. Everything around me shook and layers of dust puffed into the air.

In the split second during the noise, I thought, 'Maybe this is it,' and, 'well it was nice up to now.' I waited for the pain to kick in, but it didn't. The shock served to jolt me back to the present and awaken me from my daydreams.

The fridge chugged to a halt and my ears deafened for a few

seconds, before ringing with a tinny noise for the next half an hour. The explosion had smashed one of the strip lights, cracked a window and knocked out the electricity.

Then I noticed the bunch of kids outside laughing at us. A Georgian Bart Simpson had chucked a very powerful firecracker into the café.

I looked cautiously up at the counter and the ladies who were working in the café. They looked shocked, but started nervously smiling and laughing, and didn't seem to care too much.

We walked back to the house. The extended family had come, including the mother and her young son and grandmother. They decorated a Christmas tree and handed out a speciality Georgian food called churchkhela, made of walnuts strung together and dipped in a fruit pudding made from wine molasses. It was chewy and tasty.

I was tired, and the heat from the stove made me doze off. We slept in the back room on Soviet-style mesh spring beds, with heavy mattresses that sunk in the middle.

We were up early at 7.30 am and sipped hot, Georgian-style coffee as the morning sun beamed through the partially frosted, single-glazed windows. The sun took on a spiritual quality. Each morning it freed the earth from cold and darkness of the night before.

The three of us said goodbye to our hosts. We shook hands and hugged, but didn't stand around in the cold for long. The road was carpeted in a deep layer of frost. My body jolted and shivered and I pedalled hard to warm up. It was only minus fifteen, but first thing in the morning, with skinny cycling gear on, I felt the cold deeply in my bones.

We stopped briefly and ate cheesy pizza for breakfast from a roadside kiosk. One large hatchapuri cost only two Georgian Lari, which was about sixty pence. We continued cycling beside the still water along the coastline, sheltered by rows of pine trees, passing a few half-finished hotels.

Two men were having a barbecue on the pavement. They had

put a couple of rocks beside a small fire and rested some skewers of meat over it, which were spitting and spluttering, and smelt good. A herd of cows nonchalantly wandered across the road, enjoying the morning sun.

Some children ran out of a side street and into the road in order to throw firecrackers at me. One landed on my back and burnt a hole in my jacket. I maintained a big smile to stop myself from getting off my bike and strangling them.

The Caucasus Mountains were like an impenetrable wall in the distance, shrouded in a light-blue haze. Some wild ponies were grazing on a field of harvested maize crop. They chewed on whatever remained. It felt like nature was still in the running as far as the environment went and people lived within the natural environment rather than attempting to completely remake, command and control it.

The road continued across flat land that reminded me of the plains we had crossed in Hungary. The plains in Georgia, which run between the mountain ranges, are on a migratory path and provide a rest stop for birds flocking from Russia down to warmer climes for the winter. There are marshlands and lakes to feed and rest. I watched the white birds land, and then take off in large flocks. Their movements looked like those of swarms of insects or shoals of fish. Specks in the distance moved and morphed across the sky. I felt connected to their journey. I wondered where they would end up. 'It must be a tough challenge,' I thought.

There were horses galloping about. I'd never seen a herd of wild horses before. They looked free but wary of us. They seemed to communicate and interact with each other in a continuous and chaotic conversation. They neighed, snorted, reared up, and cantered around after each other.

We stopped for a coffee in the next restaurant that we saw. Suddenly we were drinking coffee all the time. Sylvester's habits were rubbing off on us. He also smoked, which was irritating because there was an attraction to holding something warm in the cold.

Sylvester suggested we continued to cycle into the night. He was in a hurry to get to Tbilisi for New Year. This wasn't too popular with Tom, as he had had his accident in the dark. However, the cold weather wasn't conducive to hanging around, and we had spent so long in Turkey that it made us want to get to the next destination faster.

Things weren't as we'd planned when we had started. It had taken over seven months to cross Europe and Turkey. We had expected to be in Iran by now, but we were learning a few things about travel, plans, time, and life in general. Thankfully, the world is a very interesting place, and it would be silly to rush through it.

However, there was inner conflict. I started to think that getting to Tbilisi for New Year's Eve would be a good idea and I longed to be in the company of other people.

We arrived in the town of Samtredia. Green, neon lights flashed in unfamiliar Georgian script, in otherwise unlit streets. There was a tall apartment block with dimly lit rooms. A group of drunken men swayed along the quiet road. We cycled around for a bit and then met a man called Alex: a thickset fellow with brown hair. He had a friendly, but strong-looking, face and sported a scar on his cheek. His eyes belied a strong character. He took us to the police station to leave our bikes. A policeman checked our passports through a small kiosk window.

Alexandra showed us to a restaurant. It was a small place, with five tables and a small bar. We sat with some other of his friends. They looked as scary as hell but were actually friendly and welcoming.

We ate khinkhali: traditional dumplings filled with mince, onion, garlic and herbs that contain a soupy juice. Without this vital information, I attacked one with my fork and instantly flooded my plate. I hadn't learnt the proper method of eating them yet.

53

Amateur Khinkhali Eater

Alex had a few stories to tell. He spoke some English and Sylvester translated the rest from Russian. He told us he was the local boxing champion, and his home was the Abkhazia Region. He said he had been fighting for five years, for the freedom of Georgia, and now he couldn't get back home to his region because of the continued trouble there.

My yet-non-existent knowledge of anything about Georgia, including its political situation, meant that I could only nod in wonder at the guy's macho stories. He had led us to hot food, beer and cheesy hatchapuri so nodding was the least I could do.

The big chap brought over a flagon of what I thought was vodka but turned out to be chacha, a traditional fruit brandy. We drank shot after shot and, in between each drink, Alexandra made long drawn-out toasts to family, friends, and our countries. My head was soon swimming.

We paid around seven dollars for the three of us to stay in one room in the 'hotel'. The catch was that we had to leave by eight in the morning, although I didn't know quite why. The apartment block was strange. The lobby was dark when we got there and there was no one at reception. It was dusty and draughty. Alex got the key from behind reception and showed us up to our room.

We climbed up four flights of stairs. On one flight, there was a window by the stairs. I realised it had no glass in it. There was just a gaping hole into the darkness. There were quite a few stairs missing. The concrete was worn and crumbling away. I think many people were living in the hotel. There was no reason for them to be tourists, in this dead-looking place, in mid-winter.

Perhaps they were refugees.

The room had solid beds with one blanket each. The taps in the bathroom were rusted solid and there was no water. The blue bath had streams of rust stains in it. It looked like someone had been mixing cement in it.

We chatted animatedly for a while before going to sleep. I kept turning over in the night in order to adjust the blanket over me. It was cold because I had left my sleeping bag in the police station. However, there was a roof and it was better than sleeping in the snow.

In the morning, I waited for Sylvester outside a restaurant with the bikes and watched people going about their everyday activities. The road was half constructed, with a gravel base and the kerbs in place, but no tarmac. An array of different vehicles went past; a fume-bellowing, brown-grey truck and an old Soviet van with a number stencilled on the side, indicating I didn't know what.

Long, pale legs wrapped in tight, black pencil skirts were on show as their owners braced the cold temperatures, treading carefully in high-heeled black stilettos. Men, looking as if they were in the cast of the American TV Show *The Sopranos*, wore black berets and bomber jackets.

I went to a bank to change money. It was suitably chaotic and packed inside and I assumed it must have been payday. I went in, scruffy and dirty, and milled about for a while. The concept of queuing was non-existent. Women around my chest height, wrapped up in fur coats and scarves, nattered, and appeared to be trying to convince the teller they should be allowed to go first.

I was feeling rather English and the prospect of standing in a nice, orderly queue seemed quite appealing. I obviously looked panicked, because the security guard came over to me and parted the sea of people so I could get to the front. This was a little embarrassing, but it did solve the problem quickly.

My grip on the trip's purpose had loosened, and it had started to feel a little pointless. I wanted to do some mental processing of what I'd achieved so far, so that I could decide whether I still wanted to do it.

I think that travel, in the sense of walking or cycling or other slow methods, gives one an education not afforded by any amount of academic research, theorising or reading. Not only are you able to observe the world as it is, you also process that information in the context of your own, personal, life experience. You have to confront the weaknesses in yourself. The experiences become life-defining. You immediately see how the world is different from how it is portrayed through the media, and how the fearful news we are bombarded with is not representative of reality.

The main road was well stocked, with restaurants dotted along the route to serve the constant flow of traffic to the capital. Most restaurants would have a fire outside to attract people to the warmth, which worked as I pulled up to one to warm my hands. A house with one floor converted to a restaurant was run by a family. We were invited to drink vodka and eat mandarins, which topped up my alcohol and vitamin C levels.

The valley sides were steep, covered in bare trees and mist so you couldn't see beyond the thick veil. I was surprised to see anyone but there were people selling things on the roadside, standing, exhaling white puffs of condensed breath into cold hands. Stalls sold all manner of wooden crafted cutlery and crockery; spoons, forks, bowls, and broomsticks. There were terracotta pots of all shapes and sizes, many designed as elaborate wine tumblers, with the horn-shaped drinking receptacles hanging on the side.

A group of men stood round a car bonnet drinking 'Chacha'. Cows shuffled along the roadside and pigs snuffled and foraged amongst leaves and debris.

It was starting to get dark and we were stuck on the road climb, which seemed to be getting steeper. I was chugging along in granny gear. It was the most exhausted I'd ever felt. It started to snow. Cars and lorries crept past us. No one seemed to be willing to make any rational decisions; we just pedalled and pedalled.

We pulled into a restaurant, which had big expensive cars outside. The price for a small portion of grilled pork was high, compared to the other restaurants we'd been to, but was compensated for by the roaring fire, which I thawed out next to. A large group of men were eating, with a couple of guns propped up against the wall, perhaps after a day of hunting.

It was now snowing with big fluffy snowflakes. I couldn't help but feel happy and excited: snow at Christmas time! We passed through a long tunnel, avoiding an ice formation protruding from a frozen drain at the side.

The tunnel was two kilometres long, and navigating it on a bicycle, competing with the smog from lorries, was a grim experience. I pulled my Buff over my mouth to attempt to filter the air. It's only when you travel these manmade environments without being in the comfort of a car that you realise how uninhabitable they are. They are built to accommodate machines, not humans.

It was well and truly dark now and my headtorch, although fully charged, decided that it was too cold to function. The road was fast being covered in a blanket of snow. All I could see was a sphere of snowflakes falling around my face. The sound of cars passing meant I stopped every ten metres to reassess my position in relation to the road to make sure I hadn't veered off. It was pretty dangerous and stupid in hindsight. I was worried there would be another accident.

There was no sign of Tom or Sylvester and I was annoyed that they had gone ahead, but then I came across their bikes propped against a small hut by the road, with an alluring light in the window, and I went in. Two middle-aged women were running a small restaurant on the roadside. It was a much-appreciated haven from the weather.

We wanted to order the same soup as before, but they only had one type available in a steaming pot on the stove. It was called hashi. A milky-looking, salty, watery, white-coloured juice with a lump of tripe boiled until it looked like some sort of deep-sea creature floating around in the centre. You would think that, considering the cold weather, and the long days on the bike, anything hot and warming would go down a treat. However, the soup was horrible. Even though it is widely considered the best solution for a hangover this side of Istanbul, I wasn't sold on the chewy, rubbery piece of gristle – appetisingly textured like flannel on one side and rubber arse on the other – but there was plenty of bread to mop it up with and, once you had chopped up the flesh, you could mix it with the bread – a bit like giving medication to a dog – and eat it that way.

Besides, it was difficult to complain; the two motherly ladies were very kind and ushered us in to sit beside the stove. One took my jacket and long-sleeved t-shirt and hung them beside the fire but they were too close and I realised the jacket was starting to melt, like a crisp packet in the oven. I rescued it and was less than pleased to learn that I'd gained some solid 80's style shoulder pads and a back supporting panel, caused by a chemical reaction in the material that had turned the fabric into solid plastic.

Normality had long ceased to exist in my life. Now I was pedalling at 10pm in the dark along an icy road, snow sticking to my beard, the visible land beside the road carpeted in a deep white blanket. Feeling in my behind, thighs and wrists was numbed by the cold.

A police car emerged, flashing behind us. They insisted on escorting us through the next town. Christmas lights hung across the street and police lights followed us in a surreal parade. Houses were shrouded in darkness and only shady souls wandered the pavements. Little kiosks selling vodka were available every hundred metres or so, so you never had to stagger far to get stocked up.

The police took us to a Turkish brothel to sleep for the night, which was nice of them. A small bar contained a couple of truck drivers watching Russian music videos on the TV. Whilst we were trying to get a good deal on a room, one of the men left to negotiate himself a cheap price for a lap dance.

We weren't going to pay twenty dollars a night so we plodded back out of the door, passing the entrance to one of the rooms on our way. I peeked in. A group of drunken men in a red-lit room with pink walls were dancing and madly waving their bottles, whilst a woman wearing an elaborately decorated belly-dancing outfit shook and pranced about amongst them like an out-of-sync spinning top. Turkish pop music blared from the tinny sound system.

Back on the road, we pedalled some more before arriving at another Turkish truck driver's 'hotel'. Once we'd negotiated our bikes between the long articulated lorries parked outside, we met the helpful proprietors who gave us a small room for fifteen dollars for the three of us. It was one of many strange little hotels along the roadside: cheaply built and badly designed, with tacky signs, and unoriginal names like 'Hotel Villa' or 'Hotel Istanbul'.

We drank a chay downstairs in the bar. There was strange artwork on the wall; a peculiar composition of nipples and the Turkish flag. A shiny brown fabric was draped down from the ceiling like a big quilted duvet, which I imagine would be quite a good hallucination-inducing sight after a bottle of vodka.

54

New Year's Eve Eve

Unease under the surface of our group dynamic soon bubbled up into a petty argument, but I was getting bored by this point. No one had the energy to argue. Instead, we ate khinkhali in a restaurant for breakfast.

A headwind blew over the open plains as we neared the town of Gori. I started to get angry as I found myself in the midst of some seemingly suicidal driving. Five cars attempted to overtake at once. I shouted, 'Learn to drive!' and 'Die!' at each car that went past.

As I reached the top of a long, gradual climb, I looked out across a mist-draped valley before descending down into the city. Gori is a grey and dull looking place, with an ominous military base and numerous army personnel wandering about.

We turned off the main road, sixty kilometres before Tbilisi, to visit the birthplace of Stalin and its museum. I thought the place looked like a large tomb, or an administrative building. It looked like many others from the Soviet era: lacking originality, rather than remaining true to an archetypal style. Thought and creativity in building design must have been difficult to push in Soviet times.

Sylvester managed to maintain that we were too slow for him, announced he would see us in Tbilisi, and buggered off. In fact, he didn't speed up, but Tom and I did slow down to a comfortable pace and I wondered why we'd bothered rushing at all.

We stopped for a second along the incredibly dangerous road – it seemed like a miracle we hadn't been flattened a long time ago – and a Vauxhall estate skidded to a stop beside us, in a cloud of dust and gravel. Out jumped a man.

Could this be the first nasty robber we would meet, that everyone had warned us about?

In his grubby hand, he clenched a note with a message from two Dutch cyclists who were cycling to Tajikistan. They had written down their email addresses for us to contact them when we reached Tbilisi.

As it got dark, it became a challenge to navigate the tyre-width area of tarmac. We kept a steady pace, but it seemed like we would never reach Tbilisi as the hours wandered past. Dark shadows of hills loomed ahead. We turned off the road into another little restaurant and found Sylvester eating stew next to the stove. Hare and tortoise did spring to mind. We decided to cycle together rather than being antisocial, although Sylvester had now given Tom and myself the fond name of the 'English wankers'.

Outside the restaurant was the Georgian version of a highway service station. There was a row of identical kiosks selling vodka, sweets, and tobacco. The capitalist economic model didn't apply here. Each babushka had a kiosk selling the same wares and it was left up to chance or a slightly more favourable positioning of the kiosk as to who sold the most goods.

The road eventually turned into a modern-looking European highway lined with streetlights. My legs went round automatically. Streetlights emitted an orange glow. There were no cars at one in the morning; there was no sign of the city other than the road getting bigger. 'The last climb, maybe,' I thought, reaching the top of a hill. It looked as if we had reached the outskirts.

The road followed the river, under a couple of tall old bridges, and finally I emerged round a corner to a sign showing 'Tbilisi'.

We stopped briefly for a meat pasty in a kiosk that looked like an out-of-business garden centre. We sat in a room and warmed ourselves for a few minutes beside a dangerous-looking heater-contraption, which consisted of an exposed wire filament set in a piece of concrete and plugged into the mains. The wire glowed red-hot and occasionally fizzed as if it was threatening to arc electricity at Sylvester's leg.

A 4x4 stopped and the driver offered to find us a hotel, but then, when they realised how slow we were going on bikes they sped off, never to be seen again. The road went straight down and we scoured our surroundings for a place to sleep. Behind the church? In the petrol station? Camping? The guys in the 4x4 said it was dangerous to camp – but then they would, wouldn't they, from their protective shell.

Tom asked a man standing beside a hut at a car-cutting yard. The man offered to let us to sleep in his hut, but when we got inside and started to get comfortable he asked for thirty dollars, so depressingly we packed back up again and left. By now, it was two o'clock in the morning and I was fighting off the desire to curl up in a comfortable ditch.

Sylvester was flagged down by a taxi driver who stopped and offered us a hotel room for forty Laris, so we agreed and followed him through the streets.

I passed some neon lights which read 'POLICE' and a restaurant that looked like the owner had got a job lot on fibre-optic flashing lights; the place was glowing and flashing in a myriad of oranges, greens, and other gaudy, ill-matched colours.

Trundling through the concrete jungle, I turned onto another road, then another, and made another turn. Then, abruptly, it was the end of the ride. The taxi stopped at the hotel and we went up into our room. I felt completely exhausted but I was wired on adrenalin. I had a relaxing shower, and fell into a heavy, blissful sleep.

55

Tbilisi New Year's Eve: 7.5 Months on the Road

We ate mandarins and sweets and drank Turkish coffee with the owners, then I walked to find an Internet cafe. I watched people doing their early morning activities: adults smoking cigarettes, kids playing in a park, and shops opening up.

Sylvester said he wanted to visit the Polish embassy because he liked getting stamps from each embassy and having a cup of tea with the diplomats, so we pedalled into the centre.

Tbilisi was more like a giant village than a city and it had a welcoming feeling. We asked a 4x4 driver where the embassy was and he said we should follow him. He drove very fast up the steep cobbled streets and it was near impossible to keep up with him. When we got to the embassy, I was hot and sweaty, and although it was minus ten, I stripped half-naked to cool off.

Tom had arranged to meet a Couchsurfer at the Marriott hotel that evening. The main street of Tbilisi – Rustaveli – was lit up with banners, decorations, and laser lights; at the end, Freedom Square had fibre optic lights hanging from its central pillar, creating a fifty-foot Christmas tree. There was an atmosphere of festivity. Cute girls in high heels shuffled over the ice on the pavements.

Bruno, the Couchsurfer, was extremely French: energetic, and intense. He explained that his friend, Aurélien, would take us to his flat. Aurélien was tall, with short brown hair. 'I am a photographer and English teacher. I recently photographed the political demonstrations which happened in November,' he said with a heavy French accent.

We walked up a quaint, cobbled street into a dark doorway and up the stairs to the flat, which was grand and opulent, with dark green leather sofas, dark wood furniture, and cupboards with carvings of traditional Georgian images of soldiers, coats of arms and the king. In the corner of the room was a huge, jet-black grand piano.

Vincent, the other housemate, walked in holding a bottle of vodka. 'Here Andy, drink this, it is Gomi juice!' Vincent was gregarious, with classic French looks, and a mischievous glint in his eye. His manner made me feel that to bother with any small talk or polite introductions would be an insult.

Martin and Emma were Couchsurfers from England who were also staying in the apartment. They had matching red hair and, on first impressions, looked relaxed but more reserved. I began to realise I'd been out of England for long enough that I could now see what Englishness really meant. They were students from Oxford and Durham respectively. Martin was studying English and Emma was studying music.

'Emma is researching music ethnology,' said Martin. 'We plan to travel from Georgia to Azerbaijan, India, and South Africa.' Vincent thought they were hilarious because Martin would break out into heavily English-accented French at every opportunity.

Vincent explained his love for Pastis, which is a French aniseed-based alcohol, and insisted we drink with him. 'Andy, you have never heard of Pastis! It is the drink of the south of France. Here, you must try it.' I was soon feeling merry, but then it was New Years Eve.

A party was on the cards and we piled out into the snow and into a white Lada Niva 4x4, the car of choice for the icy roads of Tbilisi. Vincent put on some Georgian music and started singing along. We picked Sylvester up from the embassy. Aurélien stopped the car in the middle of the road and turned up the radio. Vincent got out with his long black coat, black beret, and scarf and started twirling about in the freshly falling snow, his arms stretched out beside him, clapping and dancing similar to how I had seen Turkish people dance. Aurélien and I got out and joined in whilst the security guards filmed us on their mobile phones, smiling to see such a sight.

We arrived at another flat and met David. He was smoking a cigarette and looked like a fifty-year-old Parisian with thin hair. He was with another guy called Sebastien and three French girls. More alcohol was drunk, and Aurélien began playing the guitar whilst Vincent sang. 'Singing? Wow, old-fashioned fun!' I thought.

I yearned to leave the room and see what was happening in the city. 'We can go down to see the Christmas tree in Freedom Square,' said Sebastien. We ran down to the main square, which was packed with people. Soon I completely lost Sebastien and I couldn't find my way back to the party. Every house looked similar, with dark, crumbling plasterwork and shadowy porches. I decided that I would try to find my way back to Aurélien's flat, which seemed to take at least two hours.

When I got there, unsurprisingly there was no one in. I was determined not to have to sit and wait for the others to get back so I went into the restaurant next door. 'My friend lives here,' I said, pointing to the adjacent building. 'Look, there is my bike on the balcony. I have been locked out.'

'Don't worry, my friend, come here and sit with us,' said a man in the restaurant. I sat at the head of their table and was handed plates of food and glasses of wine.

I was completely drunk by now and began dancing with all of the women from the table. Sometime later, Aurélien, Vincent and David arrived at the restaurant too. We stayed until the party ended, but I was determined not to sleep. I got my mp3 player, walked up to the Polish embassy, and played some drum and bass to a security guard, then I was invited to another party, and so the night went on.

I had needed to celebrate and lose my cares, but the hangover the next day was terrible. I felt like I'd had my recent memory erased and I now had to reintroduce myself to my newfound friends and start from scratch.

I decided to take a walk to get some fresh air and find out why I had got so lost the night before. I retraced my steps past the music school. I looked closely and saw that the building's outer decoration was made of plaster mould, imitating skilled masonry. I wondered whether, during Communist times, the buildings had been hastily constructed to give the appearance of European style and elegance without thought for long-term durability.

The architectural details seemed like a token gesture to give an essence of grandeur to essentially functional spaces. Perhaps there was paranoia that if the styles varied too much then they would be punished for misusing resources or trying to compete with others.

A problem with the Soviet brand of communism was that it missed the point that people want to progress. However, one benefit was that it detracted from the oppressive impact of the institutional buildings such as the law court. On first impressions, it looked grand but closer inspection revealed an amateurish façade.

That evening, Bruno held a gathering at the flat. French people smoked and talked energetically and regularly interrupted each other's conversations. I tried to decipher the conversations but my French had been long since forgotten. I loved the sound of it though, as if everyone was late for life and making up for it by talking faster. A girl with shoulder-length black hair and big eyes played a guitar with a unique hand motion that looked more as if she was playing a heavenly harp than a humble guitar.

56

The Market

The following day Tom, Martin, Emma and I went on the metro to Varglis Moedani; the big chaotic market of Tbilisi. We wanted to pick up some cheap puffa jackets. I was still walking around in thin cycling clothes with my waterproof jacket zipped right up over the top, which was not suitable clothing for the temperatures, which were as low as minus twenty.

The market was located outside the train station, which was boarded up and derelict. It was split into different areas. One area sold clothes and shoes, another sold electrical appliances and mobile phones, and another food, and there were many other areas for a range of requirements. Most of the items on sale looked like they had been hijacked from a Chinese shipping container.

People in dark jackets shuffled about along the labyrinth of aisles. There were ramshackle, rusty, steel-framed stands, which were surrounded by blue plastic tarpaulin. Babushkas in layers of tatty clothes were selling satsumas, hand-knitted socks, and traditional Georgian hats, whilst warming themselves next to a small fire on the pavement. Some of the women looked very old and I thought they should be warming themselves with a cup of tea indoors.

We walked through the clothes section. There were tables stacked to the rafters with jeans, women's clothes, trainers, leather shoes, and various other things. There were dresses, belts and jewellery haging all around the sellers who, wedged in between his/her wares, were comically peering out.

I bought a cheap puffa jacket from a round-faced man who patiently waited while I compared different jackets. Eventually I bought one for sixty Lari (about twenty pounds) and wearing it was comparable to being in a warm sleeping bag. It was the warmest I'd felt in weeks.

In the evening, we met Bruno for a drink. 'I was living in Brazil before. A diplomat friend asked me to come and work in Tbilisi. I have an ambition to have a huge street party with the world's largest table for all my friends. Tomorrow I go to France for snowboarding, and then to Tel Aviv.' Bruno seemed to be living a fast-paced life, fuelled, mostly, by caffeine and nicotine, and I found it tiring to talk to him. He said we could stay at his flat until the seventh and then we would have to move.

I felt frustrated, confused, and empty, and negative thoughts brewed. I didn't expect to feel like that. I had been feeling satisfied with life recently but I found myself thinking and asking questions. I was frustrated with being stationary, the constant socialising, and the – on first impressions – hedonistic lifestyle of my new French friends. I was jealous of the energy. I had been living without luxuries and much human contact for the last couple of months, but this was socialising on steroids. It was a completely different style of social behaviour than I was used to.

We needed the time to rest in Tbilisi. Although it wasn't really admitted, we weren't prepared for travel across Georgia in the winter; it was too cold. We only had minus-five-rated sleeping bags.

We had arranged for new Extrawheel trailers to be sent to the WWF office in Tbilisi along with my bank card – lost two months ago in Turkey – and we also needed to apply for the Iranian visas. When anyone asked what we were doing in Tbilisi, we said we were waiting for things to arrive.

In the evening, we went to meet the Dutch cyclists who had sent us the note while we were cycling into Tbilisi a few days before. Zindze was athletic and bubbled with life. She had curly, blond locks of hair and a friendly face. Rinke was similarly beautiful, with curly hair and strength twinkling in his eyes.

'We have hitchhiked from Zestafoni to get the visa for Azerbaijan. I am going to hitch back to the Netherlands to get a new bike because my bike is a twenty-five-year-old city bike typical of Amsterdam,' said Rinke.

I couldn't imagine retracing my steps back through Europe. I thought he was crazy.

He had tales of pushing the bike up snowy mountain roads in Turkey. 'I had to fix something on it every day.' They had come all the way through Italy, Croatia, Albania, Bosnia, Serbia, Montenegro, Macedonia, Greece, Turkey, and Georgia. 'We use hitchhiking very often,' said Zindze. 'We are even using it in the city. People take us wherever we need to go.'

57

A Fruit Slicing Party

In the evening, Vincent invited us to a party to cut up huge amounts of the quince fruit, in order to make a large volume of vodka. When we arrived, Vincent was in the bathroom and the bath was full of quince. 'The fermentation process will take one month. Did you know, Andy, that the French say "Keep the wine in the cellar and the spirits in the roof?"' said Vincent.

Many hands made light work of the quince and afterwards we sat around and drank Pastis. Vincent had brought a group of people together who didn't know each other at all and got them cutting up fruit. 'I like to make alcohol, Andy,' said Vincent. 'I spent some time studying the properties of absinthe whilst travelling in Costa Rica and the Balkans.' He made it sound like a science but I think he just liked drinking it a lot.

'What were you doing before you were in Tbilisi?' I asked.

'I worked as a builder in Switzerland and in a Bulgarian village as a teacher. I love the Balkan music and dancing.'

I met a girl called Fanny and her friend Vanessa. 'I am from St. Pierre, a French island off Canada. I am studying at Montpellier University in Southern France,' said Vanessa. 'Travelling by bike is very good. I want to travel to South America.' Fanny offered to let us stay with her and invited us to meet them at a restaurant later on in the week.

The next day, Tom prepared a huge breakfast of eggs, hatchapuri, bacon, tomato, bread, tea, and wine (yes, wine for breakfast). Then, along with the others, we walked to the Nalkan Fortress: medieval ruins which overlook the city.

Tbilisi looked picturesque and full of character under the snow. We walked under the towering, Kartli's Deda, metal Soviet statue that looked like, if it fell forward, it would impale the parliament building. Next to the statue is the house of Boris Ivanishvili: a huge futuristic place overlooking the city. The state of disrepair of the city's infrastructure, crumbling architecture, and the general level of poverty, made it look particularly surreal. It was an incredibly ostentatious gesture of wealth, towering above the city to make sure everyone knew where the power was.

I asked Aurélien, 'What were the November demonstrations about?'

'They were to do with the rigging of the elections, and the small margin by which the president won,' he said.

'Do you think there will be any repercussions from the recent public demonstrations?' I asked. I had noticed suspicious yellow buses packed with police in riot gear; the same ones who were beating up protesters, and using tear gas in November. They were parked conspicuously on the road behind the parliament just in case anyone decided to spoil the party.

'I hope not,' said Aurélien. 'I think that the children's fairground rides and ice skating rink in front of the parliament buildings are something to do with keeping the people from having anywhere prominent to demonstrate.'

We moved out of Bruno's place to Sylvain's, another friend of Bruno. Berton was there. He was the chef at the French embassy. Previously he had worked at the embassies in New Delhi and Moscow. He cooked for visitors to the embassy, and had recently cooked for some celebrities and diplomats.

He was a tall, old chap with dark skin, inset eyes, wrinkles, big lips and a deep voice. He wore a long coat over a white pullover and a long scarf. We sat and had a whisky and discussed English politics.

'Tony Blair is a great showman and Gordon Brown a good economist,' I said. 'Everyone complains about politics and the alternative party never offers much of an alternative, but no one has the power to do anything about it.'

Initially we were going to a restaurant but the plan changed, so Berton announced, 'Now, I work,' and went about collecting ingredients and coming up with ideas. The result was a delicious tomato salad with vinaigrette, and pasta carbonara. I felt very inquisitive about these people, with their interesting lifestyles, and asked many questions.

58

French Girl

The next day, we said farewell to Martin and Emma and then met Vincent and Fanny on Rustaveli. We had arranged to meet another Couchsurfer called Sophie, so while we waited we went for a drink at 'The Acid Bar' with Fanny, and met Pierre and Romain. Pierre was helping on a youth program – like the Georgian version of the Scouts – and Romain was being paid to discover trekking routes for a travel company. After a few beers, Sophie arrived. Tom went home with Sophie but I decided to stay out and went with Fanny and Pierre to eat in a restaurant. It was the first time I had done something without Tom for ages and it felt good.

Tom and I left Sophie's the next morning to go to the Iran embassy, but when asking for directions we discovered that it had moved, so we gave up, and met Fanny in Freedom Square. We went to a back street restaurant for lunch. There were three Georgians playing traditional music and Fanny translated the lyrics from one of the songs: 'My darling, I wish I had your Black Death.' It was one of the most macabre things I had ever heard, but I liked it. It seemed to echo that it was better to share your demons than bottle them up.

I went looking for the Iranian embassy again after lunch. I went down into the metro and asked a policeman with a cauliflowered left ear if he spoke English, pointing to the location on the map. He tried to explain with hand gestures but it was obviously more complicated, so he asked another man, who offered to take me with him.

People will quite often go out of their way to help you. His name was Niwan. He was wearing a black Armani jacket and a black beanie hat. I emerged from the clunking tube carriage as it screeched to a halt at the station in the Saburtalo district.

I thanked Niwan and thought I might as well try the same technique again. I asked the next person if he spoke English, and to my surprise, he did. Not only that, but he knew the Iranian embassy had moved and that there had been an advert on TV about it five months ago. How he remembered that is a mystery.

He decided to go with me. He was an ethnobotanist and did expeditions to the Svaneti mountain region in the summer for his research. He normally had to wait for funding, but this year he had been lucky and had found it quickly. In the winter, he wrote about antiques and had a collection of English books.

We found the old embassy building, which had changed and was now the Ministry of Environmental Services. I left my new friend, and on the way back to the centre found out that it was better to run over the ice than walk. I was so slow when being careful that I would rather leave it to my reactions to save myself, upping the risk slightly, but going along more effectively.

The next day we finally applied for the Iranian visa, which required two passport photos, one hundred Euros, and a completed application form. We walked up to the statue in Vake Park. It towered like a huge metal ghost at the end of the majestic, snow-laden park.

On the way back into the centre, I bought a small, leather-bound notebook from an old lady in the subway. I'd found my notebook useful since I got one in Istanbul, but now it was well and truly worn out, used up, and the pages had a tendency to drop out. I'd used the notebook for recording details, spontaneous thoughts, and 'to do' lists.

In the evening, I spoke to Zindze about her experiences travelling by bike. 'It is the tradition for Georgian girls to get married and settle down,' she said. 'More and more young people are moving away from the villages. In Turkey, we stayed with families all the time. I don't like it when people think you are crazy. In Turkey, there were some men in a lorry and they shouted and gave me that typical Turkish hand gesture as if to say, what are you doing? You are mad.' She demonstrated with a flick of her upturned hand. Later, Zindze went to an office party. She was sleeping in the office and so attended by default.

Tom cooked an amazing roast dinner and, afterwards, I read Alastair Humphries' book *Moods of Future Joys* and warmed myself by the heater. Alastair was lonely on his travels but he spoke of how he would meet somebody and it would pick up his spirits and encourage him to keep going. It made me think of kindred spirits like Sylvester and Zindze and how they affected my overall mood.

We moved out of Sophie's huge flat into Fanny's place, which was accessed by a winding wooden staircase that was a death trap in the winter because each step was iced over.

We went out for a meal and met Servane, Fanny's friend. During dinner, the restaurant turned into an impromptu Georgian dance. I got up and attempted to dance but couldn't quite conquer the aggressive arm movements, spinning, jumping, and clapping, which were done so masterfully and confidently by the Georgians.

The dancing continued outside of the bar. With a few beers consumed, Servane showed her Georgian side and decided to fight Tom on the ice. We had all only just met – was this normal behaviour? Inhibitions and reservations no longer seemed to exist.

The morning brought a trip to the Iran Embassy and a new visa in my passport. Afterwards, Tom filmed me and I dutifully showed my most amazed and excited face. I was going to Iran, which sounded so exotic and dangerous because of all the bad press the place receives in the English media. No matter how much I tried to block it out, the negative thoughts – made so strong, compulsive, and memorable in the news – tended to return and swim around in my head, which was something I would soon have to overcome.

The next day we slept in; a very attractive activity, considering that there was ice inside the windows of Fanny's flat. Our sleeping bags were barely warm enough for sleeping indoors in the current temperatures, let alone outdoors.

Tom received an email from the British Embassy saying that temperatures were dropping down to minus thirty and they advised us not to cycle. I hoped that people would help us out and host us so we wouldn't have to camp.

One part of me was looking forward to a tough challenge, whereas my rational side was plotting how best to ask people where they kept their stove so I could stop cycling and warm myself. My hands had been badly damaged by long hours leaning on the handlebars. Only over the last couple of days had I woken up in the morning and had feeling in my hands.

We visited the WWF office and picked up new versions of the bike trailers. After we left, we found buses full of police in riot gear parked outside the TV station next door. Tom went up to them and asked if they spoke English, but they just laughed and made fun of us, like a group of little boys. The atmosphere was strange walking back through the city. It felt as if people were waiting for something to happen.

59

A Really Crazy Guy on a Bike

We got up early and walked to Sophie's, where we met Zindze and hitchhiked to the technical university to see Jumbar Lehjava. Jumbar was a brickwall of a human being, sporting tree-trunk arms and a bulging chest. He was looking extremely healthy for seventy-two. He had many stories from his epic nine-year cycle through 238 countries and, in addition, held numerous records for push-ups.

His office in the university building was an archive of his journals, photos, videos, and maps. It felt as if he was part of the archive; the living embodiment of all the documentation. Unfortunately, most of it lay dormant because he couldn't get the money or resources to publicise it.

Jumbar had a Cannondale MTB with homemade ice tyres. There were screws driven in through the tyre wall to provide extra grip in the snow. His secretary wore a long, fur coat, busily answered the phone, and shuffled papers. I wondered who was calling.

Jumbar was an old man, but he had a strong life force, bred of a strict fitness regime and a rigorous pursuit of adventure and challenge. He represented a side of the Georgian psyche which is highly competitive and strives for excellence.

Jumbar's friend arrived. He was an Olympic long-jump athlete from back in the Soviet era. During Soviet times, both men had been given a house for their sporting endeavours, but when Saakashvili came to power, the houses were taken away from them.

A teenager arrived at the office. He was Jumbar's protégé. Jumbar was helping him to train to beat his own push up record, though he didn't seem too worried about being beaten, calmly saying with a big smile, 'He has a long way to go yet.'

It was difficult to comprehend Jumbar's cycling achievements. He had cycled for nine years, which certainly served as a testament to what could be achieved. It put into perspective how far I had come. However, the distance and number of countries he had covered, although impressive, never stood as something I wanted to match. I wasn't looking to go the furthest; I was looking for something else.

Jumbar was someone who devoted himself entirely to his goal. I reflected on how many transient meetings he must have had, friends he must have made, and moved on from, and family he had left behind.

In the evening, we joined Fanny and went over to Zoe's flat. Zoe was running Georgian singing lessons and Pierre, Romain, and Vincent were there. 'Singing together without embarrassment, surely not?' I hadn't sung since I was in the school choir at thirteen years old.

The following evening we went to the 'New Art bar' to see an American accordionist called Scott Taylor. It was a relaxed evening. Afterwards, Fanny and I went together to the natural sulphur bathes in the old city, housed in stone-built domes that emitted steam from air vents in the roof.

60

Frozen Lands

We left the following day. A part of me wanted to stay but I still wanted to continue the adventure on the bike. The cold air became gradually fresher as we cycled along the Mtkvari river and up out of the city. The snow and ice-laden ground reminded me that we still didn't have winter sleeping bags. I hoped we would find a warm place to stay at night.

The area near the Armenian border was beautiful. There was a snow-covered ridge and I noticed Ancient-looking headstones in a small cemetery, poking out of the snow.

The weather was clear and fresh. It felt good to be alive, but the kilometres still felt like they went by slowly and I found myself feeling a little impatient to make progress. I wished for the feeling to disappear. Progress to where? How could I be impatient over one day's riding with such a big goal?

The visa for Armenia was fifty dollars for three months, which was expensive for such a small country. There was no obvious difference between the lands on either side of the border. The first shop over the border had tonnes of snacks and sweets, but very little in the way of real food. I bought bread and what I thought was smoked ham but turned out to be a paprika-flavoured chunk of pork fat. We sat, leaning against the shop wall, chewing persistently.

The winter was slowly beginning to release its grip on the landscape. The river looked bloated from the beginning of the snowmelt. Huge chunks of ice dislodged from parts of the river that had frozen, and floated along. However, the temperature still began to drop disconcertingly in the late afternoon. As we reached the first junction, there were two options to Yerevan.

One of them, I had heard, was more mountainous, but shorter in distance, and passed beside the unstable Azerbaijan border. This is the one we chose.

We pedalled up to a village and met some locals who were hanging about beside the alcohol shop. There was a lot of action and a crowd gathered to see what was going on. A man called Adam invited us to his family home. We followed him there. His house was built from the local reddish Armenian rock. Outside the front door was a huge stockpile of wood, an oil tank, and a chicken coop.

After much smiling, shaking hands and initial primitive communication of 'It's cold', 'We are cyclists from England', we went inside and sat down. The living room had a huge rug hanging on the adjacent wall. A television blared out generic Armenian and Russian pop music. All generations of the family seemed to be present.

There were three young boys with differing personalities. One observed with cautious curiosity, the second looked indifferent, and the third, a little toddler, went about his duties: falling, crawling, being endlessly curious, and smiling open-mouthed. There were two ladies and a grandmother who looked after another small baby. There was a noticeable visual difference between Armenians and Georgians. The Armenians had softer features, longer faces and there was more of a visible mixture of ethnic ancestry.

We were ushered into the next room for a memorable meal of cheese, jam, bread, chicken casserole, vegetables, soup, cognac, and vodka. Everyone gathered round to watch us eat. It reminded me of the Turkish family in European Turkey: a solid family unit, buzzing with energy and interaction. Our host was a sergeant in the military police. We were able to gather some basic Armenian words in the notebook and he asked us about our favourite football team and other such questions.

In the morning, we had a breakfast of bread, cheese, tea, and delicious figs in syrup, and then began cycling. After twenty minutes or so, I reached the top of a climb and waited for Tom. We had an agreement to wait for each other if one went ahead.

Tom turned up after about ten minutes and asked me if I was waiting for anything. I said, 'No, are you?'

'Yes, for you to go, I want to cycle alone.'

'Okay, you can cycle ahead then, because waiting for you is starting to grate,' I said.

'It doesn't matter if it starts to grate; you have to put up with it,' he replied.

After considering the situation for a few minutes, I decided it was a good moment to cycle alone. Armenia was a small country with friendly people and some challenging hills. If Tom was intent on cycling either far behind or in front of me, it would become very frustrating to monitor him, and it seemed it would be pointless cycling together anyway.

61

You Can Go Your Own Way

'I am going to cycle alone to Yerevan,' I announced.

Tom said, 'I don't know whether that's a good idea,' but he accepted it without saying anything else. I gave him half my food.

I felt energised and independent with a slight pang of uncertainty. Was this the right choice? I felt like I had no other one. One of the reasons for travelling was to travel with my best friend; now we were going our separate ways, in an unknown country, a long way from home. Conventionally, it would have seemed somewhat foolhardy, but we had both become self-reliant and sturdy enough to be able to cope with the challenge of independence, which was a significant part of the attraction. I wanted to test out my own survival skills, fitness, and my ability to interact with people, to see whether it was possible to do all of this alone. I wanted to take ownership over my skills rather than being scared that, if we weren't together, everything would fall apart.

Tom cycled off without saying anything. I caught him up.

'Bye then,'

'Bye,' he replied.

I cycled ahead, a white Niva stopped, and the driver gave me a bag of biscuits, explaining that he was the owner of a food shop.

He wrote down the address and a message giving me a quota of money to spend in the shop. I copied the address and gave it to Tom.

'See you in Yerevan,' I said.

'Good luck.'

'You too.'

And that was it, I cycled off.

I pedalled hurriedly. It was as if I was trying to consolidate the action by getting away from Tom so I didn't have the opportunity to turn round and go back.

With a sufficient distance between us, I felt a flood of new perception. I could feel myself going off on a tangent from an existing pattern of thought. I needed to be honest with myself; concerned with what I thought of myself and not what others thought of me. It's exciting to develop as a person and then see how that manifests itself in the physical realm. I just needed to remember not to do anything stupid like fall off, break something, or offend someone.

Climbing up out of a valley into one of the villages, I pedalled underneath a telephone pylon that looked like a Jackson Pollock artwork that had been smudged and stretched out between two telegraph poles.

The trees were bare. The landscape was a mixture of wintery white and greyish brown. The residential buildings looked similar to those of the Georgians but built from Armenian stone.

I felt a little bit nervous at first, talking to local people, saying 'barev' (hello) as I went past. I made a conscious decision to connect with people more, so I made a lot more eye contact when I said hello to sense people's reactions.

I found the shop in the next village and propped up my bike outside. Suddenly it occurred to me, the first asset of there being two people: I was going to have to be careful about leaving my bike unattended.

I went into the shop and showed the note to the chap at the till. He didn't seem to understand it at all. I was coming into the shop with a piece of paper saying he should give me one thousand dram worth of food for free. It didn't appear that the owner had signed the paper, so I guess I could have written it myself. I wasn't even sure if the paper meant I could have free food.

As I wondered what to do, a girl turned up with her friend who spoke English. However, she couldn't understand me because she only understood American English. I cursed those blasted Americans, colonising everything. They were getting between me and my three dollars of food. Anyway, just when I thought the process had hit a dead end, the till man seemed to understand and bemusedly allowed me to pick out the food I wanted.

Why would the boss give away food to this scruffy foreigner? It certainly wouldn't have happened in a local express supermarket in the UK. I picked some sweets, bread, and various other things. It's amazing how much stuff you could get for three dollars in Armenia.

Half way through this process, Tom turned up.

I felt like I was trying to get away from Tom and that we would probably be at this dance all day: me going alone and then him catching me up. Anyway I didn't have long to dwell on it.

I put *The Streets,* 'Original Pirate Material', on my mp3 player. It was comforting to hear their urban English storytelling, and I considered how accurate the lead singer's words were. They represented the spirit and personality of average life in England, at least as I conceived it. I felt nostalgic about the gritty underground and subversive behaviour.

I appreciated the clever lyrics, poetry, and the English humour. Perhaps subconsciously I was getting bored of being the foreigner who didn't understand the language. I longed for some proper communication.

I climbed for a long time, wondering whether Tom would catch me up again, whether my legs would suddenly just cave in and break at the prospect of being alone, or whether some gangsters would turn up and – I don't know – say hello, and invite me for hot soup and vodka. Nothing else seemed to compute.

I felt free, without constraint or nagging feelings. I was finally in my own dream of being alone, out there, with everything I needed to survive. Now that I was here, what did I do next? I realised that if I was alone my adventure would be entirely of my own construction, and that presented some pertinent questions.

Did I want to spend a long time alone with myself? My mind bubbled over with possibilities of meetings and places, and I focused on my visions of beautiful distant lands to visit, mainly because I could.

I reached the top of the climb and went to fill my water bottle from a spring. The water was trickling out onto a large stalagmite of ice, which had formed beneath it. The air temperature was obviously cold, but I didn't really feel it until I stopped, so I was always motivated to start quickly pedalling again. Sweat started to freeze on the outer layer of my thin, breathable cycling jersey. I quickly got back into the sun.

I noticed what looked like a waterfall emerging from the rock. The water was frozen solid, inanimate, and was I intrigued by its beautiful, flowing form. The shape was like tumbling water.

I reached the pass and then descended down into a large bowl-shaped area, covered with snow in all directions. It looked like there was a town in the distance, but as I got closer, I realised that it was in ruins.

Over the next hill, I saw camouflaged buildings, which I thought must be part of a military base, so I decided it would be best not to hang around for slow-moving target practice. I had *The Chemical Brothers* blaring away in my ears, with funny scratching noises, drum flourishes, and beats. My mind ran away, inspired by the lyrics of Ian Brown on 'Acid Test':

'I live my life, with no regret. What do you think about that?'

Who is this singer with his profound lyrics? How did he come into this wisdom?

There is no getting away from mountains in Armenia; one after another, they come. The road climbed again, and as I reached the top of a big mountain, I realised that soon I would have to find somewhere to sleep. I passed through a small village where three men were standing by the roadside. One of them gestured for me to stop and invited me for coffee. His home looked like a temporary shelter, but inside it was warm and cosy from the hot stove.

His wife started to make food. They had a small child, a girl toddler, who was wandering about and had a lion mask. I felt I should make a bigger effort to compensate for the fact I was alone. I played with the child and made lots of conversation with the man but I was tired and he kept giving me vodka.

I was given plates of cheese, bread, pickle, honey, and rice. After eating, I broached the subject of sleeping, and he said there was a restaurant eight hundred metres away. I explained I had no money, but did have a tent. He made some phone calls and, after a while, some other people arrived with … Tom. The likelihood of us ending up in the same village and the same house seemed low at the time, although it probably wasn't that unlikely.

I expected myself to feel happy to see Tom, but I didn't. I was frustrated. I wanted to be alone. I felt exasperated and I had to stop myself from snapping at him.

I reined myself in, not wanting to give off bad vibes to the hosts, but I felt like I really needed to be away from Tom for the sake of continuing the journey together in the future. I didn't really know what Tom was thinking, but he was probably having similar thoughts. I felt myself getting angry at his tiny little habits, like the way he kept pushing his moustache out of the way of his mouth. I think is officially called 'expedition fever' and rises from spending too long together.

The evening passed with varying amounts of uneasiness. Tom made conversation with the hosts. I claimed I was tired and went to sleep on the floor. Later, Tom left with the other men. I slept well and, in the morning, left early without seeing Tom.

I reached the town of Idjevan, which was teeming with people rushing about the markets and shops. Taxi drivers hung around by the side of their cars. People looked bemusedly at me; it was the middle of the winter, after all. I wanted to get money out, but couldn't find a bank, so I became paranoid that I would be caught short.

As I pedalled out of the town, a feeling of loneliness swept over me. For those moments, I wanted to be somewhere completely different, but I concluded that this attitude wasn't going to get me anywhere and so I got back on the road.

62

One Hell of a Breakfast

In the next town, I was invited into a petrol station to eat leftovers from their dinner. I could have slept there too, but it was three in the afternoon. I continued to Dilijan and pedalled past a house where there was a Jack Russell dog, similar to my dog at home, which yapped frantically at me. I took this as a good sign and decided to ask about sleeping. As I drew closer to the front door, I could hear music and laughter.

A man arrived; I asked him about refilling my water bottle and he invited me in. It was the birthday party of a young boy and one of the men. I was handed plates of grilled meat, and toasted with cognac and vodka. Armenian pop music belched from the speakers. The birthday boy was dancing like crazy. It was fantastic to see celebration without inhibition. Some occasions aren't about analysing or making chitchat about work, but about getting raucous, happy, and playing off the energy of friends and family.

I lost track of time. I ate too much and drank numerous shots of brandy and vodka and then I was back out in the street. I was told that I wasn't allowed to leave and would stay with the birthday family. I pedalled, pushed, fell and skidded my way up a black-ice-ridden dirt track to their house.

Their house was large but contained a simple array of items including a bed, a table, a stove, an old television and a few books on a shelf. The boy was incredibly energetic. He kept checking if I was feeling good by giving me the thumbs up.

He desperately wanted to show me something outside before I got settled, so I followed him out and we clambered up a path, which was thickly covered in ice. I had to drag myself along, using the fence as a handrail. I wondered what I was going to see that the boy was so excited about. There was something that looked like a cupboard in the rock. He opened the doors and inside was revealed a tiny chapel, with burning candles, and pictures of Jesus.

The boy stepped inside and beckoned me to do the same. He crossed himself, kissed the picture of Jesus and lit a candle, urging me to do the same, which I did. I considered myself an atheist, but there was something special and strong about the love that was cultivated by the innocent devotion that the boy had, away from the war and ignorance bred from the negative side of religion. I would say this phenomenon also happens when people follow their own path of learning and discovery towards non-religious spiritual growth.

We had already eaten but another huge spread of delicious food was laid out by the man's wife, including a giant pan of fried potatoes, bowls of tomato sauce, pickles, chillies and plates of grilled lamb. The man winked at me and assuredly tapped a glass receptacle containing a clear liquid, which I knew was vodka, as if it wasn't possible to eat without lining the stomach with strong alcohol.

The toasting started and the journey to alcohol oblivion began. The toasting was a lot less long-winded than the Georgian way, with just a few words, and then down the hatch with the vodka – 'arak', as it's called in Armenian. 'World', knock back the shot; 'young people', repeat; and, my favourite, 'Jesus', pointing to the sky and emptying the little glass, as if Jesus was an old friend and would have been drinking too, if he were here!

At some point, the boy disappeared and then turned up with a pump-action shotgun, which he handed to me. I didn't know what to do with it. Bizarrely, I had the urge to strike a pose, then dismissed that idea and gave it back to the boy.

I awoke in the morning and still felt very drunk but in an evil, dark way, like how you might imagine death to feel. It certainly didn't feel pleasant. I went to the loo and the enthusiastic child intercepted me and insisted we go for a walk together with his sledge. This was followed by a giant breakfast, consisting of the same meal as the previous night's dinner, unfortunately including vodka to which my liver objected painfully. It literally felt like my liver was hanging on by a thread.

63

Moonscape

I said my farewells and thanks and pedalled out of the village, still feeling quite drunk. The alcohol seemed to speed up time. The tunnel at the top of the climb was over two thousand metres above sea level, and took two hours, but it seemed like less because of the alcohol. I pedalled through the darkness for three kilometres. Half way, I passed a group of soldiers who were clearing a huge ice formation out of the road.

At the exit, I collapsed on the ground where I lay for a few minutes. A van stopped and a couple of men walked over to me and asked me if I wanted a lift in their van. I tried to explain I wanted to cycle but the man just pointed to his watch, said 'economy', and then drove off. Economy, yes, time is money isn't it, and you must be at the next place sooner than you leave. What about being present in the moment, rather than rushing to a future goal?

I freewheeled down the road and became very happy. The slow process of cycling brings together the elements of patience and meditation, leaving the mind to please itself. This is achieved through the fact you are moving slowly; therefore, still moving and achieving something, but not so fast that the brain has to adapt too quickly to new environments. The mind takes peace in how the surroundings become familiar and is able to break out of the state of responding to the outer physical realm. Of course, the surroundings trigger thoughts, but not so many as to become overloaded and paralysed, like looking out of a window in a car, which drifts the mind into a soup of indifference.

I descended through the rocky moonscape and stopped to talk to a shepherd with a crinkled face, small glazed eyes, and a wide grin showing wonky yellow teeth. He talked in Russian, then gestured to the sky. 'Yes, the weather is beautiful. How fortunate we are that it isn't grating us with a blizzard!' I said enthusiastically.

I coasted along and avoided dog attacks as if I was playing a computer game, until I reached the tip of Lake Sevan. I was alone apart from the dogs and the fish sellers, who stood on the roadside with their arms outstretched indicating the size of the biggest fish they had. The biggest fish they had was always as long as their arm span!

An immense body of water stretched towards the horizon and mountains. To see the frozen lake for the first time was quite something. I felt wonder for the natural environment. There were beautiful patterns in the ice and snow dusting on top of it. I felt drawn to the ice so I propped up my bike and moved closer to the edge of the lake.

I could hear strange sounds, 'whomping' and crackling noises, like the belly of a beast digesting some food, as the ice shifted, cracked, expanded and contracted. In the distance, I could see the weather was turning. There were menacing grey clouds, which promised biting wind and snow.

At the town of Sevan, the road turned into a highway. In the clutches of winter, the town itself looked grey and soulless like a film set for a Soviet war film or a dystopian, Orwellian city. It had grey tower blocks and an unusual and eerie looking Ferris wheel.

Snow blew across the road and I floated across the top on my bike. I munched through a large bag of shashlik – grilled meat – donated to me from the party. The road was a long slog. In the distance, at the foot of forbearing mountains, an array of huge industrial chimneys bellowed smoke. I passed ruins of old factories and houses, which were now being used as shelter for animals.

At one point, it was difficult to make out the topography of the land. It looked flat, but then I realised there were two very large dome shaped hills, which could only be made out by a slight concave curve giving away their form. I pedalled and pedalled and started to become excited at arriving in the capital. Slowly but surely, the bike edged along, while 4x4s and Ladas rocketed past.

I reached the top of the climb and saw a sign that the downhill would be 9km. At first, I was very happy at the prospect; then I realised how cold I could be if I was not pedalling. The inclement weather had now moved in and I was about to get a taste of a real Armenian blizzard. I started to descend, but very quickly I had to stop because I became unbearably cold. I donned all three Buff hats and my puffa jacket. Can you imagine cycling in a huge puffa jacket and still feeling cold? A voice in my head spoke to me: 'Bugger, I hadn't quite expected this.' My solution was very English: carry on and hope for the best.

The temperature in the city was minus thirty but I was still nine kilometres and one thousand metres above that and cycling through a blizzard. My beard froze to the material wrapped around my face. I had the very disturbing feeling that if I didn't keep blinking my eyelids would freeze. My fingers and toes were numb, but it felt like an adventure. I swooped down the hill as cars hooted encouragement.

64

Underground

I passed a sign for Yerevan and I began to wonder where I would stay that night. I stopped at a shop next to a man who was using a mobile phone and asked him where the centre was. He gestured on down the road but another car turned up and a man inside gestured for me to wait.

He jumped out of the car. He had a rather scary face, which looked like it had been scarred by burns, and his mouth sported a number of gold teeth. However, his manner was not that of the cutthroat gangster he resembled. He shook my hand and gestured to his mouth to indicate eating. The guy on the mobile phone helpfully reiterated, 'He wants you to go to his house to eat.'

The man ran a business selling car parts. His flat was situated in a high-rise tower block in a nearby residential district. The living room looked typical, with a cabinet filled with fancy crockery, a coffee table, dining table, sofa, and a television. He was married and had two small children: a girl and a boy. We ate peas and egg, lavashe – traditional Armenian flatbread – pickle, cured meats, and the unavoidable shots of vodka followed by tea and chocolates.

After a while, his friend arrived – who I thought he looked like an English football supporter. He had a bald head and wore a sporty, blue t-shirt. He was carrying a bottle of Armenian cognac, which he insisted I try, accompanied by traditional Armenian sausages called basturma and sujukh. Basturma was more like salami but sujukh was drier and more peppery; they were both delicious.

At around eleven o'clock, my host announced – after some

drawn out communication breakdown, digging for the right word – 'We go and visit museum.' His friend nodded dutifully in agreement. I attempted to explain that being lost in dreams soon would be extremely agreeable, but I was also eager to see what kind of museum would be open at this time of night.

We drove to a nearby residential area, which looked like an old area of the city, and parked next to a tall stone wall. My host walked up to a house, trying to call someone on his mobile phone, presumably the inhabitants, but this was to no avail so he tried a different tactic; he banged on the window and shouted. I thought he could have taken a hint and come back tomorrow morning, but he entered through a vine covered iron doorway into the backyard and started pounding on the back door. Shortly after, a little bearded man appeared and welcomed us into a room, which looked much like a normal homely front room.

What kind of museum it was had yet to materialise. Without much polite introduction, the little bearded man led us to a small wooden door, which he opened, revealing a ladder, which descended into a tunnel, which was crudely lit with small orange lamps. 'Where on earth did this tunnel lead?' I wondered.

The bearded man climbed onto the ladder and slowly descended, so we all followed. I looked around at the bare earth and could make out the marks where it had been chiselled away by some kind of hand tool.

I stepped off the ladder into a circular room, about fifteen square feet in size. It was a cave, which had been painstakingly excavated from the earth. We exited that room and went down some steps into at least two more rooms and a miniature chapel.

The man had spent twenty-two years of his life digging the tunnel. I wondered what the original reason for building it was. Perhaps it was paranoia. Perhaps it was originally a bunker to hide from nuclear war or a place to store contraband. Maybe he was crazy. However, the achievement was visibly epic: a product of focused human effort.

I awoke the next morning and ate breakfast whilst watching old re-runs of Soviet musicals on the telly. The show was presented by two attractive Russian girls. I was reminded how much more Armenia leans to Russia than Georgia and how people still think fondly of aspects of Soviet times.

I retrieved my bike from my host's workplace and left for the city centre. I hadn't organised a place to stay, which worried me a little. I tried to convince myself that the worrying was unfounded and to trust the process.

I checked my emails in an Internet café. I had an email from Tom saying he was going to visit the WWF office in the city that week and that he had tried to pick up our new winter sleeping bags from customs but they had wanted to charge us one thousand dollars for them to be released. Tom said he had hitchhiked to Yerevan in order to try to resolve the problem by asking at the British Embassy.

I decided to visit the Embassy to see if I could find out anything new about the sleeping bag situation. I had another email from Fanny who, I was happy to hear, was arriving in Yerevan in a couple of hours. She was a fun person to spend time with and made me feel at ease, yet on my toes.

I cycled up the street on which all the embassies were situated: Syrian, Korean, Kazakh, Chinese, Russian, and British. I went through a thick steel door and handed my passport over to the man behind a glass window. I was then allowed entry to 'little England in Yerevan'.

Inside, I was met by a lady in her mid thirties, with shoulder-length, light-brown hair. She looked tired and there were bags under her eyes. She was friendly but reserved. She told me that the ambassador had heard of our journey and spoken to the Armenian Foreign Minister, who had then told customs to cancel the charges. However, she wasn't sure how long it would take the issue to be completely resolved.

I left the embassy and was once again a tramp rather than a royal subject on a diplomatic meeting. I trudged down the road, wondering what to do. I spotted the British Council. Considering that it was called the 'British' Council, I decided that it was my right to go in there and act as if I owned the place. I parked my bike, wandered in and looked for someone to talk to, but everyone ignored me so I left.

I continued my brisk walk down the road. I felt energised, curious and free, if a little lacking in direction. 'Come on creative brain; ply me with exciting things to do!' I went down to the Cascade monument in the centre of Yerevan, which consisted of steps interspersed with gardens, which led up to an obelisk. I sat on one of the benches beside the giant statue of Alexander Tamanyan, the city planner of Yerevan. He is depicted poring over his plans for the city at his designing table.

A man came over to speak to me. His name was Seecard and he wasn't dressed like a normal Armenian – which would have been pointy black shoes, black trousers, and a black leather jacket – but, rather, was wearing a sports tracksuit.

We chatted for a while. He was an ex-professional footballer who now worked as a masseur. 'Wonders never cease', I thought; just as I'd pigeonholed all Armenian men as cigarette-smoking idlers, who kicked dust around the streets, I met this multi-faceted fellow. He worked at a yoga clinic and practiced yoga and aikido. He enjoyed mountain biking at Lake Sevan. He showed me where I could stay in a cheap youth hostel, and then I went to meet Fanny at the Opera House. She looked good; her cheeks were rosy from the cold. She had already arranged for us to stay at her friend's place.

We walked to a café first, where I had arranged to meet up with Tom. It was a posh place and I found Tom sitting in a shady corner surrounded by Spanish girls. It was nice to see he had found some new friends. Our meeting was cordial but there was no sign that we would be spending any time together for a while.

65

French Diplomacy

Fanny and I walked to the flat of Max and Irene, friends of hers who were diplomats at the French Embassy. They lived in a renovated apartment situated on the central Mashtots Avenue, one of the main streets of Yerevan. The street catered mainly for the oligarch, Diaspora and ex-pat communities, sporting trendy bars, restaurants and spotless supermarkets.

Max and Irene made a great couple. Irene was enthusiastic and friendly and Max was handsome and smart. We went to a party at their friends, Pierre and Myriam's place. They lived in a stylish, minimalist apartment. I greeted everyone in the French way, breaking the ice with a kiss on each cheek. We drank French wine, ate cheese and talked in the 'talk as if tomorrow you will be a mute' French way: the joy of conversation.

Another guest was Michel, a diplomat working for the EU on the relations between the Caucasus countries. He was a connoisseur of music from the eighties and was particularly keen to point out a famous French song with the lyrics 'Andy, dit moi oui, cherie, oh oh oh oo, shoo, cherie, dit moi oui'. If I had a franc for every time a French person has sung that song about my name since ... I'd have at least a couple of pockets of redundant currency.

I met an Armenian businessman and sausage importer who explained the subtle details of a good sausage: 'A cheap typical Russian sausage contains relatively little meat in comparison with a high quality Armenian sausage. The Russians just want something to wedge in their mouth to curb the stinging pain after the vodka. The quality of the sausage depends on the level of additives; the higher the quality of sausage, the higher the proportion of meat to soya, fat, colours, and preservatives.'

The Armenians were sausage connoisseurs and demanded high quality ingredients. Different standards of sausage were also coupled with different philosophies of sausage production, traditional handmade production compared to machine-made mass production, and other factors such as research and development. 'The best producers still understand they are running a business and try to strike a balance between economies of scale and quality.'

The following day, another trip to the embassy yielded nothing and I was told to come back on Monday. I began to realise that this might take longer than expected. Each day brought a bittersweet taste of guilt. I enjoyed the rest and soaking up the city, but I knew I should probably have been riding.

The next day, Fanny and I went to the market to buy food so I could cook for Max and Irene. I planned to cook paprika chicken; a recipe from The Hairy Bikers, which I thought was fitting, seeing as I was a hairy biker. The market area was a hub of activity. The adjacent street had rows of butchers and shops displaying their wares. The market itself was like an aircraft hangar, with lines of babushkas selling vegetables, herbs, meat and pulses. Everything was available at cheap prices.

My attention was caught by a man speaking loudly and badly in Armenian, attempting to barter for some produce with a babushka but who was evidently a tourist or at least not a local. It didn't appear that anyone understood his linguistic attempts! He was middle-aged, a little overweight, and had balding grey hair, but he moved around a lot when he spoke and he had a good energy.

'Hi, I'm Michael. Isn't the market great? You can get anything here and it's all fresh and very cheap.'

He had tired, but relaxed-looking eyes and spoke in a disarmingly laid-back way. On first impressions, he seemed like just another American ex-pat nutcase, but I was certainly intrigued by his gregarious appearance and his valiant attempts at the language. I told him about my journey and he invited Fanny and me to dinner.

That evening, Fanny and I went to a small, underground club called 'The Stop'. We were the only ones dancing. Continuing in the romantic vibe, we decided to accompany some of our friends to a strip club. We entered into the shady bar. Between dances from girls wearing PVC, rubbing themselves up and down the metal pole, an old man took to the stage and crooned some traditional Armenian songs. Dancing girls weren't really in my cycling budget and, once the bouncers began to realise this, we were gently, but firmly, turfed out into the street.

The next morning we got up late and walked down to the river. The late afternoon winter sun shone bright yellow over virgin snow. I felt good. There was nothing I could do about being stranded in Yerevan. The moments didn't feel heavy, and my mind wasn't distracted by any kind of agenda. Fanny and I were simply happy to spend time in each other's company.

We drove up to Lake Sevan. It was completely white and covered in a blanket of recent snow. We drove onto the peninsula where the rich politicians had their holiday homes. We were able to walk on the lake and a boy who was fishing there temporarily diverted his attention from his fishing line and tried to sell us some postcards.

For lunch, we ate freshly caught fish from the lake. I chatted with Max about the state of foreign investment in Armenia.

'The system is very corrupt. For example, there is a monopoly on the telecoms industry. It's very difficult for companies to enter the market, and with regards to customs and tax it depends who you know in the government.'

After lunch, we visited the natural spring baths near Hrazdan. On arrival, it looked like a ramshackle collection of farm buildings. We were met by a lady who led us past a comical steaming boiler contraption to a roofless barn, inside which there was a pipe, held in place by two large rocks, which sprayed hot water at high pressure. The water was more or less heading into a bath, which long ago had become thickly encrusted with sulphur deposits.

I blissfully soaked in the bath.

'Andy, are you going to roll in the snow?' said Max.

'All in good time,' I replied.

Nearing heat-induced loss of consciousness, I hauled my wrinkly body out of the water and hopped outside into the snow. I danced around in the cold air, jogging on the spot psychologically preparing myself before throwing myself down and rolling in the snow. The snow felt like it was burning my skin, which was a counter-intuitive sensation. However, it was intensely stimulating to jump back in the hot water after cooling myself right down.

In the evening, I cooked meatballs in wine and pepper tomato sauce with rice for Max, Irene, Pierre, and Myriam. I was nervous because Pierre was a chef and owned a restaurant in Yerevan. However, he finished his plate and had seconds. Success!

The morning came for Fanny to return to Tbilisi. We sat in the café at the Marshrutka (minibus) station. Fanny smoked a couple of cigarettes and we talked about what would happen in the future. I told her that if there were further delays I would probably return to Tbilisi to spend more time with her.

I felt lightness and an urgency in my actions and wanted to find out what was next in this story. However, I was thinking of the cycle journey, which was my mission and priority. Anything that threatened to stop it would have to fall by the wayside. I told myself that I hadn't travelled far enough yet to stop anywhere for long, although also I rather liked the idea because I was having so much fun.

In the hours after she left, I pondered that I could stay with her, and in the meantime, use the Internet to look for more sponsorship, explore Tbilisi further, and do future route research – by this point, I was running very low on funds. I began to support the idea in my mind. If I did go back to Tbilisi, I could try hitchhiking.

66

One Funky American

After Fanny had left, I went for dinner at Michael's house. His apartment was large, with grand chandeliers hanging from the ceiling, a polished wooden floor, high ceilings and balconies. The furniture was sparse but Michael said he had been refurbishing the place.

'My grandmother was Armenian and my Armenian name is Manoog.' He was a descendant of second generation Armenians in America. He had lived in an all-Armenian community when he was little but then moved to another area where there were no Armenians. That was when he became Americanised, he told me.

He made me the first cup of tea with milk I'd had for months. Unfortunately, it was powdered milk and Manoog put too much in because he was distracted by talking to me. Then he used an electronic stirrer, which frothed up the milk so that it looked more like hot chocolate than tea.

Manoog was extremely inspired by our trip and had many ideas for how to promote it. We visited a nearby NGO together to organise a video presentation the following Friday. Tom came over and we spent the next few days digitising and cutting footage for a short film for the presentation. One morning I arrived at the flat and Manoog was just about to go to bed. He had been up all night watching the presidential contest in the US.

I spoke to Manoog about Tom. 'When I offer my perspective on a situation, I feel like he takes it as an insult to his intelligence,' I said.

Manoog replied, 'It would be boring for him if he was with a person who said he was right all the time. I feel sorry for people who are always right. Once, a close friend of mine was, I thought, with the wrong women. He took my intervention badly and I didn't speak to that friend for 30 years. However, that friend then went on to find the love of his life and has been married to her ever since.' I felt better after talking to him. I didn't feel judged by him.

The atmosphere between Tom and I was still tense but it improved with time spent together. I knew there was a development when I cooked lunch and Tom accepted it. He sealed the peace deal by playing a new drum and bass mix by *High Contrast*, which he had downloaded. How different I felt, no longer consumed with our conflicts. It was easy to right the situation with some calm time spent together, sharing, talking and music!

Manoog organised a trip to see a jazz concert at a club called 'The Stop'. The act was a band from Brooklyn and they were friends of Manoog. They played jazz, mixed with elements of hip-hop. The performance throbbed and meandered, switched and swapped styles. The artists deliberately fell in and out of sync with the flow. I watched the cellist, who was playing a catchy bass rhythm. His face expressed the changes in the music and his delight in playing. The drummer teased the air with intricate syncopated rhythms, effortlessly executed. There were some special moments: an unexpected ride here or a snappy-snare there to wake the awareness. Their virtuosity was inspiring.

The next day was the presentation at the NGO. About twenty people turned up. I was full of energy beforehand: an intoxicating combination of excitement and fear, even though it was only a small group of people.

Surprisingly, instead of being asked questions about the most unlikely experiences of the trip, we were asked about the most mundane aspects of everyday life on the bike: where we went to the loo, how we got food, where we slept, and how to get sponsorship. It was great to be able to share some information with others.

67

pas de roues, juste un pouce

The following day, I hitchhiked to Tbilisi. I knew if I wanted it to happen I would have to make some moves. I packed minimal items into a bag and left the house after breakfast.

I decided to walk to the nearest road that led out of Yerevan. I walked up the hill so I would miss the cross-town traffic and catch traffic leaving the city. The path was thick with snow and clumps stuck to my cleats, forming lumps of ice which made it difficult to walk.

There were plenty of cars going up the hill and I felt confident about getting a ride. As each car went past, I measured up who was inside and wondered where they were going. I had a feeling, as I passed under a big old railway bridge, that I had left the city. I took this as a cue to start sticking out my thumb.

A few cars passed me without stopping. I kept reminding myself that I would need patience, but I stopped mid-thought as an ancient Soviet bus pulled up and I thought, 'Bugger, I'm supposed to be hitchhiking.' However, the bus was not yet in service, so taking it didn't break the rules. It was going up the hill towards its first pick up. The friendly old driver with grey stubble, a wrinkled face, and oil stained hands said he was heading to Abovian, which was on my way.

The bus chugged up the hill. I observed the usual road rage of cars speeding, tailgating, swerving and overtaking one another. The driver dropped me off at a bus stop at the beginning of the highway. I thanked him, got off, and had an impending feeling of, 'What next?' – The feeling of being dropped somewhere unplanned was a little disconcerting. It was a lot colder at the top of the hill and the wind whipped menacingly in long gusts, as if at any moment it could turn into a blizzard. I put on my woolly hat and gloves, slung my bag over my shoulder and impulsively started walking hurriedly along the road. However, I soon stopped myself to make a mental note that I wasn't going to walk there, so I turned around and stuck my thumb out.

What was the most efficient way to thumb? Was thumbing even the best thing here, because I had seen other people moving their outstretched arms up and down with their hand in a flat horizontal position. I soon realised that people knew what I was doing and I began to learn the language of hitchhiking. A few cars passed and someone in the car would do a crossed arms signal, which meant that there was no space in the car. This meant that if there had been space, then maybe they would have picked me up, which gave me confidence.

A couple of 4x4s with tinted windows went quickly past. There was no sign of them stopping. Maybe the driver couldn't see me because he was too high up. A few vans and small lorries went past in clouds of diesel smoke.

After a few minutes, a Volga stopped. A Volga is a typical Soviet car. It is grand, long, and moves like a boat. It contained three young men. I told the driver I wanted to go to Sevan. He agreed and I jumped in the back seat. The other passengers didn't speak English apart from one guy who spoke a little. 'I am twenty four. I was born in Russia. My parents were Armenian.' He puffed smoke to one side. 'Where are you from?'

'I am from Leicester, erm … No, that never works … Birmingham, London? …'

'Last year, did Scotland split from England?' he asked.

'I thought Scotland just had an independent parliament,' I mused. Then I realised how poor my knowledge was of that sort of thing, so I felt a little stupid.

They were going skiing for the first time. I attempted to mime the snowplough skiing position with my arms to much hilarity. They didn't look well kitted out for skiing, wearing typical leather jackets and woolly gloves. I bade them farewell at the turning to Tsakdazor. By now, I was well along the highway, and surrounded by nothing but snowy mountains.

Cars flew along, blowing drifts of snow, which looked like shifting white sands. When I watched the cars, it reminded me of the mortality of human beings; the seeming knife edge of control of a speeding vehicle and the subsequent trajectory that would occur through a small loss of concentration. The transient and temporary nature of life seemed clear.

I hitched up my coat around my neck and waited for the next car to arrive. I imagined standing there all day in the freezing cold, but after about ten minutes a man in an old Lada estate pulled up. He was in his mid to late fifties, had a friendly face and a sagging stubble-covered chin. He looked like he might have been handsome in his earlier years. He was wearing a tweed coat with a worn leather jacket over the top so that the cuffs of the jacket protruded at his wrists. His name was Armen and he spoke some English. His car was slow, with a maximum speed of about forty-five miles per hour and there was a hole in the floor, which let a draught in.

We passed Lake Sevan and he told me the story of the Lady of the Lake, a big Soviet-era statue that is beside the lake. Legend has it that the lady lit a torch so that her love interest could swim to meet her but when he was half way across the lake it started to rain, which doused the flame so her lover could no longer see where to go, and drowned.

We stopped at a petrol station so he could put gas in the car. He got out of the car and said, 'This is a good place to charge and discharge,' as he ran off to urinate in the snow. The attendant attached the tube to the gas canister mounted in the boot of the car. When he returned, he offered me an apple.

'Do you want the red apple or the yellow apple?' as if it was a magical choice.

He was an intriguing person. He had been a computer programmer during Soviet times working on 'calculating machines'. He told me that the computer he worked on had been the size of an entire room. I thought that we never learnt about Russia at school, only America. I wondered what on earth he had done with a computer that filled an entire room, and imagined wondrous mathematical equations controlling important decisions or spacecraft.

Surprisingly, he had a daughter in Spain, studying Spanish and literature, who spoke good English. He said he liked *The Beatles* and started singing 'o blad dee, o blah dah, life goes on, woooh! Da da da, life goes on! Very good band.' He said it was very difficult to get a job in Armenia and people did anything they could to support their families. The difference between city life and country life was so stark there. Kitsch, glamorous high streets contrasted against the traditional village lifestyle.

In the town of Dilijan, he had to visit someone about business. He was making a living selling machine parts. I sat, waited, and observed an old lady who was bent over almost double, hobbling down the middle of the street. She had cloths wrapped around her feet. Even the locals took a second glance at her. Then some schoolchildren ran past, bursting with energy and shouting to each other.

Armen returned to the car. 'Direct service to Vanadzor!' he exclaimed. I smiled in appreciation. He explained about the apples. The yellow one was called the Golden Six and the other was a 'something' Delicious. I suggested 'golden' but he said no. They were American apples, but one of the Soviet leaders had brought over a seed and planted it in Armenia.

Armen dropped me off at the junction after the town. I had made good progress so far, but Armen's car had been slow and the day was moving on. I walked along the roadside. A few cars passed and one man in a Mercedes 4x4 gave me a dismissive flick of his hand. 'Cars that make people act like that should be banned,' I thought.

I found myself growing frustrated and angry but I calmed myself. I told myself not to be so expectant, and to persevere. As if to quash my previous generalisation about Mercedes drivers, a new, black Mercedes pulled over and a well-dressed man ushered me inside. I stomped the snow off my feet as best I could and gingerly stepped in. He fidgeted a lot and spoke quickly and in a high-powered way at me. He had a Mercedes Ego™. He drove very fast, on the thinnest, twisting mountain roads, beside steep drops into the valley below, as if he was late for his own funeral.

I couldn't tell if he was happy to pick me up or not. I tried to ask him how far to Georgia. 'Skorka kilometre, Georgia?' He gestured five with his hand, which got my hopes up, and I thought I was close to the border. He turned off the road through a pair of ostentatious gates and pulled up at the entrance of a large building. The man owned a hotel, and invited me to eat. I was shown to a hotel room and was brought chicken and chips. I hastily ate, thanked my host, and left, because time was getting on. I didn't want to be trying to hitchhike in the dark and I had no camping equipment with me.

I started walking down the road with my thumb out but I couldn't get a ride. Then, by an unbelievable stroke of luck, the Yerevan to Tbilisi Marshrutka turned up. I flagged it down and it had space for one more person so I bundled myself into the cramped space next to a lady wearing a thick fur coat and who I noticed, when she smiled, had an impressive array of gold teeth.

This was my first experience of a Marshrutka ride. A Marshrutka is usually a white van, which has been converted into a bus and does cheap, long-distance travel – as long as you don't mind the crazy driving, lack of seat belts, and being packed together like sardines.

Half way, there was a rest stop and everyone got out and smoked cigarettes. I bought a juicy kebab from a roadside seller and then the journey resumed. The roads snaked their way along, hugging the cliff side. The driver seemed completely oblivious to the abyss down into the steep valley, without any sort of road barrier. The suspension had seen better days and it felt like someone was hitting my arse with a plank of wood whenever we went over a bump.

The mountains looked like hibernating dinosaurs. We passed a couple of derelict industrial areas, which were being reclaimed by nature: rusting and rotting away, overgrown with plants. They looked strangely beautiful.

The last sixty kilometres to Tbilisi seemed to take forever. I drifted in and out of sleep.

Arriving at the city, there was a busy highway: a dual carriageway with no barrier in the centre, so cars piggybacked on each other to overtake into the oncoming traffic, driving fast. Lights swooshed past. We reached the station and I walked through the streets towards Fanny's place. Tbilisi looked different to Yerevan. The streets were dark and the buildings seemed to be eroding faster. Maybe it was something to do with the durable Armenian granite they use for the buildings. I reached the Marjanishvili Bridge and walked up the cobbled street leading to Rustaveli. A man asked me for a lighter. I fumbled in my bag, 'No, sorry.' I usually had one to light the stove. I became aware of not being so well equipped, after having carried everything I needed to survive with me for so long.

I walked down Rustaveli, passed through Freedom Square and up into the district called 'Sololaki', where Fanny lived. I walked into the Italian courtyard and up the spiral wooden staircase. Fanny was there at the window doing the washing up. I was happy to be back in Tbilisi to explore the city and spend time with new friends.

68

There Is No Road, Only Movements

We celebrated my return by going to the Davit Gareji monastery, which is on the steppe next to the Azerbaijan border. Vincent had learnt to drive like a Georgian: using the horn regularly and driving fast. He gave me a sly grin, hooted and accelerated to pass a car trying to cut in front. We turned off the highway and soon were in a wild and hilly, snow-covered landscape which reminded me a little of the Yorkshire moors. We past a lake and everyone jumped out and ran down to the waters' edge. Vincent pointed out to a building in the distance. 'We're going to the black tower!' he said dramatically.

The Davit Gareji monastery was excavated from the side of the hillside, exposing the ochre coloured rock. There were monks occupying the place and, although I couldn't see them, I could feel their presence.

Nino, Vincent's partner, asked me, 'Are you a believer, Andy?'

I said, 'Erm … I don't think so.'

She said, 'You must at least respect this; don't you feel an atmosphere?'

I did feel something mystical about the place. It was like something from a story: a strange dwelling surrounded by wilderness; I felt like I had travelled back in time to a medieval era. The monastery was certainly a spiritual place. It was a refuge, perched on the ridge, next to the border. I bet it had many stories to tell from its history.

We walked to the top of the ridge and the panoramic view over the Azerbaijan plains spread out before me. Although Tom and I had been living outside for months, we had spent most of our time on the roads, so it was a treat for me to be in open countryside. The mountains reared up like waves frozen mid-break. I could see a flock of black sheep in a circle, down on the plain, in the hazy distance. They looked like ants. The others continued along the path and then disappeared from my line of sight and I found them in one of many caves dug into the cliff side. 'What an amazing campsite,' I said.

Vincent said, looking into the distance, 'If we started a fire, the Azeris would start shooting!'

On the return journey to Tbilisi, Vincent stopped to buy chacha from a roadside restaurant. He paused to say, 'It is very good here,' before swiftly exiting the car. He returned with an unlabelled glass bottle containing a clear liquid. He passed the bottle to David, who swigged repeatedly from it until he was suitably pickled and agreed it was good.

Back at Vincent's flat, I tried to have a conversation with David, but once I'd finished he said, 'I didn't understand a thing you just said, Andy,' and we fell about laughing. Maybe it was the chacha, but David explained that he understood the American English accent, but the British English accent, particularly mine, was impossible for him to understand. David was very friendly. He put his arm around me and, with a wink, said, 'I know you're really fluent in French, Andy.'

In the evening, I went to a singing lesson. The famous French singer Henry Salvador had recently died and Vincent played a tribute to him on the guitar. Romain had just returned from a snowboarding trip in the mountains. He talked about riding over two-metre-deep, powder snow, with not a soul in sight.

Afterwards, we went to a restaurant and we made toasts to various things: 'To us!', 'To today!', 'To nostalgia for being twenty years old!'

'Where were you when you were twenty?'

'I was in France, in a squat!'

'I was in a flat with friends!'

'I was teaching Trotskyism!'

'I was at York University!'

'In Tbilisi!'

'In Spain!'

Later, Fanny tried to teach me how to dance to rock and roll. 'Keep your elbows in, strong and confident, then spin me around and catch my hands again. Stick that leg out there. Pull that leg in … No! Not like that!'

Fanny was a great dancer. She possessed an innate rhythm, as if a metronome was ticking inside her head. The more she danced the happier she became. I found it difficult to do anything other than a sort of pedalling motion.

As an Englishman, I am aware of a certain moral pressure to keep up appearances and politeness. There is a built in susceptibility to coyness, shyness, and inhibitions when confronted with things like dancing and singing. However, I resolved that it was therefore a challenge to break down these reserved behaviours and attitudes. A man came into the restaurant beating a Georgian rhythm on a drum. Everyone cheered, and Fanny and Aurélien took to the dancefloor. Aurélien threw his arms out, fists clenched, shoulders back and head up. He lunged towards Fanny, who lightly tiptoed around him making flowing shapes with her arms in the air. The dance looked like a cross between a delicate ballet and a mating ritual.

It was a rousing night. The owner of the bar was a larger than life woman called Mancho. She had big, but tired eyes, which were heavily made up. She took to the piano whilst Vincent played the accordion and David played the guitar. Everyone was drumming on the table and stamping on the floor. I wondered whether this was a normal, French night out or whether I had just fallen in with some extraordinary people. Nevertheless, I realised I had found some of the things I set out for: friends, energy, real celebration, and a more intense way of life.

One evening we went for a drink in a bar and I met Dion, an English girl working for an NGO. We talked and I immediately noticed her 'Englishness'. Dion chatted away whilst smoking a roll up cigarette. 'I'm missing my boyfriend. He's in Engl …' She stopped mid-sentence to apologise. 'I'm sorry … I think I'm going to gush.'

I had to search through my database of English slang: 'Gush'? I think she meant she was going to cry. I found it tiring to make small talk. It seemed like a waste of time.

Over the days, I felt differently because of the change in lifestyle. I had been used to feeling super-fit and being out in the fresh air. However, now I had stopped, my body began to ache. I got headaches and felt lethargic. I felt the urge to exercise for the sake of feeling better, which I hated. I wished that my lifestyle could be active enough so I wouldn't have to exercise just to feel good. Being around lots of people and being in a city brought complicated thoughts and feelings which threatened to throw all my plans into question. My finances were getting low. The money for the new video camera went out. I looked back at my spending. Due to our discipline with spending, we had managed to stick more or less to a budget of five Euros per day, but I would need to make some cash to be realistic about my future travel plans.

One night, I had a dream. People were in a line, which I interpreted as the human population and personal life moving forward in space and time. Each person had an effect on his or her surroundings and on their direct environment. There were scientists around the people conducting tests, but I managed to escape to another place where I met an old school friend. I climbed up a tree but went too far out on a limb. I saw other branches were breaking off around me. I didn't have a way of getting down and was too tense to move. Someone on an opposite branch said, 'Make the leap to the next branch down; the tree's weight, combined with mine, and other people on the tree will make the tree bend down.' That's what happened, and I successfully got out of the tree.

In the evening, Fanny and I went to her friend Manana's house. When Fanny had first moved to Georgia, she lived for two years with her adopted family in a village called Guurdjaani. Manana's son, Rolandi was there. Rolandi was a famous actor in Georgia, playing theatres in the city and appearing in a popular

277

soap opera. He gave me some tips on Georgian dancing.

'Andy, when dancing you should imagine that you are a great man who is strong and tall. Your shoulders should be back, your head up, stomach out and backside in.'

The following morning we went to Guurdjaani, and the taxi ride was the scariest experience of my life. There were four people in the taxi. The driver was either trying to impress or scare the foreigners, and although the other Georgian in the car was trying to make out that he found it all quite funny, even he looked concerned. The driver was a cross between Dennis Hopper's characters in *Blue Velvet* and *Easy Rider*. He even had a big moustache and fake-looking sideburns. He was like a demon, hell-bent on death; he blindly overtook every vehicle we caught up with, speeding up and pulling out like a slingshot as we approached.

I consider myself an incredibly lucky person, based solely on surviving that one experience. After a while, in a very masochistic way, I may have begun to enjoy it. I had a choice between being scared of death – which hadn't yet happened – or alive and enjoying the thrill of speed. The latter at least meant seeing things in a positive light.

We arrived at Nora's house intact. Nora was the mother of Manana and Fanny's adopted grandmother. She was sinewy, slender, and very wrinkly. She paced around busily, sweeping the floor and shooing the chickens around. 'Fanny!' she squealed when we arrived, giving her a big hug and chattering away in Georgian.

The house was large but bare. The paintwork was peeling from the wooden beams and the wallpaper from the walls. The last time anything had been new was in Soviet times. Nora had a wood burner in the kitchen for heat and cooking, which she used instead of the old, electric cooker which didn't work. She boiled water for tea on a dangerous-looking heater with an exposed filament, the wires from which were poked directly into the wall socket, causing a spark when inserted. There was no central heating, no gas supply, and there hadn't been for years. The electricity was regularly cut off. It was what she was used to. She wanted mod cons and comforts but made do without. She made sure to complain about it and made sure that Fanny knew about it. I felt sorry for her, but she had a strong family supporting her, a strong spirit, and some land to grow vegetables and keep chickens on. I don't think I have ever met a woman of that age with such a powerful life force. There was even something childlike about her. It seemed like her spirit had never aged.

Fanny and I walked down the main road to the market, to buy vegetables for the borscht we planned to cook Nora. The road was very busy and the 4x4s tore along the uneven surface. All the houses were similar to Nora's: red brick, overgrown front gardens, and in varying states of maintenance. We bought fresh ingredients and then cooked the borscht over the wood burner. It was a great success. 'She says it has cured a stomach illness that she has had for ages,' Fanny said whilst giggling.

In the morning, Fanny led me out onto the balcony, 'Close your eyes, I want to show you something. Don't worry, I won't send you down a hole.' I opened my eyes to a clear view of the Caucasus Mountains. They floated like painted strokes in the sky above the morning haze, but equally looked like an impenetrable wall with Russia the other side.

We walked to a nearby monastery on a hill. The main road had worn tracks leading off it with many puddles and people pottering about. Some men were crowded around an old silver car, doing repairs, with the bonnet open. The snow was thawing out in the sun and I felt hot wearing my jacket. The changing season seemed to offer a new beginning.

We walked up above the village, where there was a better vista of the mountains. Two tall, slender men with long beards, wearing black cloaks, passed us. At the entrance to the track leading to the monastery, there was a gatekeeper with a huge dog. One of the monks followed us through, pacing along gently but purposefully. The monastery was built from huge slabs of stone. It had two towers, which Fanny said was unusual for such a building. It was a very calm place, which made me long for camping outside again.

Inside, the church was dimly lit. The interior was simple, with a few pictures, such as St. George slaying a dragon. I stood in the centre and listened for the monk, who had stealthily entered before us. It was as if he was overseeing us. There was some movement above and the sound of footsteps downstairs and he appeared, sitting down on the footsteps of a very low doorway that looked like it was only possible to get through if you were a dwarf. The tall monk, with his knees around his chin, sitting next to the dwarf's doorway, looked like something from *Alice in Wonderland*.

He observed us whilst I wandered around absorbing the atmosphere of the place. Fanny asked me to come and light a candle. I placed the candle in a holder and spotted the monk observing calmly. For a moment, I felt peace. I felt content and I wasn't thinking or questioning why. There was enough life to not need to. All I needed to do was focus on the present and the process would lead me where I needed to go.

Outroduction
(Formerly known as the Introduction)

It was a leap into the unknown. We left on our bikes on a huge adventure and had no idea what to expect. The goal was to let the complexities of life do the directing for while, tear away considerable preconceptions about the world, and grasp life's true potential.

Although I had read accounts from other cycle tourists about friendly, hospitable people, I couldn't fully shake the negative images that had been implanted in my head by the media about war and terrorism. If I had believed what I had seen in the news, I wouldn't have turned the next corner, let alone pedalled thousands of miles into an unknown world.

As the trip unfolded, I realised that there was no need to worry because I had a support crew, which consisted of everyone I met. It was the most surprising and wonderful part of the journey and it provided an amazing insight into the everyday life and philosophies of the average human being.

The hospitality Tom and I received is a testament to the goodness of human beings. The people we met were always kind and happy to help, which contrasts with the negative news stories in the media that tend to cultivate a strong paranoia in people.

When the media frames a place negatively, it can become the representative image of an entire country. I advocate that positive news should be spread as widely as possible to reinforce positive ideas and behaviour.

After I got over my fear of the unknown, I wanted to learn more deeply about the people I met. I wanted to get closer to the reality of life in the places that we visited. When people stared at us or ignored us, I wished I could get a glimpse into their thoughts. Did we make people feel nostalgic about riding bikes as children? Were we obviously tourists? Did we inspire dreams of adventure or did people think we were crazy? I wanted to understand better what those people thought of people like me.

Travelling by bike is unique compared to other modes of transport. A bicycle traveller is a mystery to most because usually only poor people ride bikes, not rich Westerners. In addition, it is a slow, arduous, and reflective mode of transport in a world bent on going faster.

People were always curious to find out more about our journey. That interest and curiosity rubbed off on me. I began to realise that what I wanted to learn about myself was also what I wanted to learn about other people and that this learning may even be reciprocal.

The secrets of life are locked up in the lifestyles of people around the world and travelling by bicycle is a fantastic way to learn from other cultures. In order to really understand and unearth these treasures, you have to be fully immersed in the experience, ideally speak the language, and definitely be willing to take the time to dig deeper.

ABOUT THE AUTHOR

Andy Welch studied a BSC in Environment, Economics and Ecology at York University and MA Design Critical Practice at Goldsmiths. After working as a mountain bike guide and a designer he cycled from England to Nepal between 2007 and 2009, lived in the Republic of Georgia, and cycled across Mongolia in 2010. He lives in London.

COMING SOON:

More books...

Andy's yearning for adventure takes him further on his journey by bike through the Caucasus, Iran, Pakistan, India and Nepal and a series of realisations about life befall him.

The Open Wilderness Guiding Book

Inspired by the Situationists' 'Theory of the Derivé' and the practice of 'being prepared', Andy has created a guide for adventure, exploration and spiritual growth in the city and beyond.

Contact Andy:
Email: andy@slowquest.co.uk
Twitter: @andrewwelch5
Online: http://www.andrewwelch.info

Printed in Great Britain
by Amazon.co.uk, Ltd.,
Marston Gate.